AF688962

Catalyst

by Tutorials

Marin Benčević, Nick Bonatsakis & Andy Pereira

Catalyst by Tutorials

By Marin Benčević, Nick Bonatsakis & Andy Pereira

Copyright ©2022 Razeware LLC.

Notice of Rights

All rights reserved. No part of this book or corresponding materials (such as text, images, or source code) may be reproduced or distributed by any means without prior written permission of the copyright owner.

Notice of Liability

This book and all corresponding materials (such as source code) are provided on an "as is" basis, without warranty of any kind, express of implied, including but not limited to the warranties of merchantability, fitness for a particular purpose, and noninfringement. In no event shall the authors or copyright holders be liable for any claim, damages or other liability, whether in action of contract, tort or otherwise, arising from, out of or in connection with the software or the use of other dealing in the software.

Trademarks

All trademarks and registered trademarks appearing in this book are the property of their own respective owners.

ISBN: 978-1-950325-70-2

Table of Contents

Book License 9

Before You Begin 11

What You Need 13

Book Source Code & Forums 15
- About the Authors 18
- About the Editors 18

Acknowledgments 19
- Content Development 19

Introduction 21
- What is This Book? 22
- Catalyst 23
- Where to Go From Here? 27

Section I: Making a Great iPad App 29

Chapter 1: The Checkbox 31
- The Sample App: Journalyst 32
- The iPad Checkbox 34
- The Mac Catalyst Checkbox 37
- Key Points 42
- Where to Go From Here? 42

Chapter 2: Migrating to Split View Controller 43
- Getting Started 44
- Integrating Split View Controller 44
- Updating the UI 48
- macOS Split Views 51
- Key Points 54
- Where to Go From Here? 54

Chapter 3: Drag & Drop........ 55
How do Drag and Drop Work?........ 56
Dropping New Photos........ 56
Dropping Inside UICollectionView........ 61
Reordering Collection View Items........ 63
Key Points........ 67
Where to Go From Here?........ 67

Chapter 4: Setting the Scene(s)........ 69
Introducing Multiple Windows for iPad........ 70
Enabling Multi-Window in Xcode........ 76
Improving the Standard Multi-Window Experience........ 80
Adding Custom Drag Behavior to Create a New Window........ 87
Trying it on the Mac........ 92
Key Points........ 93
Where to Go From Here?........ 93

Chapter 5: Adding Some Context........ 95
Introducing Context Menus........ 96
Adding a Context Interaction........ 97
Opening a New Window........ 100
Creating a New Entry........ 102
Adding an Image to an Entry........ 103
Add an Entry to Favorites........ 105
Sharing an Entry........ 108
Deleting an Entry........ 111
Trying it on macOS........ 112
Key Points........ 114
Where to Go From Here?........ 114

Chapter 6: The Keyboard........ 115
Getting Started........ 116
First Responders........ 116

Adding the Commands ... 116
Alternate Keyboard Handling ... 124
Key Points ... 125
Where to Go From Here? ... 125

Chapter 7: Preferences & Settings Bundle ... 127
Getting Started ... 128
Adding the Settings Bundle ... 129
Responding to Change ... 134
Child Panes ... 138
Key Points ... 144
Where to Go From Here? ... 144

Section II: Making a Great Mac App ... 145

Chapter 8: Making Your App Feel at Home on macOS ... 147
It Starts With an App Icon ... 148
Adding a Touch of Color ... 149
A Word on Typography ... 152
Sizing Down Window Resizing ... 152
Preferential Treatment ... 155
A Few More Odds and Ends ... 157
Key Points ... 161
Where to Go From Here? ... 161

Chapter 9: The Mouse ... 163
Getting Started ... 164
Pointer Style Providers ... 164
Adding Effects With Hover Gesture Recognizer ... 166
A Few Notes on Elements and Haptics ... 169
Accessorize ... 170
Key Points ... 172
Where to Go From Here? ... 172

Chapter 10: Barista Training: Menu Bar.................... 173
A Free Menu Bar 174
The Responder Chain 174
Beyond the Default Menu.................................... 175
Deleting Entries 178
Sharing Entries 180
Key Points 184
Where to Go From Here?..................................... 184

Chapter 11: Barista Training: Toolbar 185
Getting Started.. 186
Adding the Toolbar 187
Adding Buttons.. 189
Customizing the Toolbar 194
Responding to Actions 196
Sharing 200
Key Points 203
Where to Go From Here?..................................... 203

Chapter 12: Barista Training: The Touch Bar............... 205
Understanding the Touch Bar 206
Adding Items 207
Grouping Items.. 211
Customizing the Touch Bar................................... 213
Key Points 216
Where to Go From Here?..................................... 216

Section III: Distributing Your App................. 217

Chapter 13: Releasing on the App Store 219
Updating Existing Catalyst Apps 220
The App Store vs. Third-Party Distribution 220
Adding Your App to the App Store 221
Testing Your App With TestFlight 229

Releasing Your App 232
Selling Your macOS App Separately 233
Key Points 235
Where to Go From Here? 235

Chapter 14: Third-Party Distribution 237
Signed, Notarized and Delivered 238
Creating a DMG File 241
Notarizing Disk Images 248
Key Points 250
Where to Go From Here? 251

Conclusion 253

Book License

By purchasing *Catalyst by Tutorials*, you have the following license:

- You are allowed to use and/or modify the source code in *Catalyst by Tutorials* in as many apps as you want, with no attribution required.
- You are allowed to use and/or modify all art, images and designs that are included in *Catalyst by Tutorials* in as many apps as you want, but must include this attribution line somewhere inside your app: "Artwork/images/designs: from *Catalyst by Tutorials*, available at www.raywenderlich.com".
- The source code included in *Catalyst by Tutorials* is for your personal use only. You are NOT allowed to distribute or sell the source code in *Catalyst by Tutorials* without prior authorization.
- This book is for your personal use only. You are NOT allowed to sell this book without prior authorization, or distribute it to friends, coworkers or students; they would need to purchase their own copies.

All materials provided with this book are provided on an "as is" basis, without warranty of any kind, express or implied, including but not limited to the warranties of merchantability, fitness for a particular purpose and noninfringement. In no event shall the authors or copyright holders be liable for any claim, damages or other liability, whether in an action or contract, tort or otherwise, arising from, out of or in connection with the software or the use or other dealings in the software.

All trademarks and registered trademarks appearing in this guide are the properties of their respective owners.

Before You Begin

This section tells you a few things you need to know before you get started, such as what you'll need for hardware and software, where to find the project files for this book, and more.

What You Need

To follow along with the tutorials in this book, you'll need the following:

- A Mac running macOS Monterey (12.0) or later.
- Xcode 13.3 or later.
- An Apple Developer account. You can enroll here (https://developer.apple.com/programs/) for an Apple Developer account. For development, the free account will suffice, but if you want to distribute the apps you build, you'll need a paid account.

You can use the simulator that comes with Xcode for all the chapters.

Book Source Code & Forums

Book Source Code

The materials for this book are all available in the GitHub repository here:

- https://github.com/raywenderlich/cat-materials/tree/editions/3.0

You can download the entire set of materials for the book from that page.

Forum

We've also set up an official forum for the book at https://forums.raywenderlich.com/c/books/catalyst-by-tutorials. This is a great place to ask questions about the book or to submit any errors you may find.

"To my mom, for always pushing me to do things I'm too lazy to do."

— Marin Benčević

"To my parents, for providing the education and support that ultimately made it possible for me to write this book."

— Nick Bonatsakis

"To my wife, Angela, for believing in me, and encouraging all I do. I wouldn't be where I am without you."

— Andy Pereira

About the Authors

Marin Benčević is an author of this book. He is an image processing researcher as well as an iOS developer who likes to work on cool iOS apps and games, nerd out about programming, and he can talk for far too long with you about coffee. He also has a chubby cat.

Andy Pereira is an author of this book. He is an iOS developer in Atlanta, GA. He enjoys traveling the world with his wife, learning new cultures, and playing guitar.

About the Editors

Ehab Amer is a tech editor for this book. He is a very enthusiastic Lead iOS developer with a very diverse experience. From building games to enterprise applications and POCs, especially when exploring new technologies. In his spare time, TV shows take the majority, followed by video games. When away from the screen, he goes with his friends for escape room experiences or to explore the underwater world through diving.

Pinal Naik is the final pass editor of this book. She lives in Bangalore, India. After more than a decade in regular corporate life, she chose to start working on her own to pursue her passions. She loves to create iOS apps from scratch to finish, using advanced technologies like Machine Learning and is the owner of the apps Xplooor and Alt-Selfie. Here is her latest creation (https://apps.apple.com/app/id1542732315).When not coding, you'll find her immersed in a book, traveling or spending time with her husband and her two super-energetic boys. She appreciates the support of her husband, kids, mom-in-law, mom, her late father and her amazing team here, in making this book a reality. She hopes to inspire a lot more women to become developers and app creators.

Acknowledgments

Content Development

We would like to thank **Nick Bonatsakis** for his work as an author on the previous editions of this book.

Nick is an accomplished software engineer with over a decade of experience in mobile development across both Android and iOS. He is a passionate technologist, musician, father and husband. He currently works as an independent consultant under his own company, Velocity Raptor Inc.

vi Introduction

By Nick Bonatsakis and Marin Benčević

Since the introduction of the first iPhone, Apple has been building and maintaining two parallel operating systems: macOS and iOS. Both are based on Darwin but optimized for different types of interaction. As time passed, the apps and features on macOS and iOS started to converge slowly. It became very common for developers to create and support apps that ran on multiple types of Apple devices, from iPhone, iPad and Mac.

The trouble with building an app that runs on both iOS and Mac is that you need to learn and use two different UI frameworks: `UIKit` and `AppKit`. And, therefore need to maintain two distinct codebases. While it is, of course, possible to share some code using frameworks, the entirety of an app's UI-related code effectively needs to be done twice.

With the arrival of **Catalyst**, it's now possible to bring an iPad app to the Mac using a single, UIKit-based codebase. With minimal effort, your iPad app can function quite well on macOS, and with a bit of additional effort, can become a world-class Mac citizen.

What is This Book?

Throughout this book, you'll work with on a sample app called **Journalyst**. Starting with a basic iPhone-only app, you'll learn how to first enhance for iPad with some of the features that apply to both iPad and Mac. Once your iPad app really shines, you'll take the next step by optimizing it to run on Mac using Catalyst. Finally, you'll learn how to build and distribute your new Mac app to both the Mac App Store and independently.

Who is This Book Written for?

This book is for you if:

- You have an existing UIKit iPhone app that you want to bring to iPad or Mac without much hassle.
- You have an existing UIKit iPad app that you want to bring to Mac.

How to Use This Book

This book is organized into three sections, carrying you through optimizing an iPhone app for iPad, then bringing that iPad app to Mac, and finally distributing the Mac app. It's best read linearly, but if you already have a great iPad app, you can jump straight to the Mac section. Do note, however, that Apple has added some new iPad capabilities alongside the introduction of Catalyst that you may not be familiar with. Even if you have an existing iPad app, it'd be a good idea to review the first section before proceeding.

Catalyst

If you've made it this far, you likely know what Catalyst is. But in case you need a refresher, it is Apple's mechanism for bringing iPad apps to the Mac. Introduced in macOS 10.15, it enables you to simply check a checkbox in your UIKit-based Xcode project and begin running your app on the Mac.

Starting in macOS 10.15, many of Apple's own apps that run across iOS and macOS have been built using Catalyst, including Maps, News, Voice Memos, Podcasts, and Reminders. If you've used any of these apps on Mac and iPad, you'll note that they are similar in structure, but the apps feel quite genuine on their respective platforms. Even when you run your iPad app on Mac without modification, you'll find that it already adopts many of the Mac-standard UI idioms, it's not just your iPad app running on a desktop simulator.

Here's a look at how the Reminders app looks, first running on iPad:

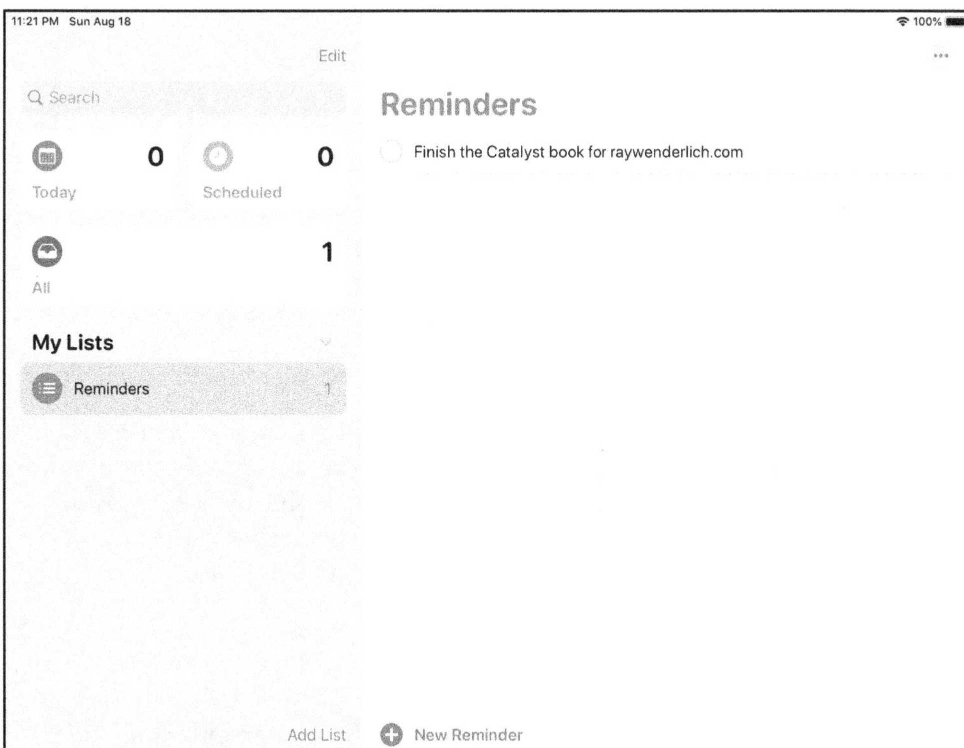

And now, on Mac:

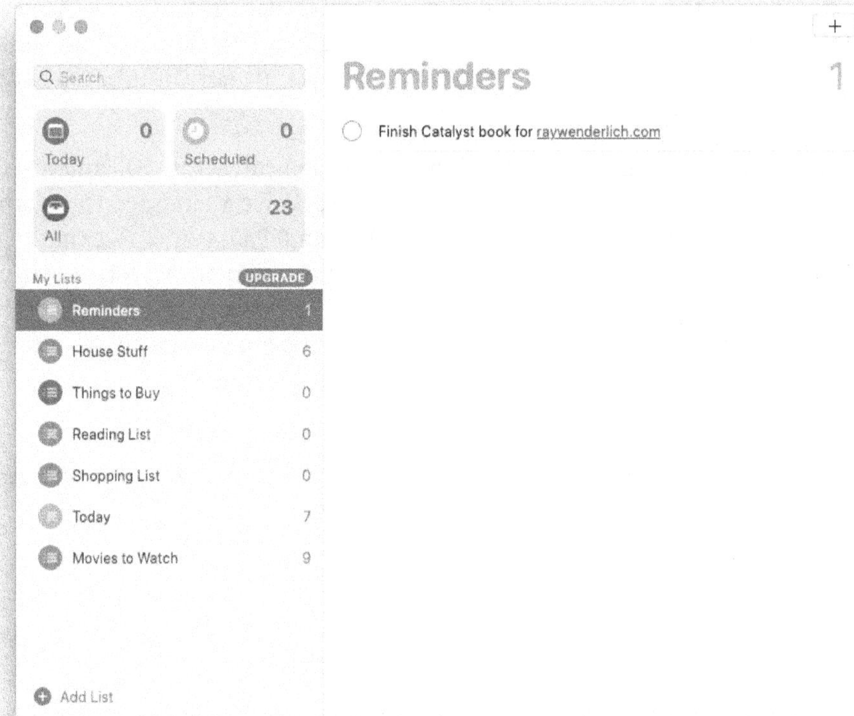

A few more things to note about Catalyst before you learn more about how it works:

First, you've probably noticed the word "iPad" used over "iOS" or "iPhone and iPad" when Catalyst is being discussed. This is not a coincidence. Catalyst is only available for apps that support iPad. This is because iPad apps have already gone through changes required to take advantage of things like a larger display, keyboard, multi-window, etc. Thus, they make a much smoother transition to the Mac.

Secondly, while Catalyst apps run on Mac, they are not AppKit apps, and can't easily accomplish some of the feats achieved by AppKit apps. Catalyst is a powerful first step towards a new way of building Mac apps, but a first step nonetheless. For this reason, AppKit is still a fully supported method for building Mac-only apps and is going to be the best approach for some classes of apps.

Lastly, when you build using Catalyst, you *may* end up with a separate Mac binary, although you're using one single codebase. You can distribute your app as a universal app binaries for iOS that run on iPhone, iPad and the Mac. You can also distribute your app separately, just like any Mac app, on the Mac App Store or independently.

Now, let's take a deeper dive into how Catalyst does what it does.

Catalyst Under the Hood

As mentioned earlier, Catalyst is not merely taking your iOS app and running it in a simulated Mac environment. Nor is it some variation of AppKit, which still exists separate from Catalyst and UIKit. So what is it then?

Well, it's UIKit running under the x86 architecture, and rendering Mac-style UI. But, it's not just UIKit. It's also many of the system frameworks you know and love, some that were already available on Mac, and some that were not. Because AppKit remains as a first-class method for creating Mac apps, Apple now has two stacks for doing so.

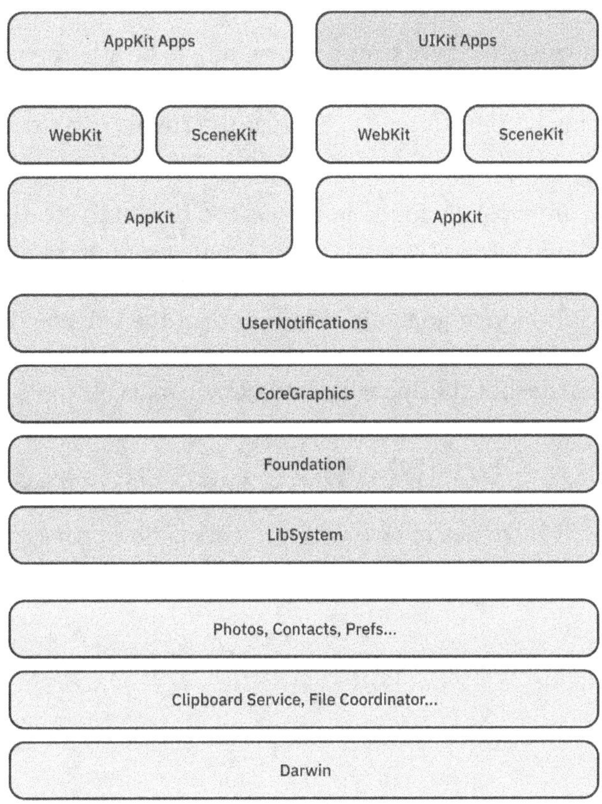

Instead of maintaining two entirely separate framework stacks, Apple has wisely unified frameworks where possible and left them separate otherwise. In the above diagram, you can see where the stacks continue to have separate components (WebKit, SceneKit, etc.), and where they converge (frameworks like Foundation and various types of user data stores).

Framework Availability

While Apple has made the experience of running iPad apps on Mac quite frictionless, not all frameworks available on iOS are available on macOS. Frameworks that take advantage of hardware features found only on mobile devices aren't available on macOS. Therefore, code that uses these frameworks must compile out when building under Catalyst.

You'll learn more about how to conditionally include or exclude code when running under UIKit for Mac later on in the book.

UI Availability

Much like with frameworks, there isn't always going to be a 1:1 analog between an iOS UI component and a Mac equivalent. As you start porting your iPad apps to Mac, you'll notice that many controls on iOS, such as `UITabBar`, don't exist on Mac. So, they must be replaced with suitable Mac-style alternatives.

Tabs, for example, are typically found in macOS toolbars at the top of windows as opposed to a dedicated lower area on iOS. The top of a window is where a user expects to find hierarchical controls on a desktop app. Whereas, for one-handed touch device use, it is more ergonomic to have tabs at the bottom. In this case, you could simply render a standard `UITabBar` when running on iOS, but move those same tabs to `NSToolbar` for the app window when on macOS.

Which Apps Should Make Use of Catalyst?

Now that you have a good idea of how Catalyst works, it's worth asking the question: Which apps make sense to be ported to the Mac? The answer, as you'd expect, is: Not all of them.

In general, any iPad app can be configured to run on Mac. But, if your app falls into one of the below buckets, it might be particularly ripe for Catalytic conversion:

- **Existing UIKit iOS apps.** If you have a large UIKit-based codebase, it might be easier to use Catalyst to bring your app to macOS instead of rewriting your whole app in SwiftUI.
- **Apps with comprehensive iPad support.** If your app is already well supported on iPad, and you've put off making a Mac app for lack of time or wanting to maintain another codebase, now might be the time to bring it to Mac.
- **Apps with old or poorly maintained AppKit counterparts.** Likewise, if you already have a Mac version of your iOS app, but it has fallen into disrepair or is out of date, it may be a good idea to sunset it in favor of a Catalyst app based on your iPad project.

Conversely, if any of the bullets in the below list describe your app, you may not need to use Catalyst:

- **Apps that make extensive use of mobile-device hardware.** An app that is entirely based on ARKit for example (like an AR-based game), would be almost entirely non-functional on Mac.
- **Apps that leverage cross-platform engines.** A game build using a tool like Unity, for example, can already be built for Mac without the use of Catalyst.
- **Apps that already have well-supported AppKit versions.** Many iOS apps already have very well done and maintained AppKit counterparts. In these cases, there isn't a huge benefit to switching to using Catalyst.
- **SwiftUI apps.** If you app is written completely in SwiftUI, you don't really need Catalyst! SwiftUI supports all three platforms out of the box.

Where to Go From Here?

Now that you've been introduced to Catalyst and have a general understanding of what it does and how it works, it's time to put it to the test. In the first chapter, you're going to check some checkboxes and find out how easy it is to get started running your app on both iPad and Mac.

Section I: Making a Great iPad App

Catalyst is all about letting you use code you've written for iOS on macOS. But not *just* any code. At least for now, you can only run code that is written for iPad on a Mac. And because most of the code will run on both platforms, before you dive in to running your app on your Mac, there are a few things you should do to make your code ready.

In this section, you'll take an app written to run on iPhone and adapt it to run on iPad. Then you'll add some features to make it behave like a first-class iPad citizen. And through the *magic* of Catalyst, these features will make your Mac app better too!

Chapter 1: The Checkbox

By Nick Bonatsakis and Marin Benčević

In the introduction, you learned about what Catalyst is, how it works and the initial considerations you'll make when using it to bring your app to the Mac.

In this chapter, you're going to get your first look at the sample app that you'll be interacting with in this book. Once you familiarize yourself with the basic functionality and architecture, you'll take your first steps toward bringing the app to macOS.

By the end of this chapter, you'll learn:

- The basic functionality and architecture of the sample app.
- The Xcode project changes needed to get your iOS app running on macOS.
- Which features Catalyst gives you for free when running on the Mac.
- Which features don't work as well out-of-the-box.

It's time to get comfortable with the sample app that'll be your companion in this Catalytic journey.

The Sample App: Journalyst

Meet the last journaling app you'll ever need; it's called **Journalyst** and it has been designed from the ground-up to be the best way to chronicle your daily adventures. Start by taking it for a quick test drive.

Open **Journalyst.xcodeproj** from the starter project for this chapter in Xcode and then build and run.

You see the main journal entry list screen:

Journal entry list main screen.

Here you can see all the journal entries you've created as well as an **add** button in the upper right that will add a new entry when tapped. Try tapping the add button a few times to see new entries get added to the list.

Next, tap any entry in the list to dive into the journal entry detail screen.

Entry detail screen.

At the top of this screen, there is a text area where you can add the textual content for this entry. Below the text area, you'll find a button that you can tap to **add images**. Finally, there is a **Share** button in the upper-right that, when tapped, will bring up the standard iOS activity view, allowing you to share the content. Spend a few moments tapping on the various controls, and then get ready to move on to the code.

In the Xcode project, expand the **Journalyst** group in the navigation pane. Once you do so, you'll see a handful of groups that house the various architectural components that make up the app, alongside the standard files you'd expect in a new Xcode project.

Here's a brief breakdown of the files:

Models

- **Entry**: A class that represents a single journal entry in the app.
- **EntryDataSource**: A datasource class that works with table view to update its data.

View Controllers

- **MainTableViewController**: A table view controller that renders the journal entries list, which is the main screen of the app.
- **EntryTableViewController**: A table view controller that renders the detail screen for a single journal entry.

Views

- **EntryTableViewCell**: A table view cell that represents a single journal entry on the main screen.
- **ImageCollectionViewCell**: A collection view cell that renders an image attachment in the image area of the single journal entry screen.

Take some time to dig into each of the above files so you can get a feel for the overall structure and data flow. The app is not overly complex, but it will serve as a great starting point for taking you through all the aspects of Catalyst.

Once you feel comfortable with the project, it's time to take your first steps towards Mac-ifying your first app.

The iPad Checkbox

"Wait, what? Weren't you migrating this app to run on the Mac? What's this iPad business about?" You may have noticed that the Journalyst app is currently configured and designed to run on iPhone only. Well, it turns out that an iPhone app, even a great one, doesn't translate well to the much larger screen of a Mac.

iPhone apps are optimized for single-window use, where you see one screen at a time on a very confined display size. They aren't typically concerned with things like drag-and-drop, multi-tasking, split views, keyboard shortcuts and all manner of other functionality commonly found in Mac apps.

iPad apps, on the other hand, are concerned with the above features, run on comparable display sizes, and thus have far more in common with Mac apps. For this reason, Apple wisely decided that, for an iOS app to run on macOS, it must be capable of running on iPad. So if you were hoping to take your iPhone-only app straight to macOS, you're in for a bit more work than you may have expected. This book will guide you through the process of both bringing your iPhone app to iPad, and then bringing that iPad app to the Mac.

Apple states that the first step in making a great Mac app using Catalyst is making a great iPad app. The more your app is designed to be a good citizen on the iPad, the easier it will be to bring it to macOS using Catalyst. So before you can check the "Mac" checkbox, you'll have to check the "iPad" checkbox.

In the Xcode project, click the top-level **Journalyst** entry in the navigation pane, select the main app target, and click the **General** tab. You see three checkboxes within the **Deployment Info** section, only "iPhone" is currently activated.

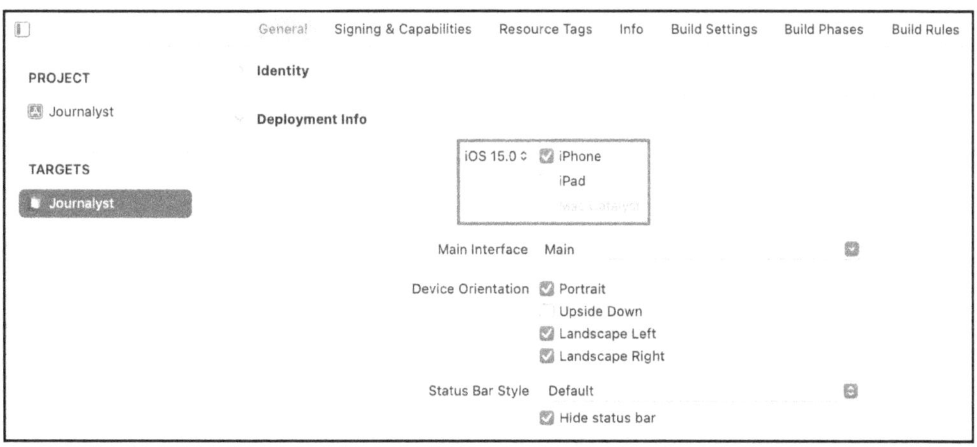

Xcode checkboxes.

Check the **iPad** checkbox. Just like that, you've added support for iPad. Select an iPad simulator as the run target then build and run to look at the fruits of your labors.

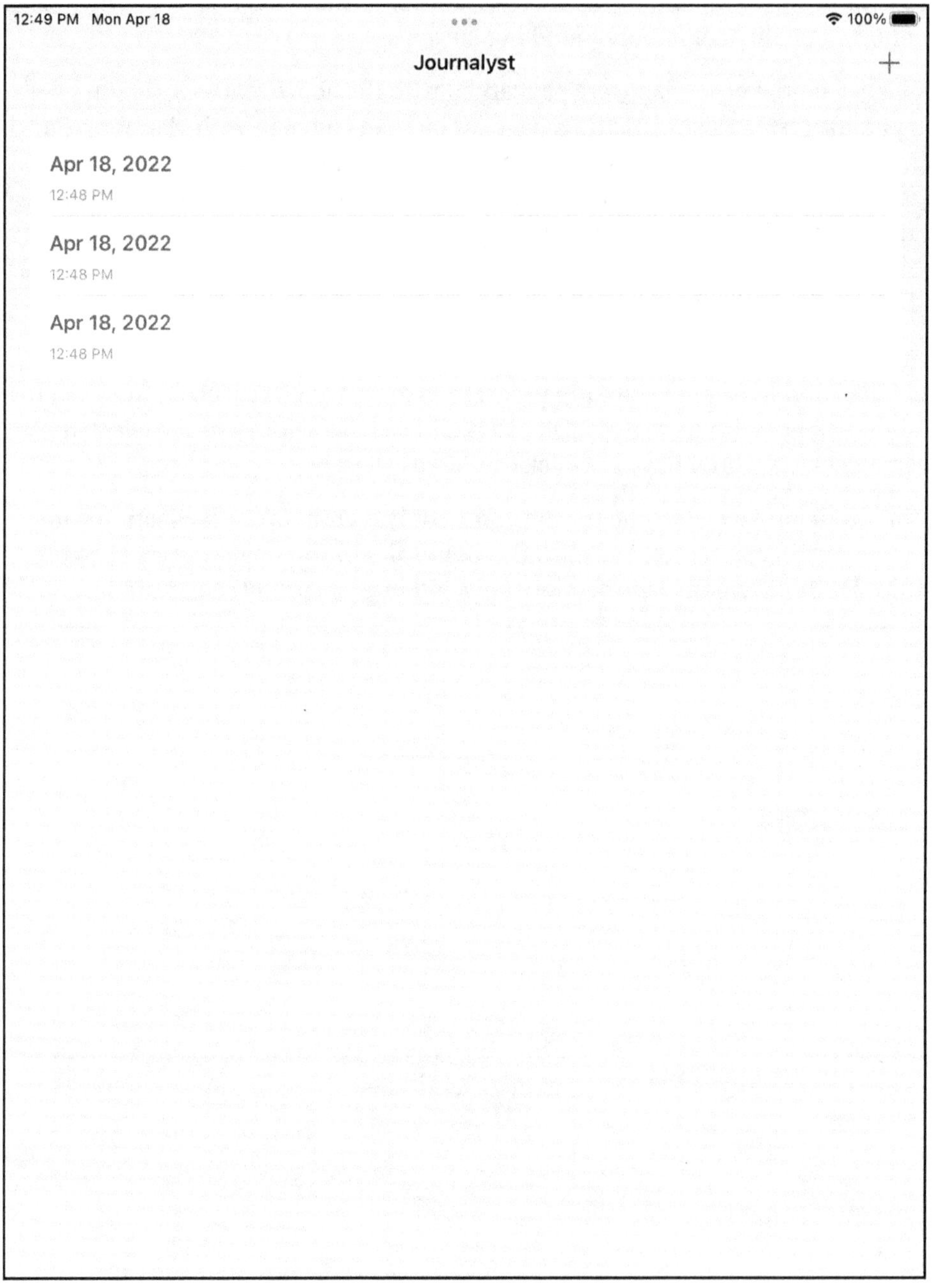

Main screen on an iPad.

And there it is! The Journalyst app running on the iPad... Looks great right? Well, maybe not so much.

Through the magic of auto-layout, nothing looks broken per se, and app features still work. However, what you see is an inflated version of the iPhone app. It doesn't look or feel like a first-class iPad citizen. You can do much better than this, and in the chapters that follow, you will.

Be aware that some features are downright broken when running on iPad. If you try to activate anything that would bring up an action sheet, such as adding an image or sharing an entry, the app will crash. You'll learn why this is the case, and how to fix it in the next chapter.

But this chapter is all about instant gratification via checkboxes, so put your dreams of creating the next hit iPad app to the side for now and prepare to see the app running on the Mac.

The Mac Catalyst Checkbox

And now the checkbox you've been waiting for! Back in the **General** tab of the **Journalist** target settings, go ahead and check the **Mac Catalyst** checkbox.

You'll notice that, this time, *unlike* when you checked the "iPad" checkbox, Xcode prompts you to make some changes to the project. Allow it to do so, and the following changes will be made:

- An entitlement for App Sandbox is added to the **Journalyst.entitlements** file. Apps that are distributed on the Mac App Store must incorporate sandboxing, which you'll learn more about in a later chapter that covers distributing your Catalyst app.
- A new run destination for **My Mac** is added to the project so that you can run the app from Xcode.
- Incompatible frameworks, app extensions and other embedded content are excluded from the Mac build. In this case, there aren't any yet.

Once you've enabled the Mac checkbox and accepted project changes, you'll notice a new dropdown to the right of **Mac Catalyst**. Go ahead and click it, then select **Optimize Interface for Mac**.

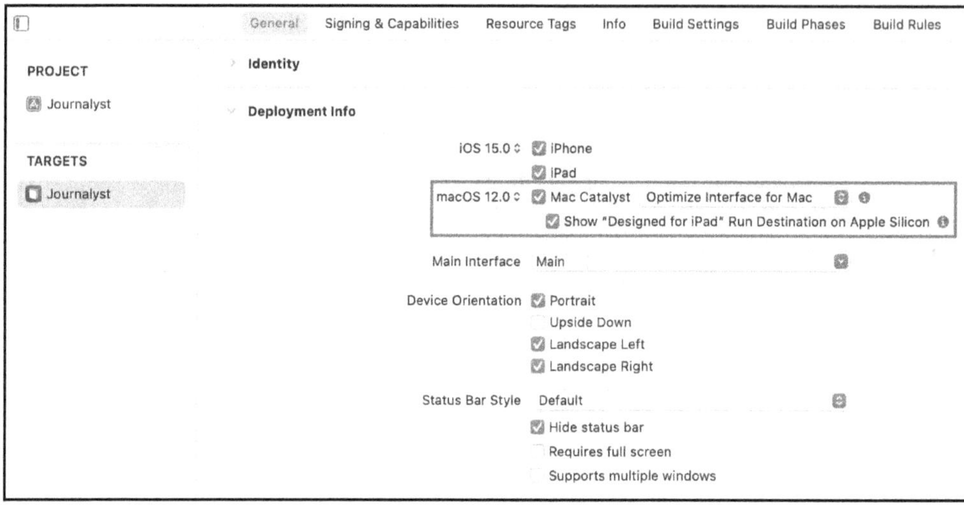

Mac Catalyst options.

From Apple's Xcode 12.2 release notes on the option:

> When bringing iPad apps to macOS, you can now use the Optimize Interface for Mac target setting to use native macOS controls and Mac resolution.

Since your ultimate goal is to make an app that looks and feels like a first-class macOS app when running on the Mac, you want the interface to be optimized accordingly.

Go to the **Signing & Capabilities** tab of the **Journalyst** target settings and under **Signing**, you'll notice you have bundle ids for iOS and Mac Catalyst platforms. Under the Mac Catalyst platform, you'll notice **Use iOS Bundle Identifier** is checked.

Go ahead and uncheck the **Use iOS Bundle Identifier** checkbox. Then, create a Mac Catalyst bundle identifier as *maccatalyst.com.yourcompany.Journalyst.*

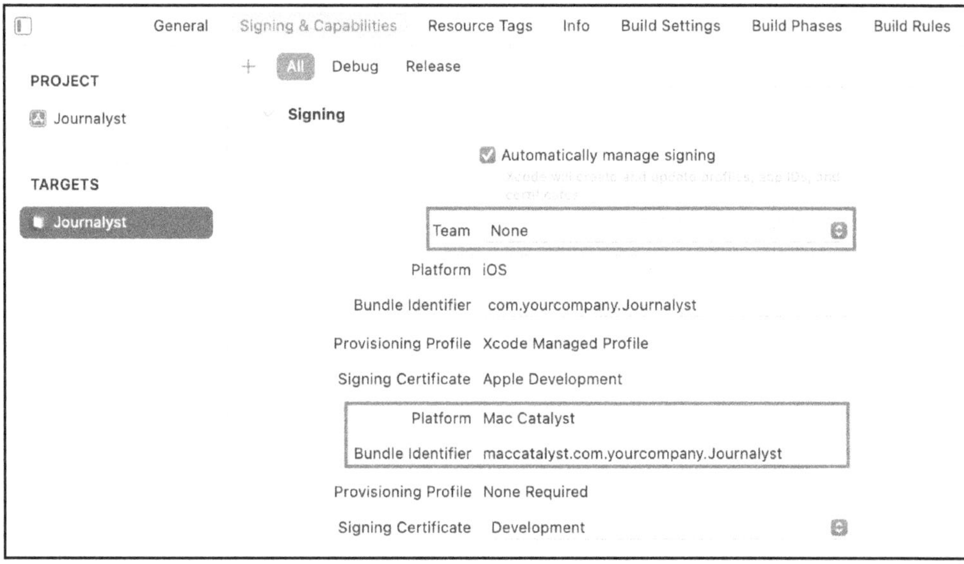

Mac Catalyst bundle identifier.

This makes sure the app you are running uses a different bundle identifier on macOS, allowing you to separately control and price your macOS app in the App Store, or distribute your macOS app outside the App Store.

The last thing you'll need to do before running the Mac app is to specify code signing information. This step isn't necessary when running the iOS app on simulators, but in this case, your Mac is a real device, so the bundle needs to be signed.

Go ahead and select a team. Make sure **Automatically Manage Signing** is enabled, and Xcode will take care of the rest.

Finally, change the run destination to **My Mac**, build and run, then bask in the glory that is your first Catalyst app!

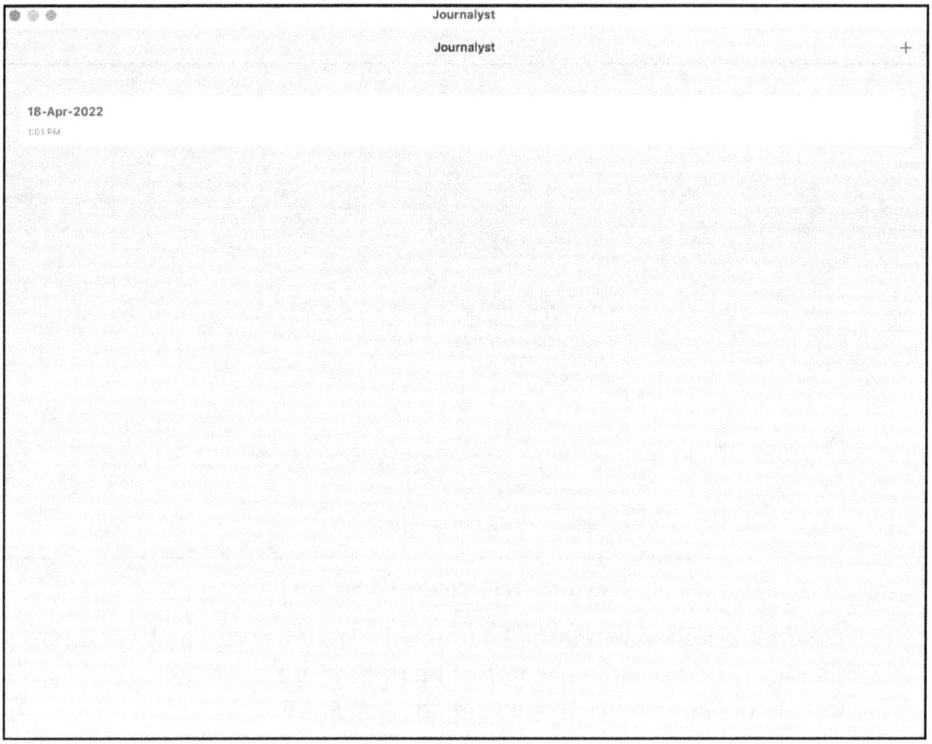

Main screen on a Mac.

Much like when you ran the app on iPad for the first time, the basic functionality is there after applying almost zero effort, but the app in its current form leaves much to be desired. Still, Catalyst gives you a whole lot of Mac goodness for free, so poke around, and you'll find that your Mac app already has the following features:

- A basic Mac menu bar.
- Support for trackpad, mouse and keyboard input.
- Support for window resizing and full-screen display.
- Mac-style scroll bars.
- Copy-and-paste support.
- Basic drag-and-drop support.
- Support for system Touch Bar controls.

But it's not all rainbows and checkboxes at this point — there's still a lot of work you'll need to do to make this app a first-class Mac experience. Some of the more notable features that are currently missing are:

- Multi-window support.
- A better navigation structure, given the larger screen size (a split view would do nicely here).
- Extended drag-and-drop support for things like dragging images into journal entries.
- Extended keyboard support for things like shortcuts.
- Extended mouse support for custom contextual menus.
- A Mac-style preferences window for app settings.
- A better look and feel for the app that aligns it more with what you commonly see on macOS.
- Better support for the menu bar, toolbar and the touch bar that go beyond what you get out-of-the-box.

That list might look daunting, but the remainder of this book guides you through the process of implementing all these features and more. The rest of the chapters in **Section 1** covers the features that you'll add to turn Journalyst into a great iPad app. **Section 2** then covers the process of turning your great iPad app into an even greater Mac app. Rounding things out, **Section 3** walks you through the finer points of testing using TestFlight, packaging and distributing your new Mac app.

Key Points

- Journalyst is a basic journaling app that you'll be improving throughout this book.
- Before you can make a great Mac app using Catalyst, you need to make a great iPad app.
- Catalyst gives you plenty of Mac functionality for free.
- To make a truly great Mac app using Catalyst, you need to go above and beyond what comes out-of-the-box, covered above.

Where to Go From Here?

In this chapter, you became familiar with Journalyst, the sample app of this book, as you learn how to bring apps from iPhone to iPad, and then to the Mac. You took the first steps along this path by configuring the app to run on both iPad and Mac by changing the Xcode project configuration. Finally, you learned about which features Catalyst provides out of the box and which ones require additional effort to enable.

Chapter 2: Migrating to Split View Controller

By Andy Pereira

The split view controller provides a way to manage two view controllers at the same time. The split view controller takes advantage of the iPad's significantly larger screen size, making it easy to display a master-detail style interface. This also makes it easy to adapt to the screen size of the device someone may be using. In this chapter, you'll convert the iPhone "master-detail" pattern found in Journalyst to a split view controller, then update the UI to take advantage of the view.

Getting Started

Open the starter project for the chapter. Select an iPad Pro simulator in the active scheme, then build and run. In its current state, the iPad version of Journalyst requires you to select an entry before you can see the details.

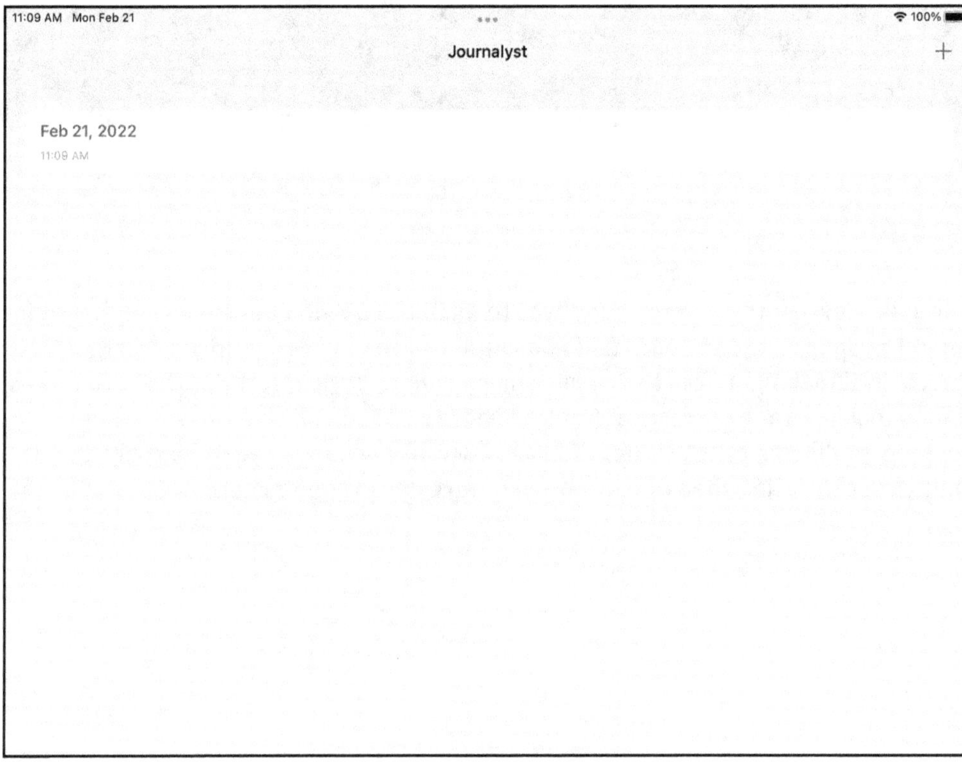

Select an entry to see it's details.

Integrating Split View Controller

Open **Main.storyboard** and select the **Entry Table View Controller** scene. From the menu bar, select **Editor ▸ Embed In ▸ Navigation Controller**.

This inserts a navigation controller and keeps the segue you had before, but you need to change a property of it. Select the segue between the Journalyst scene and your new navigation controller and in the **Attributes inspector** change the **Kind** to **Show Detail**.

The segue already has a segue action attached to it from the starter project, and you won't need to change that.

Now, open **MainTableViewController.swift** and add the following property:

```
var entryTableViewController: EntryTableViewController?
```

The segue action connection didn't need to change, but with your new navigation controller, the code it runs will. Replace `entryViewController(coder:sender:segueIdentifier:)` with the following:

```
@IBSegueAction func entryViewController(
  coder: NSCoder,
  sender: Any?,
  segueIdentifier: String?
) -> UINavigationController? {
  guard let cell = sender as? EntryTableViewCell,
  let indexPath = tableView.indexPath(for: cell),
  let navigationController
    = UINavigationController(coder: coder),
  let entryTableViewController
    = navigationController.topViewController as?
    EntryTableViewController else { return nil }
  entryTableViewController.entry
    = dataSource?.itemIdentifier(for: indexPath)
  self.entryTableViewController = entryTableViewController
  return navigationController
}
```

It's important to understand that an `NSCoder` gets passed into this method, where it's used to initialize the navigation controller found in the storyboard. Notice that once the navigation controller is initialized, an **EntryTableViewController** is already the `topViewController`.

Back in **Main.storyboard**, open the Library by clicking the **add** button at the top-right of the canvas. Then, drag a **Split View Controller** to your canvas. Delete the following scenes from the canvas attached to the split view controller:

- **Navigation Controller**
- **Root View Controller**
- **View Controller**

Next, control-drag from the split view controller to the navigation controller attached to the Journalyst scene, and select **primary view controller**. Then, connect the split view controller to the navigation controller of the entry table view scene, and select **secondary view controller**.

Finally, select the split view controller scene and in the **Attributes inspector**, set the following properties:

- **Is Initial View Controller**
- **Style** is set to **Double Column**.

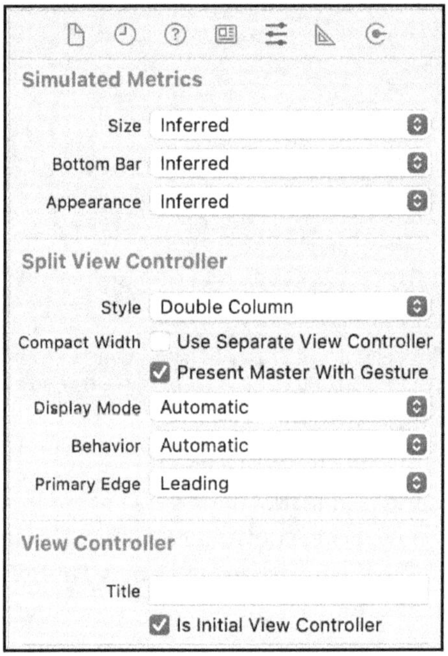

Attributes inspector of the split view controller.

You're almost there!

In **AppDelegate.swift**, add the following to the end of the file:

```
extension AppDelegate: UISplitViewControllerDelegate {
  func splitViewController(
    _ splitViewController: UISplitViewController,
    collapseSecondary secondaryViewController: UIViewController,
    onto primaryViewController: UIViewController
  ) -> Bool {
    guard let secondaryNavigationController
      = secondaryViewController as? UINavigationController,
    let entryTableViewController
      = secondaryNavigationController.topViewController
    as? EntryTableViewController else {
      return false
    }
    if entryTableViewController.entry == nil {
      return true
    }
    return false
  }
}
```

This conforms **AppDelegate** to `UISplitViewControllerDelegate`. Here, it is simply configuring the behavior of how the split view controller will handle the view on the right hand side of the controller.

Last, add the code below to the main body of **AppDelegate**:

```
func application(
  _ application: UIApplication,
  didFinishLaunchingWithOptions launchOptions:
    [UIApplication.LaunchOptionsKey: Any]?
) -> Bool {
  if let window = window,
     let splitViewController
       = window.rootViewController as? UISplitViewController {
    splitViewController.preferredDisplayMode = .automatic
    splitViewController.delegate = self
  }
  return true
}
```

Here, you set the `preferredDisplayMode` of split view controller to automatic. This wraps up the work needed to get your split view controller to work.

Build and run. Rotate the simulator orientation to **landscape** and your app is now updated with a split view controller!

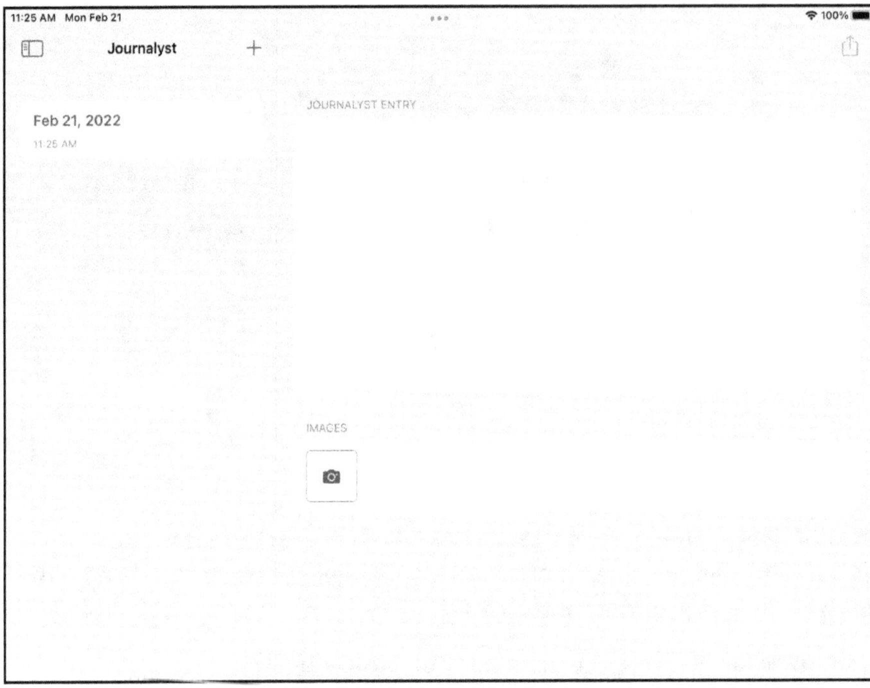

Journalyst with a split view controller.

Updating the UI

Even though you have a working split view controller, you'll notice that not everything is working smoothly. The first entry in the list does not automatically get shown in the **EntryTableViewController**. To get that working, open **MainTableViewController.swift** and add this code to `viewDidLoad`:

```
if let splitViewController = splitViewController,
   let splitNavigationController
     = splitViewController.viewControllers.last
       as? UINavigationController,
   let topViewController
     = splitNavigationController.topViewController
       as? EntryTableViewController {
  entryTableViewController = topViewController
}
```

This will give the view controller access to the **EntryViewController** present on the right side of the screen.

Next, replace `populateMockData` with the following:

```
private func populateMockData() {
  reloadSnapshot(animated: false)
  if let entryTableViewController = entryTableViewController,
     let entry = entries.first,
     entryTableViewController.entry == nil {
       tableView.selectRow(
         at: IndexPath(row: 0, section: 0),
         animated: false,
         scrollPosition: .top
       )
     entryTableViewController.entry = entry
  }
}
```

Now, whenever the data is initially loaded, the first entry in the table view will get selected automatically.

Build and run everything again. You see the time of the first entry appear at the top of the **EntryTableViewController** navigation controller.

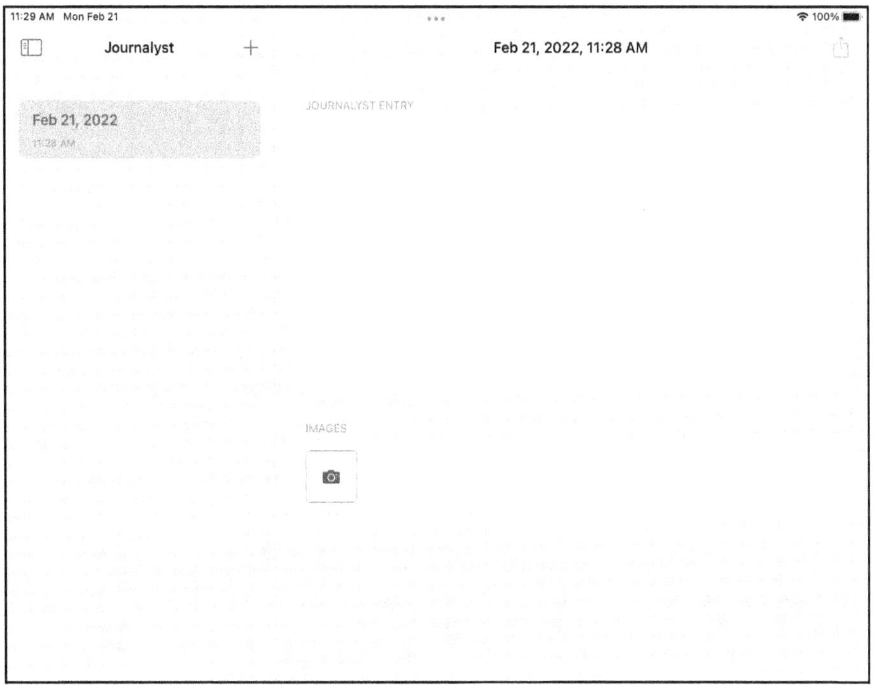

Selecting first entry in Journalyst.

We're getting close, but there are still a few more pieces to consider. Currently, text added to an entry doesn't save, and adding an entry image or trying to share an entry causes a crash.

Open **EntryTableViewController.swift** and add the following to the `UITextViewDelegate` extension:

```
func textViewDidEndEditing(_ textView: UITextView) {
  entry?.log = textView.text
}
```

Now, when you switch entries in the left-hand side, the text contained in the text view will be saved to the entry you were previously editing.

Next, you need to fix image and sharing functionality. When the app is running on an iPhone, the system will handle showing the activity controller and action sheet for you. However, on iPad you need to do a little more for it to work.

Because iPad wants to present the action sheet in a `UIPopoverPresentationController`, you'll need to tell it where to present from. In `addImage(_:)`, add the following just before the last line of the method:

```
if let sender = sender,
   let popoverController =
     actionSheet.popoverPresentationController {
  popoverController.sourceRect =
    CGRect(
      x: sender.frame.midX,
      y: sender.frame.midY,
      width: 0,
      height: 0
    )
  popoverController.sourceView = sender
}
```

Here, you check if there is a popover presentation controller, and then set the `sourceRect` and `sourceView` properties. Now, when you tap the **camera** button, the modal will be presented from it.

Last, add the following in `share(_:)`. Once again, place this code just before the last line:

```
if let popoverController =
  activityController.popoverPresentationController {
  popoverController.barButtonItem =
  navigationItem.rightBarButtonItem
}
```

While very similar to the previous additions for `addImage(_:)`, in this case, the **share** button is in a navigation bar. Therefore, you simply set the `barButtonItem` of the popoverController. Now, both modals will work properly.

Build and run. Now, add some text to a journal entry, add a few images and then share.

Everything is in working order:

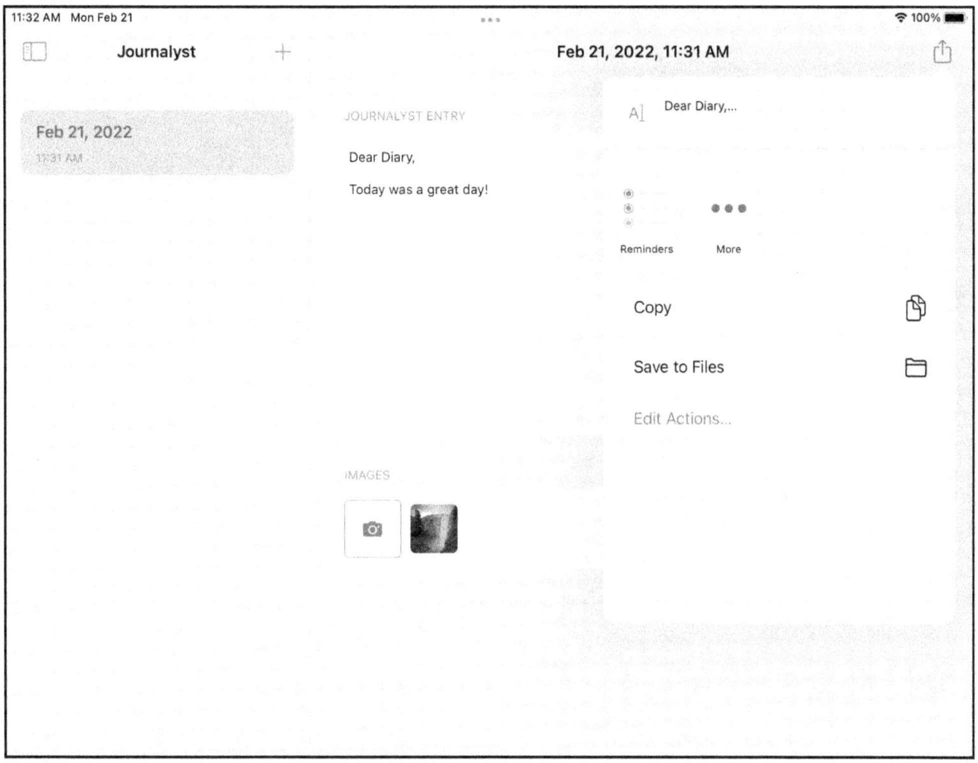

Adding images and sharing.

macOS Split Views

In traditional macOS apps, split views have long been the standard way of presenting a UI in a similar way to the split view controller. Catalyst makes it easy to take a split view controller and turn it into something that looks right at home on a Mac.

To see what the app looks like on a Mac, change the device in your active scheme to **My Mac**, then build and run again and add a few more journal entries:

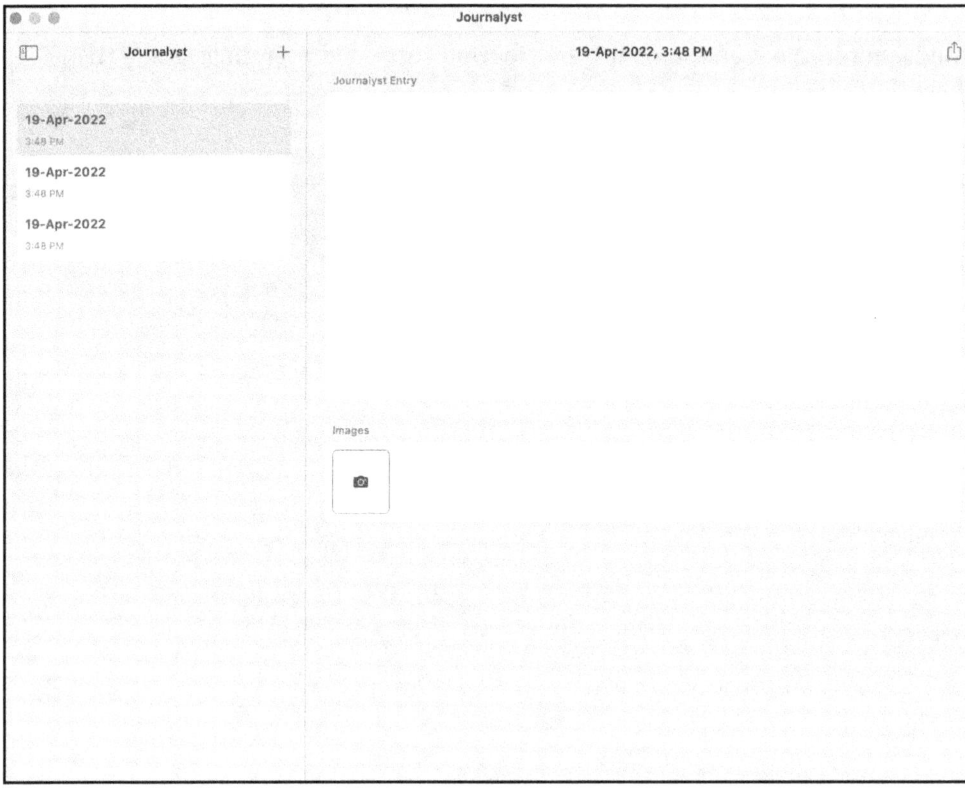

Split view controller works on a Mac.

You see the app looks almost exactly the same as it did on iPad.

> **Note**: Don't forget to set your team in your project's settings for **Signing & Capabilities**.

There are a few pieces of the user interface that aren't quite right, like the entry table view. Typically, the side views on Mac have some transparency. The first thing you can do to address this is set the split view controller's primary background style.

Open **AppDelegate.swift** and add the following to the end of the `if let` block, right after setting `splitViewController.delegate`:

```
splitViewController.primaryBackgroundStyle = .sidebar
```

This style will not have any affect on iPad or iPhone apps, but will make your app feel much more at home on a Mac.

Build and run one last time, and again, add a few entries. You'll see there's a much better look and feel now:

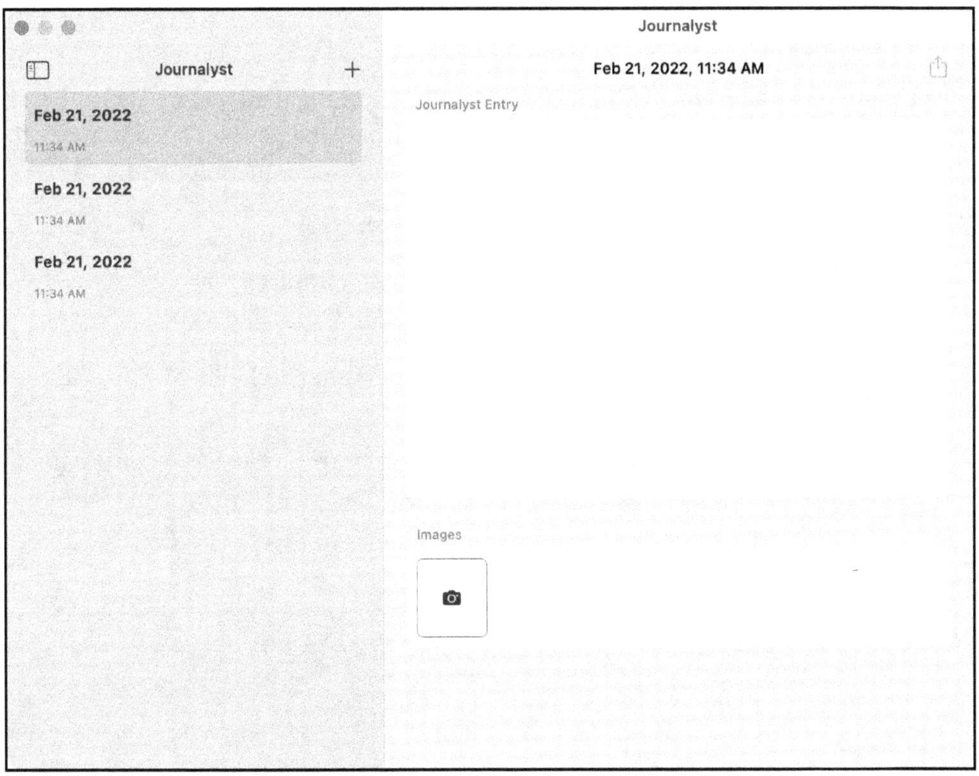

Background style of a side bar changed in Mac.

Key Points

- Split view controllers make it easy to create an iOS and macOS app from the same codebase.
- Popovers on iPadOS and macOS are handled identically.
- There is minimal work to make a split view controller look proper on macOS.

Where to Go From Here?

This chapter got you from an iPhone-only app to a working iPad and macOS app that feels right at home on each platform. You learned what changes you need to make to handle the different platforms, and how much Catalyst will handle for you.

You can learn more about the following subjects here:

- **UISplitViewController**: Check out Apple's documentation (https://developer.apple.com/documentation/uikit/uisplitviewcontroller).
- **IBSegueAction**: Watch WWDC 2019 video (https://developer.apple.com/videos/play/wwdc2019/210/).
- **Catalyst**: Read Apple's human interface guideline (https://developer.apple.com/design/human-interface-guidelines/ios/overview/ipad-apps-for-mac/).

Chapter 3: Drag & Drop

By Marin Benčević

On macOS, dragging and dropping files is such an integral feature that we typically just take its presence for granted. It's so useful that Apple decided to bring it over to the iPad in iOS 11. With Catalyst, you can go full circle and bring the iPad's drag and drop *back* to macOS. Everything old is new again, right?

In this chapter, you'll update the app so your users can add new photos to their diary entry by dragging them from other apps and dropping them into the entry view. You'll also update the entry photos collection view to allow reordering the photos by dragging and dropping.

How do Drag and Drop Work?

Before you start working, you need to get familiar with the basics of drag and drop. Now, theory can be a *drag*, however, quite useful in understanding the concept.

Each drag and drop action has two sides: The dragging side and the dropping side. The objects on both of these sides are `UIViews`. To enable dragging, you need to add a **drag interaction** to a view. When iOS detects that a drag is being attempted on a view, the drag interaction uses a **drag interaction delegate** to determine which **drag items** will be dragged. This delegate can also customize the look of these items as they're being dragged.

The whole point of drag and drop is to share data between apps. The **drag items** being passed around are not the actual data. Instead, they contain a way to *get* the data once the drop happens.

On the other side, a **drop interaction** uses a **drop interaction delegate** to determine what will happen when the item is dropped into the destination view. The drop interaction delegate can also animate the destination view whenever the dragged items enter the destination view or change position inside the view.

Overseeing all of this is a **drop session.** Drop session is a manager, but the good kind of manager: It lets you work without getting in your way, but always has answers ready to any pressing questions you might have. The session knows which items are being dragged, how to get their contents, where they're being dropped to and other useful contextual information.

To enable drag and drop on your views, all you need to do is add the interactions and implement the delegate methods. Once you do that for your iPad app, it will work on macOS automatically. It also works on iOS, but only inside your app.

OK, that's the theory. Let's *drop* right in and get into some code!

Dropping New Photos

Open the starter project from the provided materials of this chapter. Build and run on an iPad. Take a look at the entry photos collection view. Currently, you can only add new photos by clicking the camera icon and choosing a photo. On macOS and the iPad, it's common to select a bunch of photos from the Photos app and just drop them into the destination app. You'll make this happen.

Before you can start working on drag and drop, there are a few project-specific changes you need to make. When the app loads, it first launches the *main* table view controller, which in turn creates a new *entry* table view controller with a new entry. At the time of writing, in some cases, the split view controller will only load the *entry* table view controller, without loading the master. In those cases, the entry will be `nil`. To work around this issue, you'll force the app to always perform some setup after it launches.

Open **MainTableViewController.swift** and add a new method to the class:

```
func prepareForPresentation() {
  loadViewIfNeeded()
  populateMockData()
}
```

This method performs the necessary setup actions that populate your app with an empty entry.

Next, open **AppDelegate.swift** and add the following code at the end of the `if` block inside `application(_:didFinishLaunchingWithOptions:)`, right after where you set `primaryBackgroundStyle`:

```
if let mainNavigationController
     = splitViewController.viewController(for: .primary)
     as? UINavigationController,
   let mainViewController
     = mainNavigationController.viewControllers.first
     as? MainTableViewController {
  mainViewController.prepareForPresentation()
}
```

The above code fetches the main table view controller and calls the method you added earlier every time the app launches. This makes sure entry table view controller always has an entry to work with.

With that out of the way, you can get started on dropping photos into the app!

Open **EntryTableViewController.swift** and at the bottom of `viewDidLoad` add the following code:

```
let interaction = UIDropInteraction(delegate: self)
textView.interactions.append(interaction)
```

As mentioned before, for dropping to work you need to add a `UIDropInteraction` to a view. In this case, you'll allow dropping photos inside the text view of the entry screen.

Next, at the bottom of the file, add the following extension to implement `UIDropInteractionDelegate`:

```
extension EntryTableViewController:
  UIDropInteractionDelegate {
  func dropInteraction(
    _ interaction: UIDropInteraction,
    canHandle session: UIDropSession
  ) -> Bool {
    session.canLoadObjects(ofClass: UIImage.self)
  }
}
```

As you enable drag and drop, you need to first declare the kinds of things that can be dropped inside the view. In this case, you'll only accept the drop if the session has at least one drag item that's a `UIImage`.

Now implement the following method inside the extension:

```
func dropInteraction(
  _ interaction: UIDropInteraction,
  sessionDidUpdate session: UIDropSession
) -> UIDropProposal {
  UIDropProposal(operation: .copy)
}
```

As items are dragged inside a view, this method is called repeatedly. This method returns a **proposal** of what *could* happen if the user were to drop the items right now. In the proposal, you define what kind of drop operation this would be with a value from the `UIDropOperation` enumeration. In this case, you return `.copy` which means that the dropped item will be copied from the source app to your app, and the user will see a + sign while dropping.

Other possible values of this enumeration include:

- `.move`: Tells the user that the item will be moved.
- `.cancel`: Says that the drag will be canceled.
- `.forbidden`: Used when the drop is *usually* enabled for this view, but there's something about the combination of dragged items and destination view's state forbidding this in a specific case. For instance, there might already be an existing item there which needs to be deleted for the drop to work.

> **Note**: During a drag interaction, `dropInteraction(_:sessionDidUpdate:)` gets called many, *many* times. Make sure you're not doing any long-lasting work in there.

The last piece of the puzzle is to define what happens once the user drops the dragged items. Add the following method inside the `UIDropInteractionDelegate` extension:

```
func dropInteraction(
  _ interaction: UIDropInteraction,
  performDrop session: UIDropSession
) {
  session.loadObjects(ofClass: UIImage.self) {
    [weak self] imageItems in
    guard let self = self else { return }
  }
}
```

This method gets called when the user releases the dragged items into the view. To get the dragged photos, you can ask the session to load all the dragged items of type `UIImage`.

Once the images are loaded you can add them to the entry and update the collection view. Add the following code inside the closure:

```
if let images = imageItems as? [UIImage] {
  self.entry?.images.insert(contentsOf: images, at: 0)
}
self.reloadSnapshot(animated: true)
```

Here, you're casting the received array to `[UIImage]`. Once you have the photos, you prepend them to the entry and add a number of items at the start of the collection view equal to the number of photos that were just dropped. `reloadSnapshot` will automatically animate the changes you make to the collection view's data source.

> **Note**: `loadObjects` can only be called inside this delegate method. You can't access a drag item's data before or after this point. The completion handler is always called on the main queue, so there's no need to use dispatch here.

Build and run the project on an iPad. The easiest devices to test on are 11-inch or larger iPad Pros. Enter split-screen with **Photos** by dragging its icon from the dock to the right-hand side of the screen. Find some nice vacation photos and drag the photos over to the **text view** of the entry screen:

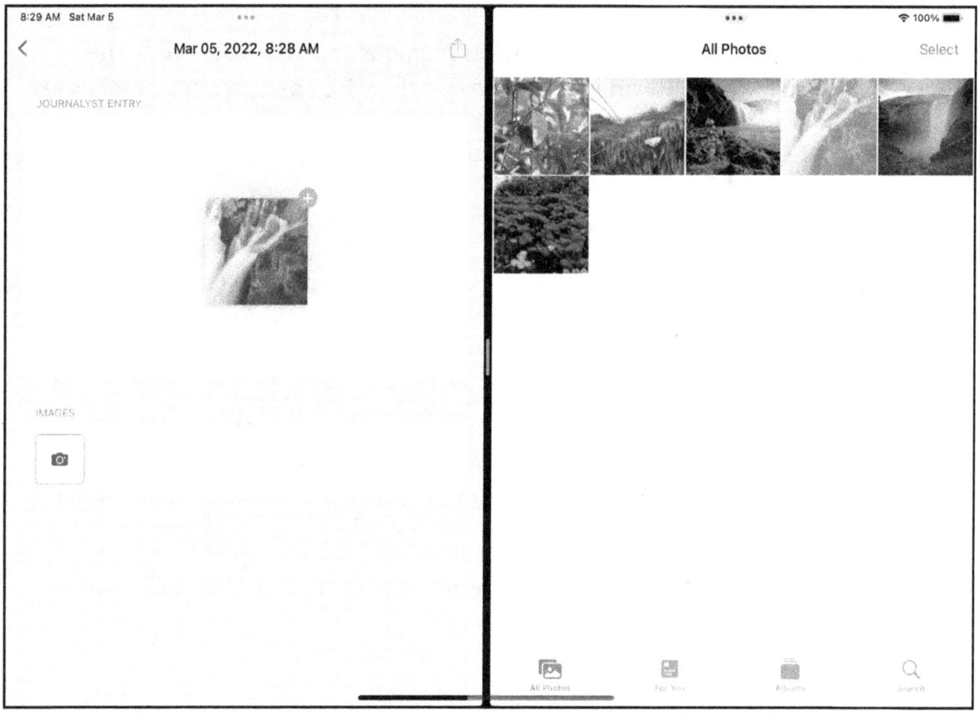

Drag a photo from Photos to the text view.

You see the photos appear in the collection view:

Photo appears in the collection view.

Dropping photos like this is much easier than going through an image picker and looking for the perfect photo. Now that the user can drop photos into the text view, you'll next allow them to drop photos directly into the collection view.

Dropping Inside UICollectionView

Dropping photos in the text view is convenient when you want to add a bunch of photos to the entry, but it would be nice to let the users drag photos into specific positions directly inside the collection view. You'll also show an animation of the existing photos parting to allow space for the newly dropped photos.

Thankfully, `UIKit` includes drag and drop APIs specific to table and collection views. While you will work on adding drag and drop to a collection view, the same process is valid for table views with minor method name changes.

Still in **EntryTableViewController.swift**, start by adding the following line to the end of `viewDidLoad`:

```
collectionView.dropDelegate = self
```

`UICollectionViewDropDelegate` is very similar to the delegate you implemented earlier in this chapter, except it has additional features specific to collection views.

Add the following extension to the bottom of the file to implement the delegate:

```
extension EntryTableViewController:
  UICollectionViewDropDelegate {
  func collectionView(
    _ collectionView: UICollectionView,
    canHandle session: UIDropSession
  ) -> Bool {
    session.canLoadObjects(ofClass: UIImage.self)
  }
}
```

This is the same implementation as before. You're only interested in `UIImage` instances.

Next, implement the following method in the extension:

```
func collectionView(
  _ collectionView: UICollectionView,
  dropSessionDidUpdate session: UIDropSession,
  withDestinationIndexPath destinationIndexPath: IndexPath?
) -> UICollectionViewDropProposal {
  UICollectionViewDropProposal(
    operation: .copy,
    intent: .insertAtDestinationIndexPath
  )
}
```

This method, like the one you implemented before, returns a proposal. For collection views, there's one additional piece of information: The **drop proposal intent**. The intent defines what would happen to the collection view if the user dropped the items right now.

You return `.insertAtDestinationIndexPath` which makes the collection view part the items to the left and right of the cursor, and show an empty space where the dragged items will be dropped. This signals to the user that the items will be dropped at that specific position.

Another possible value of this enumeration is `.insertIntoDestinationIndexPath`. This tells the user that the dropped items will be dropped *inside* the cell. This is useful for things like nested cells or cells that contain items inside them.

Finally, implement the method that performs the actual drop:

```
func collectionView(
  _ collectionView: UICollectionView,
  performDropWith coordinator:
  UICollectionViewDropCoordinator
) {
  let destinationIndex = coordinator.destinationIndexPath ??
  IndexPath(item: 0, section: 0)
}
```

A difference between the delegate you implemented earlier and this one is that the collection view delegate gets a **collection view drop coordinator**. This coordinator has a reference to the drop session, but also includes collection view specific contextual information, like which index path the user is dropping to. You'll use this information to add photos to specific indices in the `entries` array.

Add the following code to the method:

```
// 1
coordinator.session.loadObjects(ofClass: UIImage.self) {
  [weak self] imageItems in
  guard let self = self else { return }
  if let images = imageItems as? [UIImage] {
    // 2
    self.entry?.images.insert(
      contentsOf: images,
      at: destinationIndex.item
    )
  }
  // 3
  self.reloadSnapshot(animated: true)
}
```

This code is similar to the one you wrote earlier from dropping into the text view. Here's what's going on:

1. First, ask the session to load all `UIImage` objects.
2. Then, insert those objects into the destination index you fetched earlier.
3. Once you update the array, just like before, you call `reloadSnapshot` to make sure that the collection view animates those changes.

Build and run. Drag over a few photos to the collection view.

Once you have at least one photo, when dragging another one across the collection view you'll notice the items move to show an empty space where the item will be dropped.

Dropping a photo inside collection view.

If you drop the item, it will animate into position. That's a pretty cool effect with no manual animation code. Thanks, `UIKit`!

Now that you have dropping in your collection view, why not add dragging as well? Read on to find out how!

Reordering Collection View Items

Speaking of the work `UIKit` does for you, if you implement both dragging and dropping for a collection or table view, it will automatically support reordering the elements. That's why your next task is adding drag support to the collection view. By the end of this section, you'll be a real *drag* expert!

Add the following line to `viewDidLoad`:

```
collectionView.dragDelegate = self
```

Just like there's a collection view specific drop delegate, there's also a drag delegate. Begin the implementation of the protocol with the following extension at the bottom of the file:

```
extension EntryTableViewController:
  UICollectionViewDragDelegate {
  func collectionView(
    _ collectionView: UICollectionView,
    itemsForBeginning session: UIDragSession,
    at indexPath: IndexPath
  ) -> [UIDragItem] {
    guard let entry = entry, !entry.images.isEmpty else {
      return []
    }
    let image = entry.images[indexPath.item]
    let provider = NSItemProvider(object: image)
    return [UIDragItem(itemProvider: provider)]
  }
}
```

For dragging to work, there's only one required method you need to implement. This method gets called when `UIKit` detects a dragging interaction is about to begin, and it asks you for the items that are being dragged. Thankfully, the delegate method includes the dragged index path as a parameter, making the task of finding the image much easier.

You check that there *is* an image to drag, and then get the image at that index path. If there is no image, you return an empty array, which stops the drag interaction and lets `UIKit` interpret the drag as a regular touch or mouse event.

The item providers define how data will be transferred from one app to the other. Some existing `UIKit` classes like `UIImage` already implement the required methods for this, so you can easily create a provider just by passing the image.

With the drag delegate implemented, you need to make a few changes to your existing code to support rearranging items. Change the implementation of `collectionView(_:dropSessionDidUpdate:withDestinationIndexPath:)` to the following code:

```
if session.localDragSession != nil {
  return UICollectionViewDropProposal(
    operation: .move,
    intent: .insertAtDestinationIndexPath)
```

```
} else {
    return UICollectionViewDropProposal(
      operation: .copy,
      intent: .insertAtDestinationIndexPath
    )
}
```

A **local drag session** is a drag session that was started inside your app. If the session is local, you return a `.move` drop operation because the items will be moved from one index path to another. If it's not a local session, you return `.copy` like before.

Next, when the user is rearranging items, you first need to delete the original item and then add it to its new position. Add the following lines to `collectionView(_:performDropWith:)`, right before the `loadObjects` call:

```
if coordinator.session.localDragSession != nil {
  for item in coordinator.items {
    guard let sourceIndex = item.sourceIndexPath else {
      continue
    }
    self.entry?.images.remove(at: sourceIndex.item)
  }
}
```

If this is a local drag session, go through each item to be dropped. Each item contains a source index path, i.e. the index path it was dragged from. You remove the dragged image from the source index in the images array. This ensures users don't accidentally duplicate items when trying to rearrange them.

Build and run. Like before, add a few photos to the collection view. Then try to drag one of the photos from the collection view to another position. You'll notice when you drag, it disappears from its original position, and a parting animation happens when you move over a different position. Once you drop it, the collection view animates it into that position:

Re-ordering photos in the collection view.

You just made your app's user experience much better by allowing users to drag, drop and rearrange photos with a smooth look and feel, and all with minimal code.

And *guess what*, this works on macOS without any code changes. If you don't believe, set the active scheme to **My Mac** and run the app. Find some vacation photos in the Finder and drag them to the app.

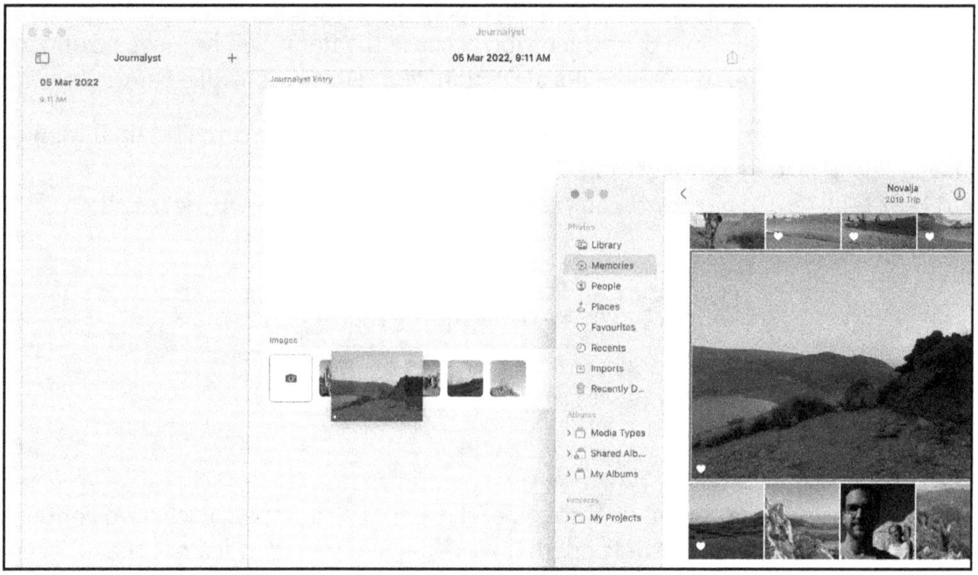

Drag and drop works on the Mac.

As a developer, there's nothing better than features working without any extra code. Even better, you can now also rearrange the collection view items in your iOS app!

Now you know how to implement drag and drop! Hope this chapter didn't *drag* on for too long.

Key Points

- Add drag and drop to custom views by adding a **drag** or **drop interaction** to the view and implementing the necessary delegate methods.
- Use a **drag session** to get the dragged items and load the dragged data.
- For table and collection views, it's enough to implement the collection or table view specific drop and drag delegate methods.
- An iPadOS implementation of drag and drop works on macOS and iOS, but on iOS, it only works within one app.

Where to Go From Here?

In this chapter, you implemented a basic implementation of drag and drop. You can go even further by including custom animations while the user is dragging items across your views. You can also customize how item previews look while they're being dragged. You can see an implementation of that in the WWDC 2017 session called Mastering Drag and Drop which you can find here (https://apple.co/2vOhvYA).

For collection and table views, you can make the user interface smoother by utilizing placeholder cells. When the user is dragging over the table or collection view, you can show placeholder cells with loading indicators. Once the items are loaded, the cell gets updated. You can see this in action in the WWDC 2017 session called Drag and Drop with Collection and Table View, which you can find here (https://apple.co/2JzzTOw).

Chapter 4: Setting the Scene(s)

By Nick Bonatsakis and Marin Benčević

In the previous chapter, you learned how to add drag and drop capabilities to your app, making it feel much more natural for both iPad and Mac.

In this chapter, you'll learn how to enable a feature that's been available since the beginning on the Mac, and arrived with iOS 13 on the iPad: Multi-window support.

By the end of this chapter, you'll learn:

- What multi-window support is and why you'd want to enable it for your app.
- How to enable basic multi-window support in Xcode and in your app.
- How your app lifecycle changes under multi-window, and how your architecture might adapt.
- How to add custom support for drag and drop window creation.

Ready to dive into the exciting world of multiple windows? Awesome! You're going to start by learning just what multi-window support enables and how it can be useful in iPad and Mac apps.

Introducing Multiple Windows for iPad

In 2007, Apple unveiled the next generation of computing with the introduction of the iPhone. Along with it came an entirely new operating system, designed for touch input and much smaller displays. `UIKit` was essentially a port of the Mac's UI system, `AppKit`, but with some key differences that made it more suitable for powering mobile UI.

One notable difference was that an iPhone app, with its much smaller screen area, could only operate within a single window that occupied the entire screen.

Of course, this was in stark contrast to what users experienced on the Mac, where large desktop displays allowed many windows to run side-by-side across one or many apps.

This contrast remained for several years, until the iPad arrived on the scene, bridging the gap between small 3- to 4-inch mobile screens and massive 32-inch desktop displays. Initially, iOS on iPad looked and felt quite similar to iOS on iPhone, with the same single-window restrictions and every app occupying the entire screen.

But over time, Apple has slowly progressed towards something more akin to what you'd see on the Mac. First, it added the ability to run apps side-by-side. Then it introduced tabs in apps like Safari. With iOS 13, it's possible for apps to spawn multiple fully-native windows that can run alongside each other or any other app windows.

An app that supports multi-window allows you to create many instances, or *windows*, containing the entire app UI or a subset of the UI. Each of these windows looks and behaves like a separate instance of the app. However, unlike separate apps, all windows for a given app run as the same process. You'll learn more about this later.

Why Multi-Window?

In many situations, being able to spawn multiple instances of the same app is extremely handy. Consider the following use-cases that are only possible with multi-window support:

- **Messages**: Carrying on two or more conversation threads without having to switch back and forth.
- **Pages**: Working on two documents side-by-side when you want to reference information in the first while working on the second and drag and drop content between the two.
- **Mail**: Writing a message in one window and searching previous messages for contacts or other information in the second window.
- **Safari**: Researching a topic across two different websites, side-by-side at the same time.

Generally, any app that lets a user view or create many instances of the same type of content is a good candidate for multi-window support.

Mac users, and now iPad users, will expect your app to function just as well, if not better, than the built-in Apple apps. If you want to build a first-class experience, take the time to enhance your app with support for multiple windows.

Multi-Window in Action

There are many ways to spawn and interact with multiple app windows on iPad. Some come with the system. Others are specific to individual apps. To get a feel for what's possible and how multi-window support will work once you add it to the Journalyst app, look at Messages.

Grab the nearest iPad or iPad Simulator and start by opening the **Messages** app. If you've ever used apps on the iPad in multi-tasking mode, where you run two different apps side-by-side, you'll know that you can swipe up from the bottom edge to reveal the dock. Go ahead and do so, then hold and drag the Messages icon to the right of the screen and drop it when you see the drop zone.

Multiple Messages app on the iPad.

You now have Messages in a side-by-side split screen. Both windows are fully functional, as if you had two Messages apps running at once.

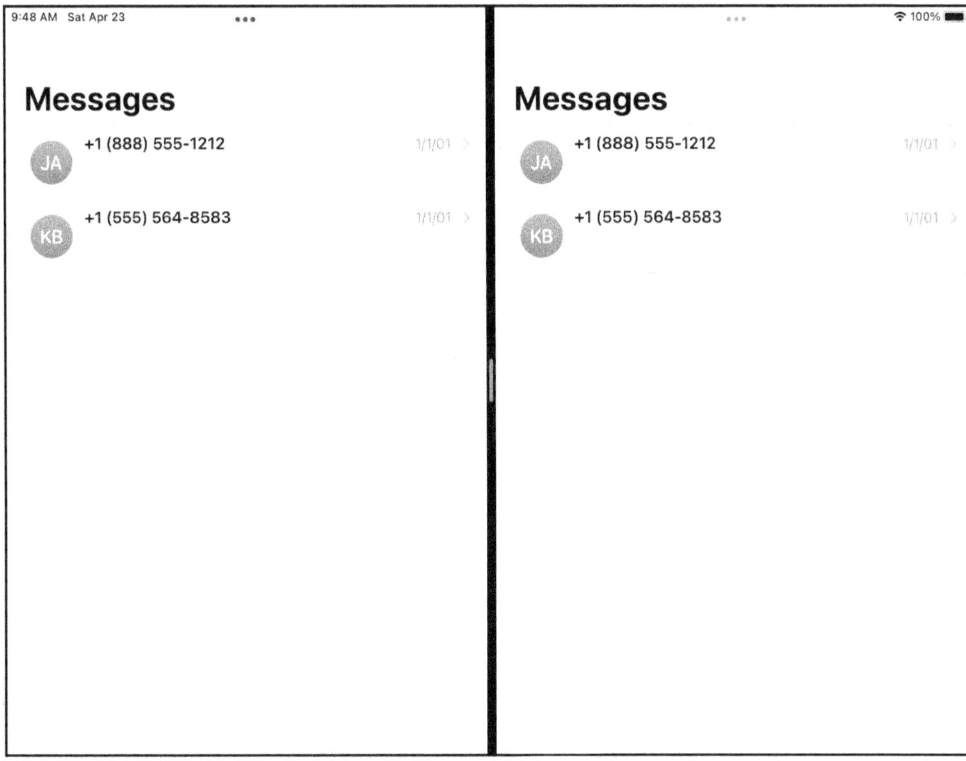

Messages running side-by-side.

Notice the separator in the middle of the screen and the handle-looking control. Touch and hold on the handle and drag all the way to the right edge of the screen, seemingly dismissing the second window. But wait! You didn't dismiss that window, you just detached it into a fully separate window.

Swipe up from the bottom of the screen again to bring up the dock once more, then tap and hold on the Messages app icon until you see a contextual menu pop up. Tap **Show All Windows** and you'll see a view of all the windows for this app, including the one you spawned and then swiped off to the right.

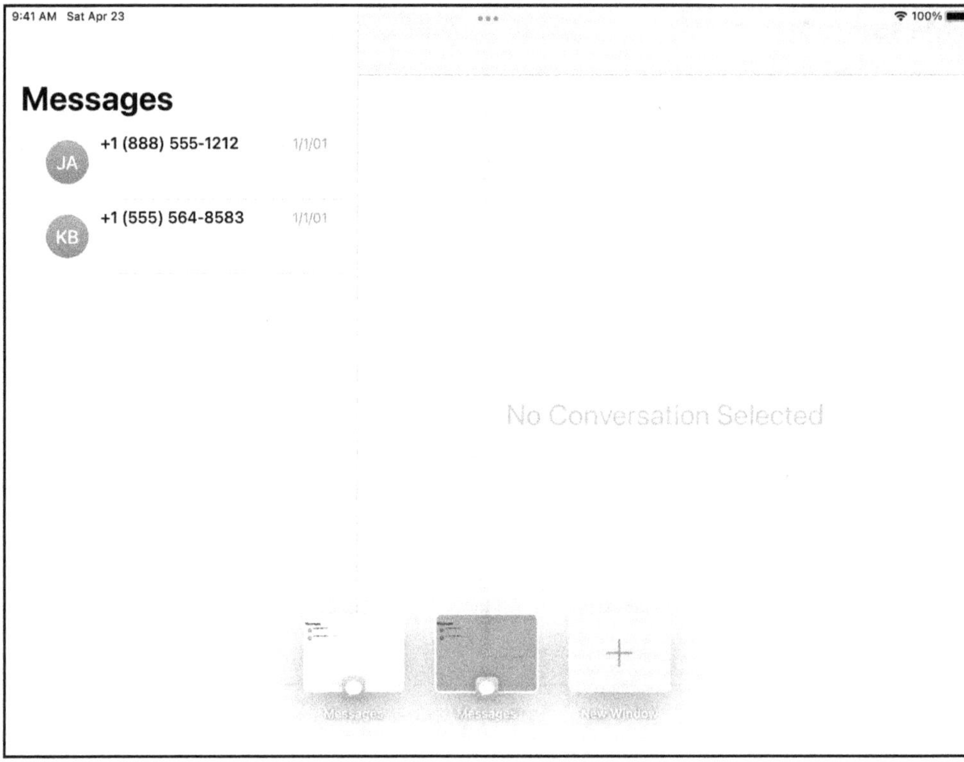

Show All Windows.

You'll notice here that there's also a + button you can use to create new windows. Try tapping it to see it in action.

> **Note**: Tapping three dots at the top of Messages also shows all open windows. Then, you can add a new Messages window.

Finally, tap one of the windows to get back into Messages. Tap and hold on one of the conversations in the sidebar for a moment, drag it to the right edge of the screen, then drop it once you see the drop zone indicator.

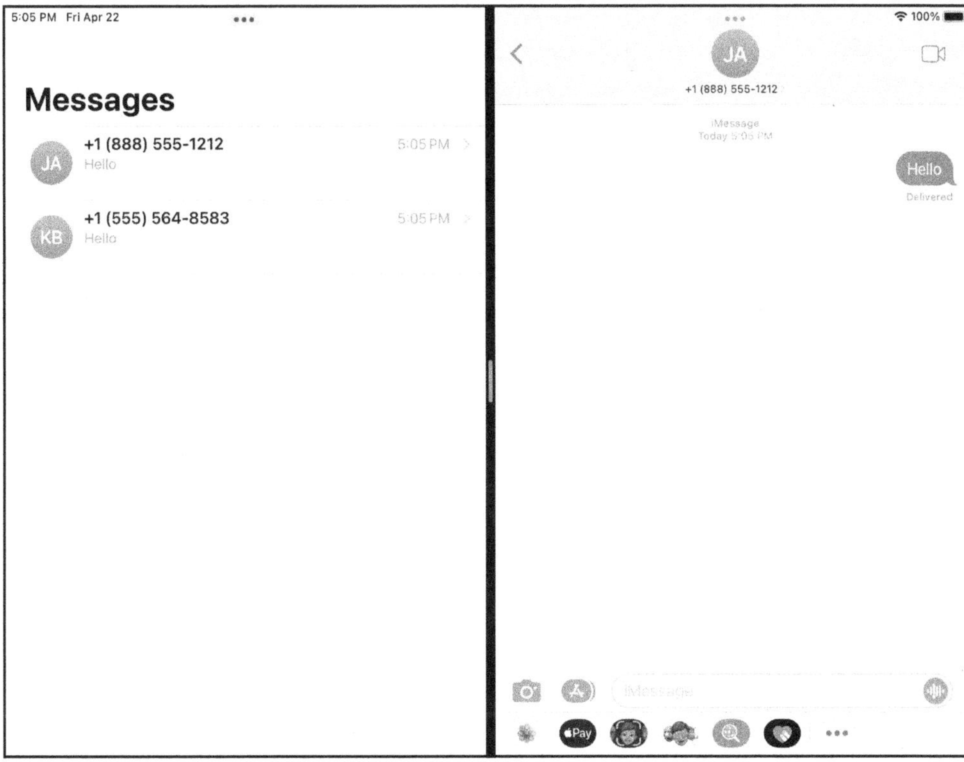

Messages with contacts on one side and conversation on the other side.

You now see that conversation on the right side of the screen, while you still have a fully functioning Messages app on the left. The other multi-window controls are part of the baseline support, but this one needs some additional work because, as you might expect, the interaction is specific to the content in the Messages app.

If the idea of adding these features to Journalyst excites you (hint: It should), then strap in, because you're about to do just that!

Enabling Multi-Window in Xcode

Open the starter project for this chapter in Xcode and head over to the project settings. Click the **Journalyst** target and make sure you're on the General tab. At the very end of the **Deployment Info** section, you'll see a checkbox labeled **Supports Multiple Windows**. Go ahead and check it to, you guessed it, enable multi-window support.

Enable multiple windows in Xcode.

Now open **Info.plist** and you'll notice that Xcode has added a new entry, **Application Scene Manifest**. The dictionary contains only one sub-entry called **Enable Multiple Windows** and it's set to `YES`.

You might think this would be enough to add basic multi-window support. But if you were to run the app now on an iPad, you'd see nothing but a big fat empty screen.

To understand why that is, you'll need to learn a bit about how the standard app architecture changes in a multi-window environment.

Introducing Scenes

In the pre-multi-window world, the entry point to every app was the app delegate. Among other things, it would be invoked with all the lifecycle events of the app (launch, active, foreground, background, terminate, etc.). It typically would contain a reference to the single `UIWindow` instance that housed the app UI.

In an app that supports multi-window, the app delegate is still the main entry point. However, you can now have many windows, and you need to be able to manage and notify each of them of lifecycle events independently. To do all that, you need to add a new abstraction. That abstraction is called a **scene** and it has the following components:

- **Scene**: Represents a single instance of your app's UI, including basic information and state changes.
- **Scene Delegate**: Responds to state changes and events from a scene.
- **Scene Session**: Manages the scene process, including configuration and state restoration.

When you enable your app for multiple windows, the system will continue to invoke app-level lifecycle events such as `didFinishLaunching` and `willTerminate` on the app delegate. However, a scene will now handle all lifecycle events and information associated with an instance of your app's UI.

When you launch your app, the system will now create a scene session and its associated scene to represent the first instance of your app, much like it would create a single `UIApplication` instance for the entire app.

To respond to UI-instance-level lifecycle events, the system will now invoke a custom scene delegate implementation that you provide, much like your app delegate did previously. With each additional scene your user initiates, the system will create another instance of this stack, allowing your app to manage each of its windows independently.

Adding a Scene Delegate

Now that you've learned how scenes allow you to effectively manage multiple instances of your app's UI, it's time to finish enabling multi-window support for your project.

Back in Xcode, create a new Swift file and name it **SceneDelegate.swift**, then add the following code:

```
import UIKit

class SceneDelegate: UIResponder, UIWindowSceneDelegate {
  var window: UIWindow?
  func scene(
    _ scene: UIScene,
    willConnectTo session: UISceneSession,
```

```
        options connectionOptions: UIScene.ConnectionOptions
    ) {
        if let splitViewController =
          window?.rootViewController as? UISplitViewController {
          splitViewController.preferredDisplayMode =
          .oneBesideSecondary
        }
    }
}
```

There's not a lot going on in the above code, just a reference to the scene's `UIWindow` instance and the addition of `scene(_:willConnectTo:options:)`. This gets called whenever you create a scene and connect it to the scene session. For now, that's all you need in the scene delegate. There's just one more thing you need to add before you're done with basic multi-window support.

Open **Info.plist** once more, copy the below snippet to the clipboard, then highlight the **Application Scene Manifest** entry. Then expand it and paste to add the new sub-entry.

```
<?xml version="1.0" encoding="UTF-8"?>
<!DOCTYPE plist PUBLIC "-//Apple//DTD PLIST 1.0//EN"
  "http://www.apple.com/DTDs/PropertyList-1.0.dtd">
<plist version="1.0">
  <dict>
    <key>UIWindowSceneSessionRoleApplication</key>
      <array>
        <dict>
          <key>UISceneConfigurationName</key>
            <string>Default Configuration</string>
      <key>UISceneDelegateClassName</key>
        <string>Journalyst.SceneDelegate</string>
      <key>UISceneStoryboardFile</key>
        <string>Main</string>
        </dict>
      </array>
  </dict>
</plist>
```

If you expand the configuration fully, you'll see an Application Session Role that consists of an array of items, each containing the configuration for a particular scene type. In this case, there's only one entry in the list representing the default configuration that you use whenever you create a new scene. However, the app can define roles for specific window configurations.

The following describes each key-value:

- **Configuration Name**: The identifier for this scene configuration.
- **Delegate Class Name**: The class that implements the scene delegate, which you'll use for an instance of this scene configuration.
- **Storyboard Name**: The name of the storyboard you'll use to create an instance of this scene.

With the above configuration change in place, build and run. Long-press on the app icon, show all windows and you'll find that you can now use the system UI to create new windows.

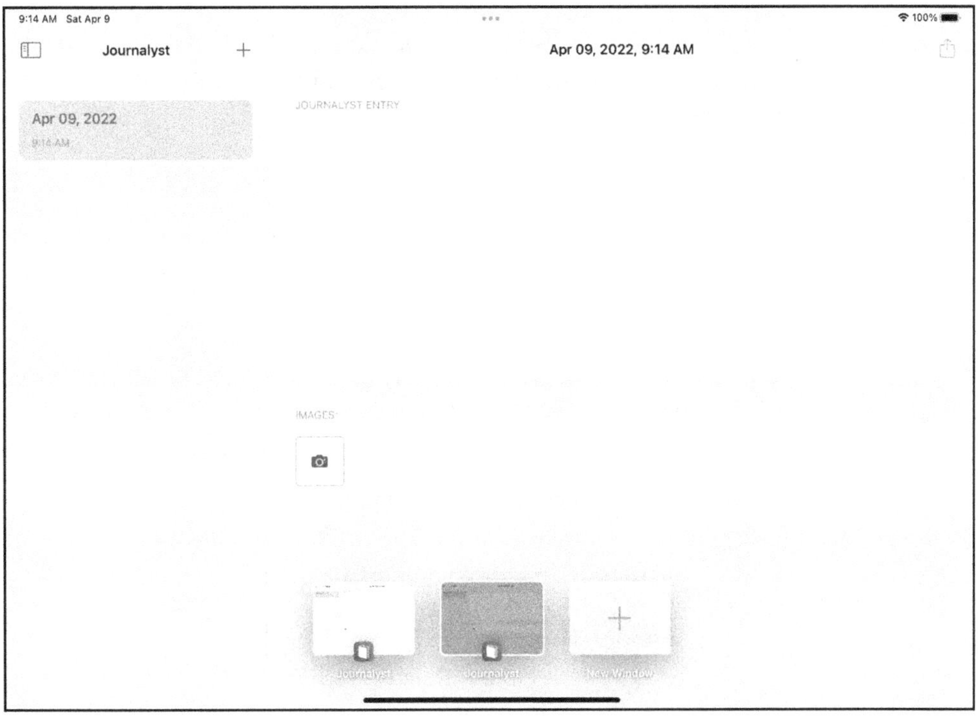

Multiple Journalyst windows.

Things are looking great, but if you start playing with the app across several windows, you might start to notice that a few things are off. In particular, try bringing up the app in two side-by-side windows by revealing the dock and dragging the app icon to the right edge. Once you have both windows in place, go back to the main table view controller and try adding some new entries in the left window. Gasp! The right window's entry list doesn't change in the slightest.

Well, that's certainly a day-wrecker, but no worries! You're about to learn why this problem occurs and, more importantly, how to fix it.

Improving the Standard Multi-Window Experience

Remember that when iOS creates a new scene for your app, it's instantiating an entirely new and parallel instance of everything required to build your UI. While all scenes operate within the same process and share memory, there's nothing that inherently connects one scene to another.

Before you learn to resolve the data issue, introduced by moving to multi-window, you'll need to understand how the Journalyst app currently propagates data changes from its data layer to the UI layer, when a user adds an entry.

Open **MainTableViewController.swift** and look at the `addEntry` method:

```
@IBAction private func addEntry(_ sender: Any) {
  DataService.shared.addEntry(Entry())
  reloadSnapshot(animated: true)
}
```

The above method gets called whenever you tap the **Add** button on the entries list sidebar. There's nothing overly complex going on here; you persist the entry to an in-memory data store via `DataService.shared.addEntry` and then call `reloadSnapshot` to refresh the `UITableView` state.

Now, open **DataService.swift** and take a peek at its `addEntry` method:

```
func addEntry(_ entry: Entry) {
  entries.append(entry)
}
```

Again, nothing too crazy here. You're just adding the new entry to the data service's internal data structure (in this case, an array).

The following diagram shows the data flow within each app scene; it should help clarify where the issue lies.

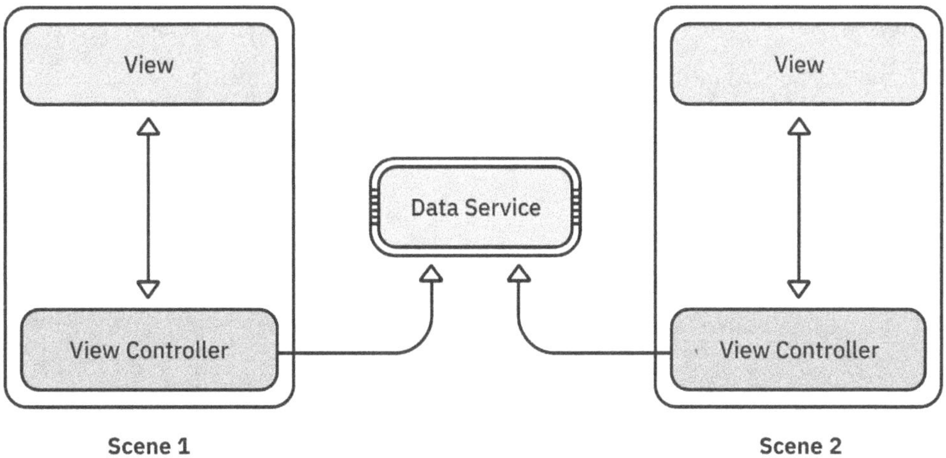

Multiple windows diagram.

Here, you see that you're dealing with two identical, but entirely disconnected stacks. Data flows between the view controller and the view only within each separate scene. Data only flows into the Data Service, but not out. The view controller in the first scene initiates the adding of the entry and triggers the table refresh only in its own instance of `MainTableViewController`. Meanwhile, over in the second scene, there's an entirely separate instance of `MainTableViewController` that's never notified of the data change, and thus never reflects it.

Now that the data issue is apparent, you'll write some code to fix it. One common way to connect disparate components in an iOS or Mac app is through the use of `Notifications` and `NotificationCenter`. Here, you're going to leverage notifications to ensure that data changes get communicated across all scenes.

Start by opening **DataService.swift** and adding the following code before the `DataService` class definition:

```
extension Notification.Name {
  static var JournalEntriesUpdated =
  Notification.Name(
    "com.yourcompany.Journalyst.EntriesUpdated"
  )
}
```

The above code adds a new notification type by extending `Notification.Name` and adding the property `JournalEntriesUpdated`. This notification will be issued every time the data in any scene changes so that other scenes can observe and respond accordingly.

Next, modify `addEntry` and `removeEntry` to look like the following:

```
func addEntry(_ entry: Entry) {
  entries.append(entry)
  // 1
  postUpdate()
}

func removeEntry(atIndex index: Int) {
  entries.remove(at: index)
  // 2
  postUpdate()
}
```

And add the `postUpdate` method below:

```
private func postUpdate() {
  // 3
  NotificationCenter.default.post(
    name: .JournalEntriesUpdated,
    object: nil
  )
}
```

Now, you're getting into some more meaty code, so take a moment to review what you did:

1. You call `postUpdate` to notify observers when the user adds new entries.
2. Next, you add the same `postUpdate` call to notify observers when the user removes entries.
3. Finally, you implement `postUpdate` by posting the notification you created earlier via `NotificationCenter`.

Great, now whenever the user adds or removes entries, this code will inform any observers of `JournalEntriesUpdated`. To close the loop, you'll need to subscribe to these updates in the appropriate places.

Open **MainTableViewController.swift** and start by removing the explicit calls to `reloadSnapshot` from `addEntry` and `tableView(_:trailingSwipeActionsConfigurationForRowAt:)` as follows:

```
@IBAction private func addEntry(_ sender: Any) {
  DataService.shared.addEntry(Entry())
}

override func tableView(
  _ tableView: UITableView,
  trailingSwipeActionsConfigurationForRowAt
  indexPath: IndexPath
) -> UISwipeActionsConfiguration? {

  let deleteAction = UIContextualAction(
    style: .destructive,
    title: "Delete"
  ) {_, _, _ in
    DataService.shared.removeEntry(atIndex: indexPath.row)
  }

  deleteAction.image = UIImage(systemName: "trash")
  return UISwipeActionsConfiguration(actions: [deleteAction])
}
```

You're about to drive UI updates by observing the data change notification you added, so you won't need to issue those updates explicitly anymore.

Next, add this code to the end of `viewDidLoad` to observe the data update notification.

```
// 1
NotificationCenter.default.addObserver(
  self,
  selector: #selector(handleEntriesUpdate),
  name: .JournalEntriesUpdated,
  object: nil
)
```

Then add `handleEntriesUpdate` to handle the change as follows:

```
@objc func handleEntriesUpdate() {
  // 2
  reloadSnapshot(animated: false)
}
```

The above code adds the `MainTableViewController` as an observer. Specifically:

1. First, you subscribe to the `JournalEntriesUpdated` notification to receive updates whenever data changes.
2. Then, you call `reloadSnapshot(animated:)` whenever the notification handler triggers, to update the view.

Build and run, bring up the dock, and drag to create a side-by-side view once again. Go back to main screen. Tap the **Add** button in either of the two scenes and watch in awe as the list in the other scene magically refreshes.

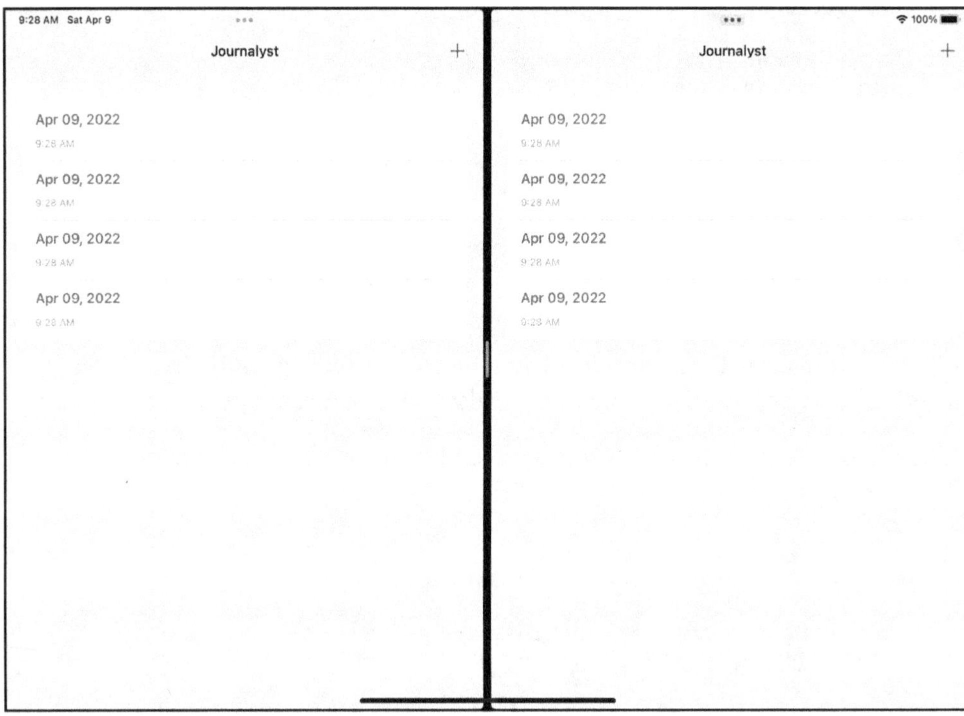

Add Entry reflected in multiple windows.

The app feels great now, so maybe you should go celebrate with a delicious dessert? Marzipan perhaps? Well, not so fast. There's still one more data issue lurking in your app that you'll need to address before kicking back with a treat.

With the app still running, enter some text on an entry in the first scene, then select a different entry. You'll notice that the cell for the entry updates with a preview of the text, but only in Scene 1.

To understand why this bug is happening, start by opening **EntryTableViewController.swift**. You'll notice this file includes the following delegate protocol declaration:

```
protocol EntryTableViewControllerDelegate: AnyObject {
  func entryTableViewController(
    _ controller: EntryTableViewController,
    didUpdateEntry entry: Entry
  )
}
```

Look at `viewWillDisappear(_:)` in `EntryTableViewController`, you'll see that whenever this view controller disappears (leaves the screen), it notifies its delegate of the data change.

Open **MainTableViewController.swift** and look at the extension that implements `EntryTableViewControllerDelegate`:

```
extension MainTableViewController:
  EntryTableViewControllerDelegate {
  func entryTableViewController(
    _ controller: EntryTableViewController,
    didUpdateEntry entry: Entry
  ) {
    reloadSnapshot(animated: false)
  }
}
```

In short, whenever the user updates an entry, the table view issues a snapshot reload to ensure the list reflects the latest data. But once again, recall that changes specific to a given view controller, or a group of view controller instances in one scene, do not carry over to instances in other scenes.

So how might you fix this issue? Yup, the same way you fixed the first data problem: By using notifications.

First things first, get rid of all references to `EntryTableViewControllerDelegate`, including the extension and assignments in `MainTableViewController` and the declaration and usages in **EntryTableViewController.swift**.

Next, open **DataService.swift** and change the `updateEntry(_:)` method to look like this:

```
func updateEntry(_ entry: Entry) {
  // 1
  var hasChanges = false
  entries = entries.map { item -> Entry in
    if item.id == entry.id && item != entry {
      // 2
      hasChanges = true
      return entry
    } else {
      return item
    }
  }
  // 3
  if hasChanges {
    postUpdate()
  }
}
```

Reviewing the changes you made:

1. First, you add a flag to track whether the provided entry represents an update or not.
2. You then track when it detects an entry change by assigning a value to `hasChanges`.
3. Finally, if it did detect a data change, you issue a data change notification by calling `postUpdate`.

Since you are already handling the data change notification in `MainTableViewController`, that's all you have to do.

Build and run, one more time. Go back to main screen on both sides. Try changing an entry in one scene while watching the list in the second scene. As soon as you leave the entry screen on **Scene 1**, you'll see the list preview for that entry updated in **Scene 2**.

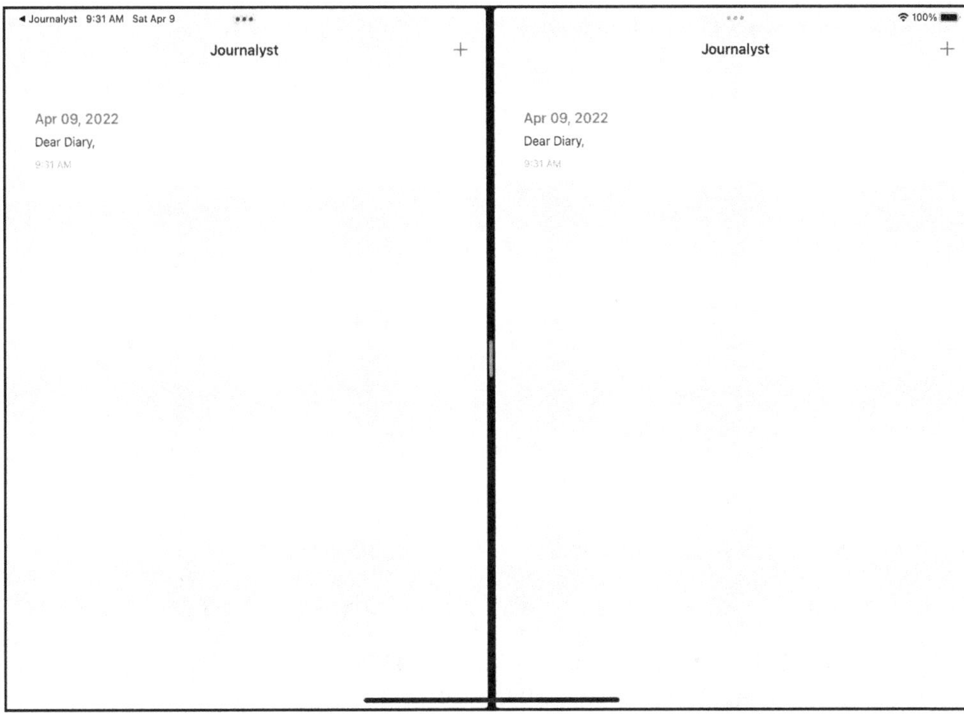

Entry details updated in Scene 1 reflects in Scene 2.

Nicely done! Your Journalyst app now has solid support for basic multi-windowing. But you're not one to settle for "basic", so you're going to implement one more feature that will take the scene support in this app to the next level.

Adding Custom Drag Behavior to Create a New Window

Recall that when you explored multi-window support in the Messages app at the beginning of this chapter, you tried out a custom mechanism for spawning new scenes. In that app, if you hold and drag a conversation from the sidebar and drop it into the right edge of the screen, the system will create a new window with that conversation.

If you thought that interaction was pretty nifty, then you're in luck, because you're about to add it to Journalyst. When you're done, you'll be able to similarly hold, drag and drop a journal entry from the sidebar to start a new window with that entry's detail.

Start by opening **Entry.swift** and adding the following extension:

```
extension Entry {
  // 1
  static let OpenDetailActivityType
    = "com.yourcompany.EntryOpenDetailActivityType"
  static let OpenDetailIdKey = "entryID"
  // 2
  var openDetailUserActivity: NSUserActivity {
    // 3
    let userActivity = NSUserActivity(
      activityType: Entry.OpenDetailActivityType
    )
    // 4
    userActivity.userInfo = [Entry.OpenDetailIdKey: id]
    return userActivity
  }
}
```

The above code adds some functionality to `Entry` around `NSUserActivity`:

1. First, you declare several static properties for various identifiers you'll use later.
2. Next, you declare a computed property for an `NSUserActivity` that represents opening the detail screen for a journal entry.
3. You initialize the activity with the unique identifier you declared earlier.
4. Finally, you store the ID for the journal entry you want to show when you spawn a new window via this activity in `userInfo`.

Next, you need to add the drag behavior that initiates the interaction, so open **MainTableViewController.swift** and add the following extension:

```
extension MainTableViewController: UITableViewDragDelegate {
  // 1
  func tableView(
    _ tableView: UITableView,
    itemsForBeginning session: UIDragSession,
    at indexPath: IndexPath
  ) -> [UIDragItem] {
    // 2
    let entry = DataService.shared.allEntries[indexPath.row]
    let userActivity = entry.openDetailUserActivity
```

```
    // 3
    let itemProvider = NSItemProvider()
    itemProvider.registerObject(userActivity, visibility: .all)
    // 4
    let dragItem = UIDragItem(itemProvider: itemProvider)
    return [dragItem]
  }
}
```

The above code might look a bit unfamiliar, so here's a breakdown of what it does:

1. `UITableViewDragDelegate` gets called when a drag interaction begins and allows you to specify the content involved in the operation.
2. Here, you fetch the `Entry` object that the user has long-pressed on and use `entry.openDetailUserActivity` to obtain an `NSUserActivity` representative of that entry.
3. Next, you create an instance of `NSItemProvider` and register the user activity object.
4. Then you create a drag item with the item provider and return it. This will ultimately expose the user activity to the system when the user drags the entry to the edge of the screen.

Now, you'll need to declare `MainTableViewController` as the drag delegate for the table view. Add the following code to the end of `viewDidLoad` to accomplish this:

```
tableView.dragDelegate = self
```

The last thing you need to do to enable your custom drag window interaction is to handle the incoming user activity in the scene delegate. You do this by configuring the new scene based on the provided entry ID.

Open **SceneDelegate.swift** and replace the entire implementation with the following:

```
import UIKit

class SceneDelegate: UIResponder, UIWindowSceneDelegate {
  var window: UIWindow?
  func scene(
    _ scene: UIScene,
    willConnectTo session: UISceneSession,
    options connectionOptions: UIScene.ConnectionOptions
  ) {
    if let splitViewController = window?.rootViewController
      as? UISplitViewController {
```

```
      splitViewController.preferredDisplayMode =
      .oneBesideSecondary
    }
    // 1
    if let userActivity
      = connectionOptions.userActivities.first {
      // 2
      if !configure(window: window, with: userActivity) {
        print("Failed to restore from \(userActivity)")
      }
    }
  }

  func configure(
    window: UIWindow?,
    with activity: NSUserActivity
  ) -> Bool {
    // 3
    guard activity.activityType == Entry.OpenDetailActivityType,
      let entryID = activity.userInfo?[Entry.OpenDetailIdKey]
        as? String,
      let entry = DataService.shared.entry(forID: entryID),
      let entryDetailViewController
        = EntryTableViewController.loadFromStoryboard(),
      let splitViewController = window?.rootViewController
        as? UISplitViewController else {
      return false
    }

    // 4
    entryDetailViewController.entry = entry
    // 5
    let navController = UINavigationController(
      rootViewController: entryDetailViewController
    )
    splitViewController.showDetailViewController(
      navController,
      sender: self
    )
    return true
  }
}
```

That's quite a lot of code, so walk through it, step by step:

1. First, you check the `connectionOptions` for the presence of user activity. In the previous section, you configured the drag interaction to expose an `NSUserActivity` containing information about the target journal entry; here, you'll receive this activity.

2. Next, you call `configure`, passing the window and the user activity, and log a message in the case of failure.
3. Inside `configure`, you start by ensuring that the activity type matches `Entry.OpenDetailActivityType`. You then obtain the entry object, instantiate an instance of `EntryTableViewController` for displaying the entry and obtain a reference to the main split view controller.
4. You now configure the entry view controller to display the obtained entry object.
5. Lastly, you wrap the entry view controller in a navigation controller and present the navigation controller as the split view controller's detail content.

Now, when you drag and drop an entry on the edge of the screen, the system will relay your user activity, housed in the drag item, to the scene delegate. There, it will configure and present the entry detail immediately.

Go ahead and build and run to give it a try.

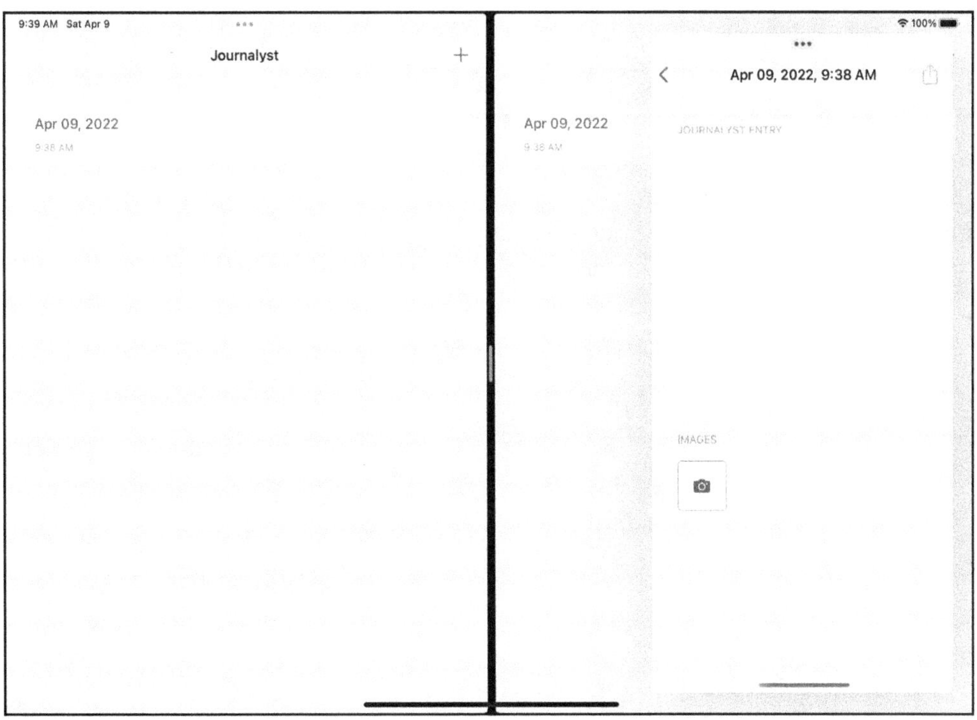

Drag and drop an entry.

Trying it on the Mac

The hard work you put in to make your app support multi-window for iPad has an added bonus: It'll work seamlessly when you run the app on Mac. Open Xcode, select the **My Mac** destination and set your team. Then build and run.

Once the app is running, just press **Command** + **N** and boom!

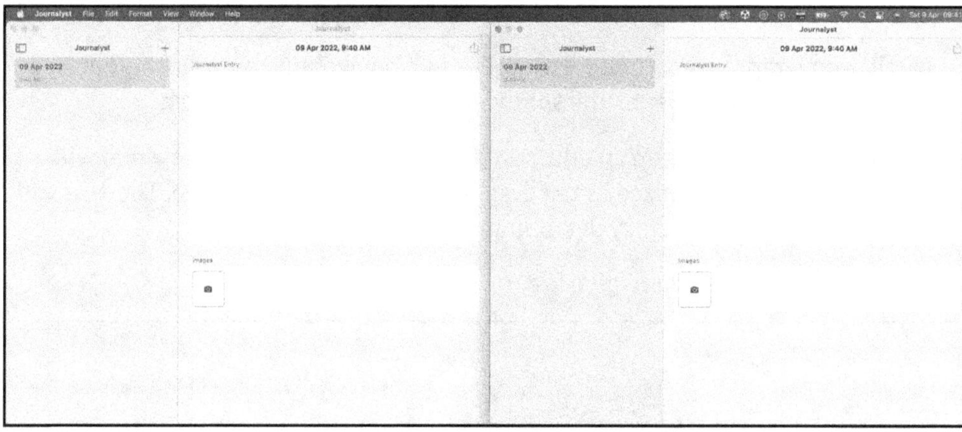

Multiple windows running on the Mac.

In a later chapter, you'll learn how to add a menu item for spawning a new window, much like you'd find in many Mac apps. But for now, pat yourself on the back and maybe indulge in that tasty dessert you promised yourself earlier.

Key Points

- Multi-window is a powerful way to be more productive on iPad and users expect to see it on Mac.
- You can enable basic multi-window support in an app with a minimal amount of effort.
- Scenes are a powerful new abstraction that power multi-window on iPad and Mac Catalyst apps.
- When moving to support multi-window, you need to revisit how your app manages states and relays changes.
- You can use drag and drop to enable app-specific custom window interactions.

Where to Go From Here?

In this chapter, you learned what multi-window support is, why you might want to incorporate it into your app, and how to do just that. You also learned about some of the issues that you might introduce when adopting scenes and how to resolve them. Finally, you learned how to go beyond the OS-provided multi-window support by adding a custom window interaction using drag and `NSUserActivity`.

In the next chapter, you'll learn how to add powerful **contextual menus** to your app so that it's more efficient on iPad and feels even more at home on the Mac.

Chapter 5: Adding Some Context

By Nick Bonatsakis and Andy Pereira

In the previous chapter, you added multi-window support to your app using scenes.

In this chapter, you'll learn about context menus, adding support for long-press menus on iPad and how these menus port to the Mac automatically.

By the end of this chapter, you'll learn:

- What contextual menus are and how they enhance your app's experience.
- How to add basic support for context interactions.
- How to implement basic menu items.
- How to make menu items dynamic.
- How to implement hierarchical menus.

Ready to experience the exciting world of contextual menus? Great! It's time to get started.

Introducing Context Menus

You might want to jump right in and start coding, but before you get started, you'll need some context around the topic at hand (pun certainly intended). Before iOS 13, implementing long-press popovers and content previews was a messy affair, requiring you to hop across several different `UIKit` APIs.

Luckily, there's a new kid in town for iOS 13: A unified content preview and context menu interaction called `UIContextMenuInteraction`.

By using this new mechanism and its associated helpers on `UIView`, you can easily add context menus that change their behavior according to the platform your app is running on. On iPad, you trigger context menus with a long-press gesture. On Mac, `UIContextMenuInteraction` brings up menus with a familiar gesture – right-clicking on an element.

Look at this feature in action in the Shortcuts app for iPad. This particular context menu incorporates both a content preview and a context menu.

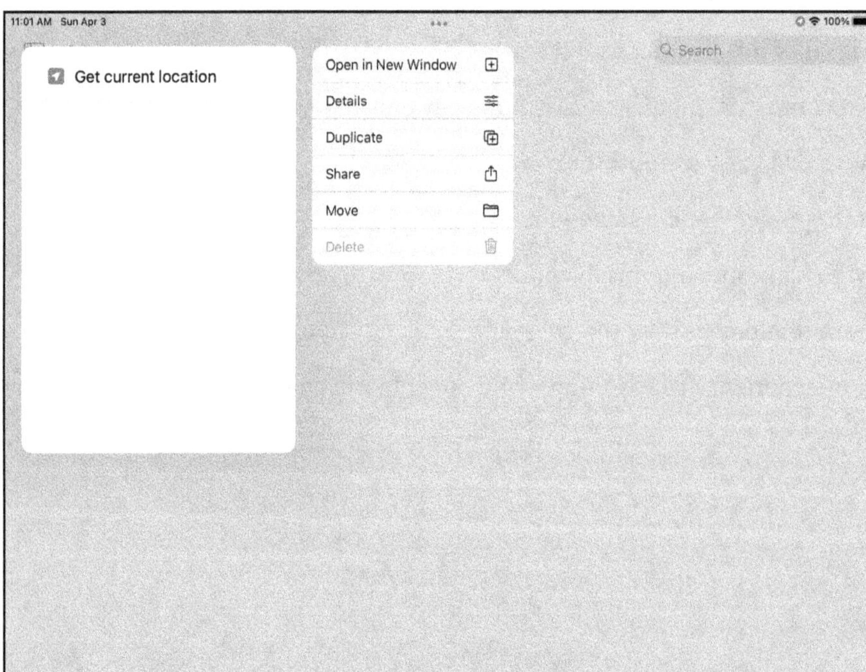

Context menu example.

Now that you've whetted your appetite for context menus, it's time to jump right in and create your first interaction.

Adding a Context Interaction

The most sensible place to enable the Journalyst app's context menus is in the sidebar. Why? Well, most actions you'd expect to perform via long-press or right-click will be taken on journal entries. Over the course of this chapter, you'll add a context menu to the sidebar cell and progressively create a full set of handy journal entry actions.

Open the starter project of this chapter and go to **MainTableViewController.swift**. In `diaryDataSource`, add the following right before the `return` statement:

```
let contextInteraction
  = UIContextMenuInteraction(delegate: self)
cell?.addInteraction(contextInteraction)
```

In the above code, you create a new instance of `UIContextMenuInteraction`, passing `self` as the delegate. You'll implement the delegate method in the next step. Then you associate this interaction with the table view cell by calling `addInteraction`, which is a method common to all `UIView` subclasses.

Now, add the following to the end of the file:

```
extension MainTableViewController:
  UIContextMenuInteractionDelegate {
  func contextMenuInteraction(
    _ interaction: UIContextMenuInteraction,
    configurationForMenuAtLocation location: CGPoint
  ) -> UIContextMenuConfiguration? {
    // 1
    let locationInTableView =
      interaction.location(in: tableView)
    // 2
    guard let indexPath = tableView
      .indexPathForRow(at: locationInTableView)
    else { return nil }
    // 3
    let entry = DataService.shared.allEntries[indexPath.row]
    // 4
    return UIContextMenuConfiguration(
      identifier: nil,
      previewProvider: nil
    ) { _ -> UIMenu? in
        // 5
        var rootChildren: [UIMenuElement] = []
        // 6
        let noOpAction = self.createNoOpAction()
        // 7
        rootChildren.append(noOpAction)
```

```
        // 8
        let menu = UIMenu(
          title: "", image: nil,
          identifier: nil, options: [],
          children: rootChildren
        )
        return menu
    }
  }
}
```

There's a decent amount of code here, look at it, step-by-step:

1. When the system calls this delegate method, the `CGPoint` it provides is in the coordinate space of the view that the user interacted with directly – in this case, the `UITableViewCell` instance. To obtain the index path of the cell, you need the point in terms of the table view's coordinate space, so the first thing you do is obtain that information via the `location(in:)` method of the `interaction` instance.

2. Next, armed with the target coordinate in the table view's coordinate space, you attempt to grab the index path for the cell that the user interacted with and bail if it's not found. Returning `nil` from this method indicates to the system that it shouldn't activate a context menu for the given interaction.

3. Next, you fetch the entry for the given cell by using the index path you obtained in step 2. You'll need the entry object to perform actions on it in the next parts of this chapter.

4. Next, you return an instance of `UIContextMenuConfiguration`. Passing `nil` as an identifier will cause the system to generate a unique ID automatically. You also pass `nil` for `previewProvider` since you are only going to be adding a menu, not a content preview. The closure here returns the `UIMenu` instance that implements the menu.

5. Next, you create a mutable array to house the list of top-level menu items. A `UIMenu` consists of one or more instances of `UIMenuElement` subclasses.

6. Then, you call a method that returns `UIAction` .

7. Then, you add the action to the list of root elements.

8. Finally, you create the root `UIMenu`, passing it an empty title and the root elements list as the children.

Next, add the following method to the same extension:

```
// 1
func createNoOpAction() -> UIAction {
  let noOpAction = UIAction(
    title: "Do Nothing",
    image: nil,
    identifier: nil,
    discoverabilityTitle: nil,
    attributes: [],
    state: .off
  ) { _ in
    // Do nothing
  }
  return noOpAction
}
```

1. Here, you create a method returning `UIAction`, which is a subclass of `UIMenuElement`. This action has a bare-bones configuration with just a title. The trailing block in the initializer is called when the user activates the action, for instance, the user clicks or taps the menu item. In this case, it does nothing.

Build and run, then long-press on a journal entry in the sidebar. You see the following:

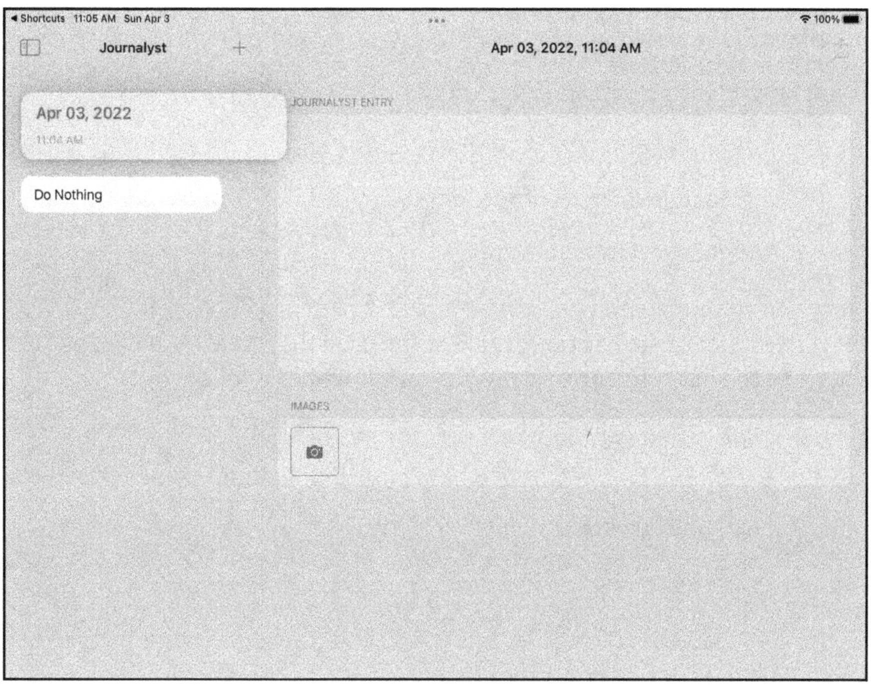

Basic context menu.

Sweet! Your first context menu. It's not much to look at yet, and it doesn't do anything particularly useful. But you're about to change that...

Opening a New Window

In the previous chapter, you learned about scenes and how they support multi-window configurations in your apps. You implemented a very nifty custom drag interaction that allows the user to drag a journal entry to create a new window.

An app with great UX often offers the same action via several paths, so that a user is more likely to discover and learn how to perform that action. Context menus are a great place to offer these alternate paths, as users are familiar with long-pressing and right-clicking. Wouldn't it be neat to add a menu action for opening an entry in a new window? Why, yes; yes, it would.

First, remove `createNoOpAction` that you created. Add a new method as follows:

```
func addOpenNewWindowAction(entry: Entry) -> UIAction {
  // 1
  let openInNewWindowAction = UIAction(
    title: "Open in New Window",
    image: UIImage(systemName: "uiwindow.split.2x1"),
    identifier: nil,
    discoverabilityTitle: nil,
    attributes: [],
    state: .off
  ) { _ in
    // 2
    self.createNewWindow(for: entry)
  }
  return openInNewWindowAction
}
```

Back in `contextMenuInteraction`, remove the code that creates the `noOpAction` and adds it to the `rootChildren` array. Replace it with the following:

```
let openInNewWindowAction =
  self.addOpenNewWindowAction(entry: entry)
// 3
rootChildren.append(openInNewWindowAction)
```

The code is similar to the action you added previously, but there are a few things that are different. Here's some more detail about what's going on:

1. As before, you create a new instance of `UIAction`. The most notable difference here is that you pass `UIImage(systemName: "uiwindow.split.2x1")` as the image parameter. This is how you reference an icon from the **SF Symbols** package that Apple introduced in iOS 13.
2. Next, instead of an empty block, you call a method, `createNewWindow(for:)`, that will do the work of creating a new window and passing it the entry.
3. Finally, as before, you add the action to the `rootChildren` array for inclusion in the root menu.

Next, go ahead and implement `createNewWindow(for:)` as follows:

```
func createNewWindow(for entry: Entry) {
  UIApplication.shared.requestSceneSessionActivation(
    nil,
    userActivity: entry.openDetailUserActivity,
    options: .none,
    errorHandler: nil
  )
}
```

Just one line of code is all it takes to get this one done. You call `requestSceneSessionActivation(_:userActivity:options:errorHandler:)` on the shared `UIApplication`, passing it `entry.openDetailUserActivity`, to preconfigure the new window and display the provided entry.

Build and run to see the fruits of your labor. Tap **Open in New Window** to see this action work in all its glory.

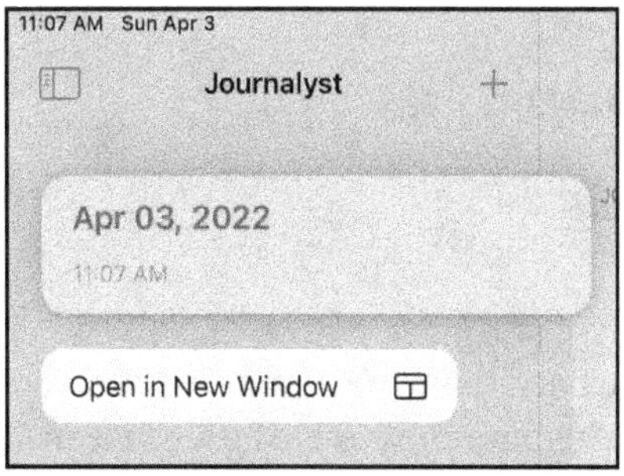

Open in New Window context menu.

Creating a New Entry

Oftentimes, apps that manage lists of data include a menu action that lets its users create a new instance of a given entity. Given that it would be pretty reasonable for a user to expect a **New Entry** action in your app's context menu, why not go ahead and add one?

Start by adding the following:

```
func addNewEntryAction(entry: Entry) -> UIAction {
  let newEntryAction = UIAction(
    title: "New Entry",
    image: UIImage(systemName: "square.and.pencil"),
    identifier: nil,
    discoverabilityTitle: nil,
    attributes: [],
    state: .off
  ) { _ in
    self.createEntry()
  }
  return newEntryAction
}
```

Add the following to `contextMenuInteraction`, after you append `openInNewWindowAction`:

```
let newEntryAction = self.addNewEntryAction(entry: entry)
rootChildren.append(newEntryAction)
```

This code is similar to the code you used to add the **Open in New Window** action. It configures the action, implements a handler, calls a method, `createEntry`, to do the work of creating the new entry, then finally adds the action to the list of root menu children.

To finish, implement `createEntry` as follows:

```
func createEntry() {
  DataService.shared.addEntry(Entry())
}
```

Nothing too crazy here, just another one-liner, this time creating a new entry via the `DataService` class. Since the data flow is tied together using `NotificationCenter`, that's all you need to do to make a new entry and show it in the UI.

Build and run once more, then check out the context menu again. You are now able to create new entries in a snap.

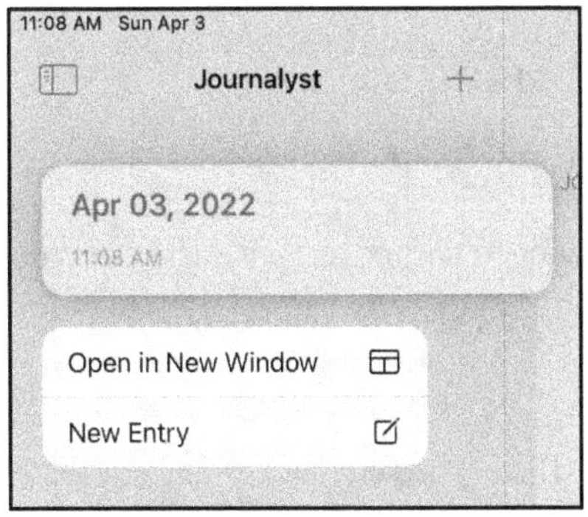

New Entry context menu.

Adding an Image to an Entry

Another action that would be pretty useful to have in the context menu for journal entries is the ability to directly add images. Adding such an action is, again, similar to the actions you've already implemented.

Start by once again adding the following:

```
func addImageAction(entry: Entry, indexPath: IndexPath)
  -> UIAction {
  let addImageAction = UIAction(
    title: "Add Image",
    image: UIImage(systemName: "photo"),
    identifier: nil,
    discoverabilityTitle: nil,
    attributes: [],
    state: .off
  ) { _ in
    self.addImage(to: entry, indexPath: indexPath)
  }
  return addImageAction
}
```

Then, add the following to `contextMenuInteraction`, after you append `newEntryAction`:

```
let addImageAction = self.addImageAction(
  entry: entry, indexPath: indexPath
)
rootChildren.append(addImageAction)
```

Again, there's nothing new here compared with the previous few actions, so jump right into implementing `addImage(to:indexPath:)` as follows:

```
func addImage(to entry: Entry, indexPath: IndexPath) {
  // 1
  let cell = tableView.cellForRow(at: indexPath)
  // 2
  photoPicker.present(
    in: self,
    sourceView: cell
  ) { image, _ in
    // 3
    if let image = image {
      var newEntry = entry
      newEntry.images.append(image)
      DataService.shared.updateEntry(newEntry)
    }
  }
}
```

The above code is a bit more involved than the previous few action handlers, so reviewing it in detail:

1. You obtain a reference to the `UITableViewCell` that activated the interaction.
2. Next, you call `present` on `PhotoPicker` to launch an action sheet that allows the user to select an image from either their library or the camera, if it's available. You pass `UITableViewCell` here so that when the app runs on iPad and Mac, the action sheet is anchored to that element.
3. Finally, if the user selects an image, you handle it by creating a mutable copy of the entry, adding the image to it and then persisting the change to the data service.

Build and run, then activate the menu again and you'll find that you can now add images to a journal entry directly from the sidebar.

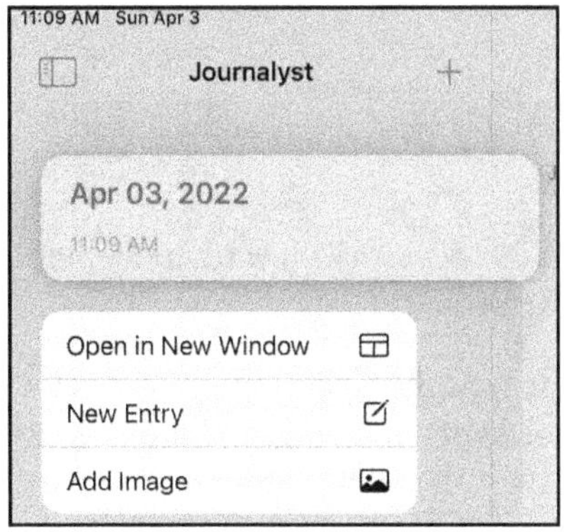

Add Image context menu.

Add an Entry to Favorites

The next menu action you'll implement allows a user to add and remove a journal entry as a favorite. At present, there isn't a way to filter by favorite entries. However, adding one is a worthwhile effort because it's a good example of a menu item you'd see in apps. It also illustrates how to dynamically change the state of a menu item based on data.

Before you add the menu item, you'll need to tweak the journal entry model and the UI associated with it to support favorites. First, open **Entry.swift** and add the following property to the struct:

```
var isFavorite = false
```

Then change the implementation of == to incorporate the new property as follows:

```
static func == (lhs: Entry, rhs: Entry) -> Bool {
  return lhs.dateCreated == rhs.dateCreated &&
    lhs.log ?? "" == rhs.log ?? "" &&
    lhs.images == rhs.images &&
    lhs.isFavorite == rhs.isFavorite
}
```

Finally, you'll want to add a visual indicator to the entry cells so your users can see at a glance if an entry is a favorite. Open **EntryTableViewCell.swift** and add the following to the `didSet` block on `entry`:

```
accessoryView = entry.isFavorite
  ? UIImageView(image: UIImage(systemName: "star.fill"))
  : nil
```

The above code sets the cell's accessory view to an SF Symbols star icon if the entry is a favorite; otherwise, it's set to `nil`.

You're now ready to add the new menu action. Jump back to **MainTableViewController.swift** and add the following to `UIContextMenuInteractionDelegate`

```
func addFavoriteAction(entry: Entry) -> UIAction {
  // 1
  let favoriteTitle
    = entry.isFavorite ? "Remove from Favorites" : "Add to
Favorites"
  // 2
  let favoriteImageName
    = entry.isFavorite ? "star.slash" : "star"
  // 3
  let favoriteAction = UIAction(
    title: favoriteTitle,
    image: UIImage(systemName: favoriteImageName),
    identifier: nil,
    discoverabilityTitle: nil,
    attributes: [],
    state: .off
  ) { _ in self.toggleFavorite(for: entry)
  }
  return favoriteAction
}
```

Then, add the following to `contextMenuInteraction`, after you append `addImageAction`:

```
let favoriteAction = self.addFavoriteAction(entry: entry)
// 4
rootChildren.append(favoriteAction)
```

Here's what this code is doing:

1. First, you create a title variable that prompts the user to "Add to Favorites" if the entry is not a favorite, or "Remove from Favorites" if it already is.
2. You create a variable to represent the icon you want to use: A star if the action is "Add to Favorites" or a star with a slash through it for the "Remove from Favorites" action.
3. Now, you create the menu action, passing it the variables you defined and calling `toggleFavorite` in the handler.
4. Finally, as always, you add the action to the root children array for inclusion in the menu.

To finish up this action, implement `toggleFavorite` like so:

```
func toggleFavorite(for entry: Entry) {
  var newEntry = entry
  newEntry.isFavorite.toggle()
  DataService.shared.updateEntry(newEntry)
}
```

In the above code, you make a mutable copy of the provided entry, toggle the `isFavorite` property and persist the change to the data service.

Build and run, then bring up the context menu again. Toggle the favorite state of an entry and you see both the entry cell and the menu option change.

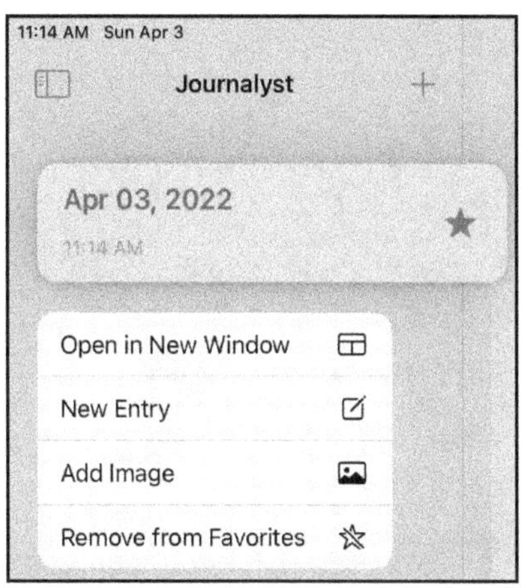

Add to Favorites or Remove from Favourites context menu.

Sharing an Entry

Your journal entry context menu is really starting to take shape now, but you're not done yet. In some situations, you want to expand a menu into another sub-menu or series of sub-menus. Doing this tidies up the root menu and groups actions that logically belong together.

To learn how to add one of these nested menus, you're going to add a **Share** menu item that triggers a sub-menu with several share options.

Still inside **MainTableViewController.swift**, add the following to `UIContextMenuInteractionDelegate`:

```
func addShareMenu(entry: Entry, indexPath: IndexPath)
  -> UIMenu {
  // 1
  let copyAction = UIAction(
    title: "Copy",
    image: UIImage(systemName: "doc.on.doc"),
    identifier: nil,
    discoverabilityTitle: nil,
    attributes: [],
    state: .off
  ) { _ in self.copy(contentsOf: entry) }
  // 2
  let moreAction = UIAction(
    title: "More",
    image: UIImage(systemName: "ellipsis"),
    identifier: nil,
    discoverabilityTitle: nil,
    attributes: [],
    state: .off
  ) { _ in self.share(entry, at: indexPath) }
  // 3
  let shareMenu = UIMenu(
    title: "Share",
    image: UIImage(systemName: "square.and.arrow.up"),
    identifier: nil,
    options: [],
    children: [copyAction, moreAction]
  )
  return shareMenu
}
```

Then, add the following to `contextMenuInteraction`, after you append `favoriteAction`:

```
let shareMenu
  = self.addShareMenu(entry: entry, indexPath: indexPath)
```

```
// 4
rootChildren.append(shareMenu)
```

This code looks similar to the code for creating a regular menu action. Here's a detailed breakdown of what it does:

1. First, you create a menu action to copy the contents of an entry. This is the first menu item for the sub-menu.
2. Next, you create the second sub-menu action, a menu item that brings up the system share sheet for more options.
3. You then create the share menu for inclusion in the root menu, passing the two sub-menu actions as children.
4. Finally, you add the share menu to the root children array so that it gets included in the root menu.

Next, implement the two methods that do the work for the share sub-menu actions like this:

```
func copy(contentsOf entry: Entry) {
  guard entry.log != nil else { return }
  // 1
  UIPasteboard.general.string = entry.log
}

func share(_ entry: Entry, at indexPath: IndexPath) {
  // 2
  var items: [Any] = []
  if let log = entry.log {
    items.append(log)
  }
  if !entry.images.isEmpty {
    items.append(contentsOf: entry.images)
  }
  // 3
  let activityController = UIActivityViewController(
    activityItems: items,
    applicationActivities: nil)
  // 4
  guard
    let popoverController =
      activityController.popoverPresentationController,
    let cell = tableView.cellForRow(at: indexPath)
  else { return }
  popoverController.sourceView = cell
  popoverController.sourceRect = cell.bounds
  // 5
  present(
```

```
      activityController,
      animated: true,
      completion: nil
    )
  }
```

Taking the above code, step by step:

1. First, you implement `copy(contentsOf:)` by setting the system paste board's string to the journal entry text.
2. You implement `share(_:at:)` by first declaring an array for the activity items and then populating the array with the entry text and images.
3. Now, you create a new instance of `UIActivityViewController` with the activity items.
4. You then configure the activity view controller's presentation to anchor on the relevant cell if it's running on larger-screen platforms.
5. Finally, you present the share sheet activity as you would any other view controller.

Build and run yet again and you'll find a new **Share** menu item. Tap the menu item to bring up the sub-menu as below.

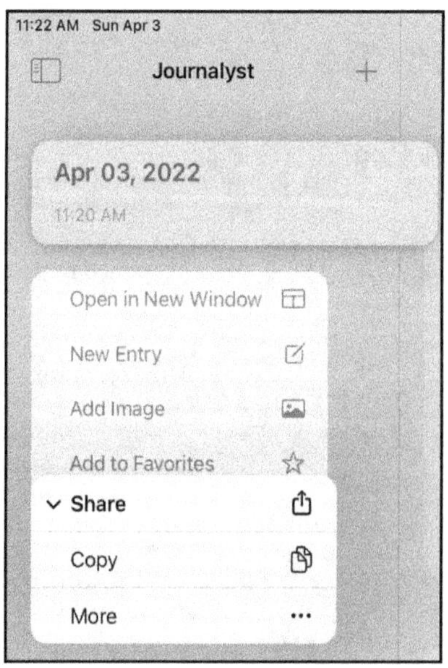

Share context menu.

Deleting an Entry

There's just one more action to go before you have a fully-armed and operational context menu. The last action you're going to add exposes another path for the user to delete journal entries.

Continuing in **MainTableViewController.swift**, add the following to `UIContextMenuInteractionDelegate`:

```
func addDeleteAction(indexPath: IndexPath) -> UIAction {
  let deleteAction = UIAction(
    title: "Delete",
    image: UIImage(systemName: "trash"),
    identifier: nil,
    discoverabilityTitle: nil,
    attributes: .destructive,
    state: .off
  ) { _ in self.removeEntry(at: indexPath) }
  return deleteAction
}
```

Then, add the following to `contextMenuInteraction`, after you append `shareMenu`:

```
let deleteAction = self.addDeleteAction(indexPath: indexPath)
rootChildren.append(deleteAction)
```

This code's almost identical to all the other menu actions you've implemented, but there's one difference worth noting: You pass `.destructive` as an attribute. This will give the menu title and icon a red color and clearly indicate to the user that this action is destructive and potentially dangerous.

Now, add the following to delete the entry when the user activates this menu action:

```
func removeEntry(at indexPath: IndexPath) {
  DataService.shared.removeEntry(atIndex: indexPath.row)
}
```

There's nothing complicated about the above code, it just removes the entry via the data service. Once again, data changes will propagate to the UI via notifications, so this is all that's needed to implement this action.

Build and run one last time and you'll see the finished menu, complete with the ability to delete an entry.

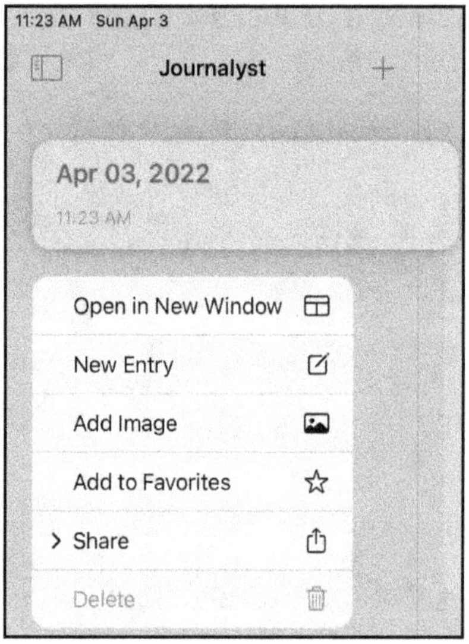

Delete context menu.

Trying it on macOS

Now that you've gone to the trouble of implementing context menus for iPad, you'll find that you get the same support for free when running on Mac.

On the Mac, the menus' look and feel automatically adjust to align with standard Mac menus. Your users will have a familiar experience.

Switch your run location to **My Mac** and build and run. Right-click a journal entry in the sidebar and explore the various actions and sub-menus.

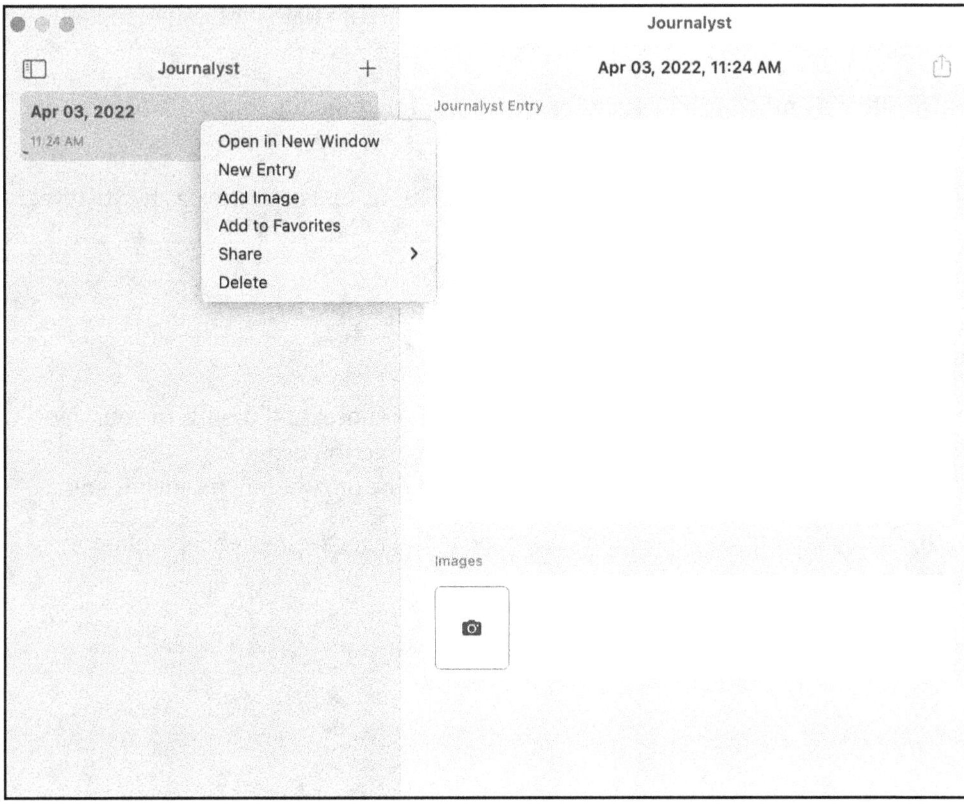

Context menu shown in Mac.

Key Points

- Context menus are a powerful way to expose alternate paths for common app actions.
- iOS offers a unified mechanism for creating context menus that work on iPad and Mac.
- Context menus can be as simple as singular actions or as complex as multi-level hierarchical menus.

Where to Go From Here?

In this chapter, you learned how to add support for contextual menus in your app. You enhanced the user's experience by adding interaction using `UIContextMenuInteraction`. You added not *just* one or two, but six such menus.

In the next chapter, you'll continue to enhance the user's experience, by adding **Keyboard shortcuts** to your app.

Chapter 6: The Keyboard

By Andy Pereira

The physical keyboard is something that has always been part of the personal computer experience. But, when iOS was introduced, it *almost* seemed like the idea of a software keyboard would take over. Luckily, for those that like a real keyboard, Apple introduced support not only for physical keyboards on iOS but keyboard shortcuts.

While keyboards shortcuts might go *overlooked* on iOS apps, macOS users expect them. In this chapter, you'll learn how to add shortcuts, what modifier keys are, and how to combine them with key combinations to quickly perform tasks in your app.

Getting Started

Open the starter project for this chapter. It's best if you can run this app on a physical iOS or iPadOS device, with a physical keyboard paired with the device. Using the simulator works too, but you *may* notice some performance issues.

First Responders

Before you add the shortcuts, it will help to understand a little bit about the responder chain and the first responder. `UIViewControllers`, `UIViews` and `UIApplication` are all classes that can receive and handle events, otherwise known as responder objects.

Since you can add keyboard shortcuts to any of these kinds of classes, you'll need to tell the system which responder is the class in the responder chain that will receive the keyboard event first. This is referred to as the first responder.

To start, open **RootSplitViewController.swift** and add the following:

```
override var canBecomeFirstResponder: Bool {
  true
}
```

Now, when you perform a keyboard shortcut, `RootSplitViewController` is able to receive and respond to it.

Adding the Commands

Keyboard shortcuts can be performed by *simply* pressing a single key on the keyboard or multiple keys. They can also be used in conjunction with modifiers keys, like **Command**, **Control** and **Option**. You're adding three shortcuts that each use modifier keys.

Open **RootSplitViewController.swift** and add the following:

```
@objc private func addEntry(sender: UIKeyCommand) {
}

@objc private func goToPrevious(sender: UIKeyCommand) {
}
```

```
@objc private func goToNext(sender: UIKeyCommand) {
}
```

For now, these don't do anything. You need them because keyboard shortcuts need actions to call. You'll come back to this later in the chapter.

Now you start adding key commands. Add the following in **RootSplitViewController.swift**:

```
override var keyCommands: [UIKeyCommand]? {
  let newKeyCommand = UIKeyCommand(
    input: "N",
    modifierFlags: .control,
    action: #selector(addEntry(sender:))
  )
  newKeyCommand.discoverabilityTitle = "Add Entry"
  return [newKeyCommand]
}
```

Here, you've added a key command for adding a new entry. It's important to know what's happening:

- `input`: This is the actual key that will trigger the action to be called.
- `modifierFlags`: In this example, you've added `.control`, which means your shortcut will be performed by pressing **Control-N**.
- `action`: This is the method called when the shortcut is performed.
- `discoverabilityTitle`: Holding down **Command** shows the Discoverability window or layer. It lists all the keyboard shortcuts available in the current application. Adding the `discoverabilityTitle` is required to list the shortcut in the Discoverability window.

Overriding `keyCommands` is how you inform the responder chain what key commands the current responder supports. It is important to note that the system reserves certain key commands for itself, which you *may not* want to override. For example: Cut, Copy and Paste's key combinations are reserved for the system and you *may not* want to change these for yourself. Because **Command-N** is *reserved* for opening a new window, you *use* the modifier to make **Control-N** create the entry.

> **Note**: `wantsPriorityOverSystemBehavior` is `UIKeyCommand`'s new property, introduced in iOS 15. This property is `false` by default. When set to `true`, it prioritizes key commands over text input or focus movements.

Build and run, and hold down **Command** to make the Discoverability window appear.

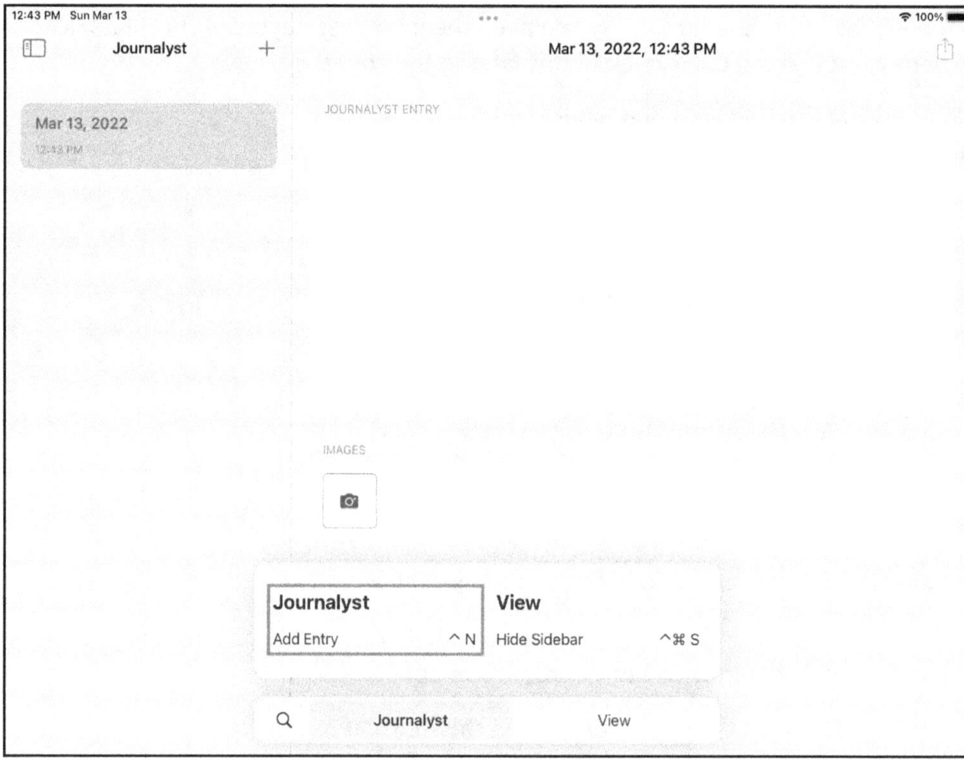

Discoverability window appears.

If you are having trouble with keyboard shortcuts within the simulator, you may need to use the **Capture Keyboard** functionality. You can select this in the toolbar of your iPad simulator, as shown below:

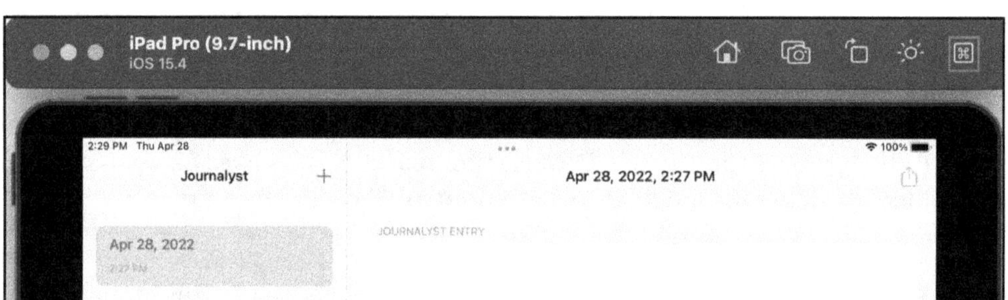

Capture Keyboard in iPad simulator.

To exit keyboard capture mode, you can select the button again, or press **Escape**.

> **Note**: When you run on an iPad simulator, because of the way the app is designed, it's best to work on this chapter with simulator in **Landscape** orientation.

To get the application to add an entry when using the key combination, add this line to `addEntry`:

```
DataService.shared.addEntry(Entry())
```

Build and run, and then press **Control-N**. You now see a new entry shows in the list.

To set the remaining key commands, replace `keyCommands` with the following:

```
override var keyCommands: [UIKeyCommand]? {
  let newKeyCommand = UIKeyCommand(
    input: "N",
    modifierFlags: .control,
    action: #selector(addEntry(sender:))
  )
  newKeyCommand.discoverabilityTitle = "Add Entry"
  let upKeyCommand = UIKeyCommand(
    input: "[",
    modifierFlags: [.command, .shift],
    action: #selector(goToPrevious(sender:))
  )
  upKeyCommand.discoverabilityTitle = "Previous Entry"
  let downKeyCommand = UIKeyCommand(
    input: "]",
    modifierFlags: [.command, .shift],
    action: #selector(goToNext(sender:))
  )
  downKeyCommand.discoverabilityTitle = "Next Entry"
  return [newKeyCommand, upKeyCommand, downKeyCommand]
}
```

The final two key commands allows the user to select the previous or next entry in the entry list. While almost the same as `newKeyCommand`, these take multiple modifier keys to perform. It requires **Command-Shift-[** to be pressed to go back in the list, and **Command-Shift-]** to move forward.

While you can decide which modifiers are used, remember to keep the combinations simple enough for your user to remember.

Build and run, and hold down **Command** to show the Discoverability window. You now see all three of your keyboard shortcuts:

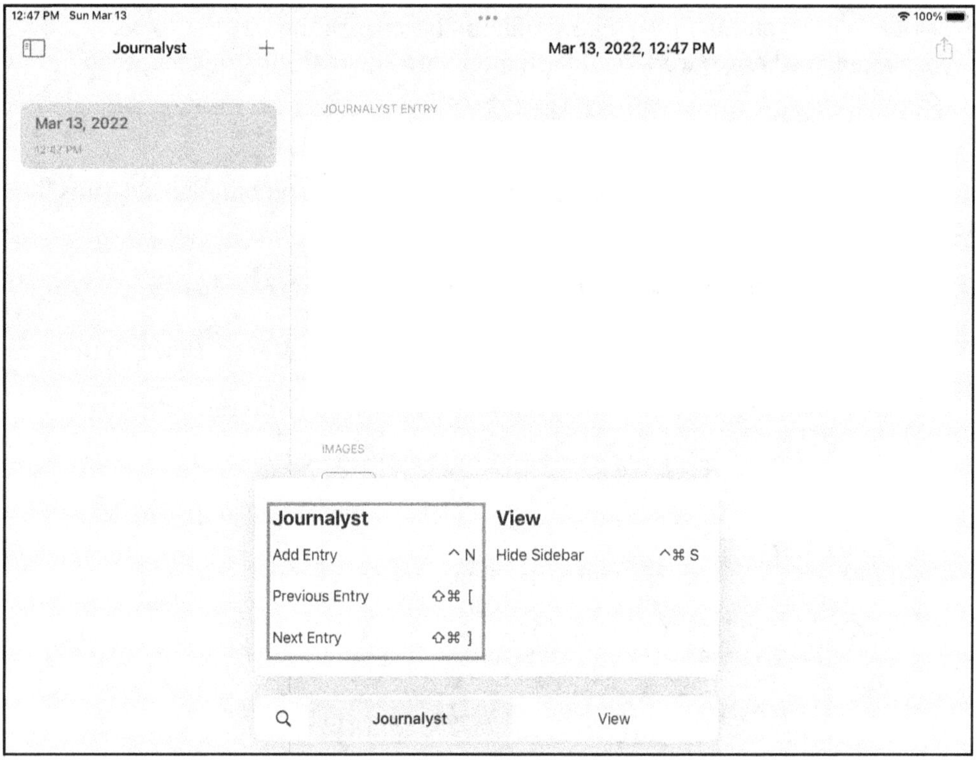

All shortcuts shown in Discoverability window.

Now, your last step is to actually do something when the keys are pressed. Still continuing in **RootSplitViewController.swift**, add this code to `goToPrevious(sender:)`:

```
guard let navigationController =
  viewControllers.first as? UINavigationController,
  let mainTableViewController =
  navigationController.topViewController
    as? MainTableViewController else { return }
mainTableViewController.goToPrevious()
```

The code above calls main view controller's method to go the previous entry in the list.

And add this code to `goToNext(sender:)`:

```
guard let navigationController =
```

```
    viewControllers.first as? UINavigationController,
    let mainTableViewController =
    navigationController.topViewController
      as? MainTableViewController else { return }
  mainTableViewController.goToNext()
```

Similarly, you can now go to the next entry in main table view controller's list.

Now, open **MainTableViewController.swift**, and add the following:

```
func goToPrevious() {
  guard let index = indexOfCurrentEntry(),
    index > 0 else { return }
  let previousIndex = index - 1
  let indexPath = IndexPath(
    row: previousIndex,
    section: 0
  )
  tableView.selectRow(
    at: indexPath,
    animated: false,
    scrollPosition: .middle
  )
  performSegue(
    withIdentifier: "ShowEntrySegue",
    sender: tableView.cellForRow(at: indexPath)
  )
}

func goToNext() {
  guard let index = indexOfCurrentEntry(),
    index < DataService.shared.allEntries.count - 1
  else { return }
  let nextIndex = index + 1
  let indexPath = IndexPath(
    row: nextIndex,
    section: 0
  )
  tableView.selectRow(
    at: indexPath,
    animated: false,
    scrollPosition: .middle
  )
  performSegue(
    withIdentifier: "ShowEntrySegue",
    sender: tableView.cellForRow(at: indexPath)
  )
}
```

When performing the **Previous Entry** and **Next Entry** shortcuts, these methods will handle going to the previous and next entries.

Build and run, and use the keyboard shortcuts. Press **Control-N** to add a few entries, and **Command-Shift-[** and **Command-Shift-]** to move through the list.

Last, add the final keyboard shortcut to delete an entry. Back in **RootSplitViewController.swift**, add the following at the end of `keyCommands` *replacing* the existing `return` line:

```
let deleteKeyCommand = UIKeyCommand(
  input: "\u{8}",
  modifierFlags: [.command],
  action: #selector(removeEntry(sender:))
)
deleteKeyCommand.discoverabilityTitle = "Delete Entry"

return [
  newKeyCommand,
  upKeyCommand,
  downKeyCommand,
  deleteKeyCommand
]
```

This adds the shortcut to delete an entry when pressing **Command-Delete**. To display the macOS system symbol for Delete, and respond to it being pressed, you use the Unicode symbol for `BACKSPACE`, which is **8**.

Then, add the following in the same file:

```
@objc private func removeEntry(sender: UIKeyCommand) {
  guard let navigationController = viewControllers.first
    as? UINavigationController,
    let mainTableViewController
      = navigationController.topViewController
      as? MainTableViewController else { return }
  mainTableViewController.deleteCurrentEntry()
}
```

`deleteCurrentEntry` does the *actual* work of deleting the selected entry in the list.

Finally, add the following to **MainTableViewController.swift**:

```
func deleteCurrentEntry() {
  guard let index = indexOfCurrentEntry() else { return }
  DataService.shared.removeEntry(atIndex: index)
  var indexPath = IndexPath(
    row: index,
    section: 0
  )
  guard tableView.numberOfRows(inSection: 0) > 0 else {
    performSegue(withIdentifier: "ShowEntrySegue", sender: nil)
    return
  }
  if index == tableView.numberOfRows(inSection: 0) {
    indexPath = IndexPath(
      row: index - 1,
      section: 0
    )
  }
  tableView.selectRow(
    at: indexPath,
    animated: false,
    scrollPosition: .middle
  )
  performSegue(
    withIdentifier: "ShowEntrySegue",
    sender: tableView.cellForRow(at: indexPath)
  )
}
```

The last thing you've added here supports responding to the keyboard shortcut and deleting the entry that is selected in the table view.

The examples in this chapter used an input that directly relates to what you see on the keyboard or its Unicode symbol. However, there are constants defined for a few keys which you'll need to use if you want to respond to Escape or any of the directional arrows:

- `UIKeyCommand.inputUpArrow`
- `UIKeyCommand.inputDownArrow`
- `UIKeyCommand.inputLeftArrow`
- `UIKeyCommand.inputRightArrow`
- `UIKeyCommand.inputEscape`

Alternate Keyboard Handling

The previous section handled adding keyboard shortcuts in a way that enabled discoverability for the user. However, you may not want to inundate your users with all the key commands you would like to support, especially if there are multiple options available.

Open **MainTableViewController.swift**, and add the following to the main class body:

```
override var canBecomeFirstResponder: Bool { true }

override func pressesBegan(
  _ presses: Set<UIPress>,
  with event: UIPressesEvent?
) {
  for press in presses {
    guard let key = press.key else { continue }
    switch key.keyCode {
    case .keyboardUpArrow,
         .keyboardLeftArrow: goToPrevious()
    case .keyboardDownArrow,
         .keyboardRightArrow: goToNext()
    default:
      super.pressesBegan(presses, with: event)
    }
  }
}
```

This is an older way to handle keyboard input. Here, you're simply listening for when keyboard presses begin and respond to the desired keyCodes. In this example, you've added the ability to use the up, down, left and right keys to cycle through entries in the sidebar.

Key Points

- Providing keyboard shortcuts is essential for macOS users, and is becoming more expected for iPadOS users.
- `UIKeyCommand` makes setting up keyboard shortcuts easy, and works across iOS and macOS.
- Ensure you handle typical shortcuts for keys that aren't automatically supported by the operating system.

Where to Go From Here?

Your app is now set to handle shortcuts. While Catalyst will automatically handle these keyboard shortcuts, you'll learn later, how to make sure these shortcuts are shown in the Menu bar.

You can learn more about `UIKeyCommand` on Apple's website (https://developer.apple.com/documentation/uikit/uikeycommand).

There's more you can learn about the responder chain, as well, from Apple's website (https://developer.apple.com/documentation/appkit/nsresponder).

Also, check out Apple's documentation (https://developer.apple.com/documentation/uikit/uikeycommand/3780513-wantspriorityoversystembehavior), to learn more on `wantsPriorityOverSystemBehavior`, the new property introduced in iOS 15.

Chapter 7: Preferences & Settings Bundle

By Andy Pereira

Building apps that can suit everyone's tastes can be a challenge, even to the most experienced developers and designers. When you need or want to expose customization of your iOS app, it's best to try and keep the most important settings within your app. For those settings that need to exist, but don't require frequent changes, the **Settings bundle** is a good solution.

The Human Interface Guidelines (https://apple.co/2HY5vtf) caution against putting frequently used settings within the iOS Settings app. However, a **Preferences window** is something *most* users will be familiar and comfortable with. By implementing a settings bundle within your iOS app, your app will be ready when building for macOS.

Getting Started

To begin, open the starter project for this chapter. Select any iPad for the active scheme, then build and run. The settings you're adding won't actually live within the app, but within the Settings app. Tap the **Home** button on the simulator, and open **Settings**. Right now, you'll see only the default settings.

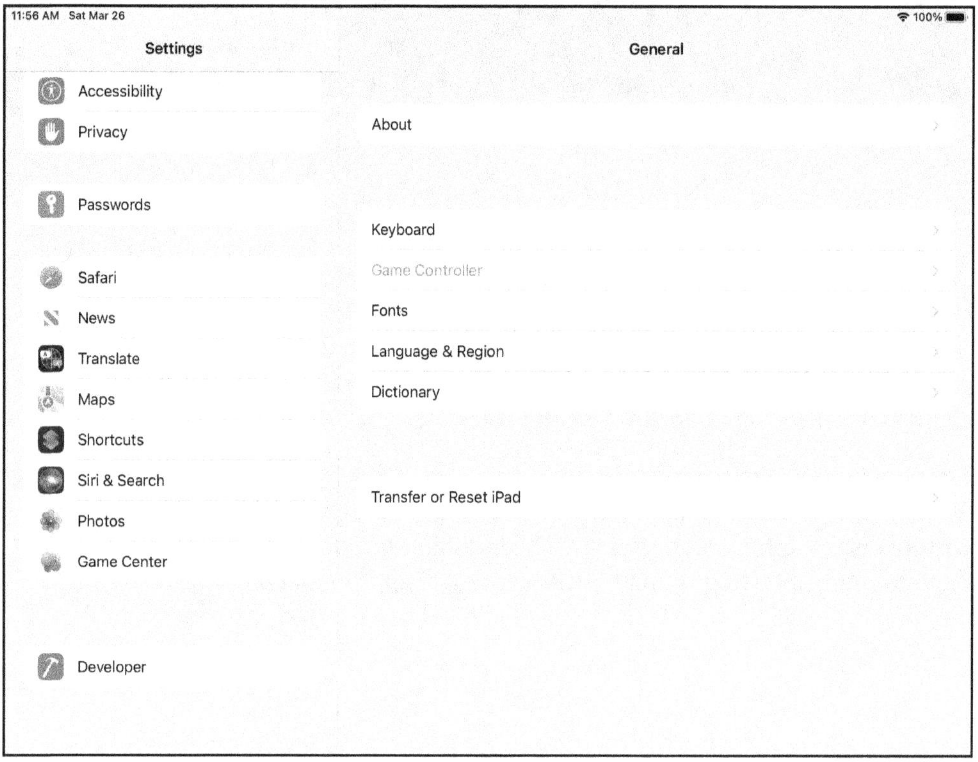

Settings in simulator.

You'll add a few preferences to this app:

- Currently, when the app runs with the system in dark mode, it will make the text view dark. Sometimes, users might prefer the area they type or read to be lighter. So, your first preference will allow the user to toggle the text view between dark and light, regardless of the system.
- Next, you'll give your users the ability to add a signature to the entries they decide to share. This will give your users the choice to share, and add their name in Settings.

Adding the Settings Bundle

To add your app and its settings to the system Settings app, in your project, select the **Journalyst** group, and then **File ▸ New ▸ File...**. Under the **Resource** header, select **Settings Bundle**.

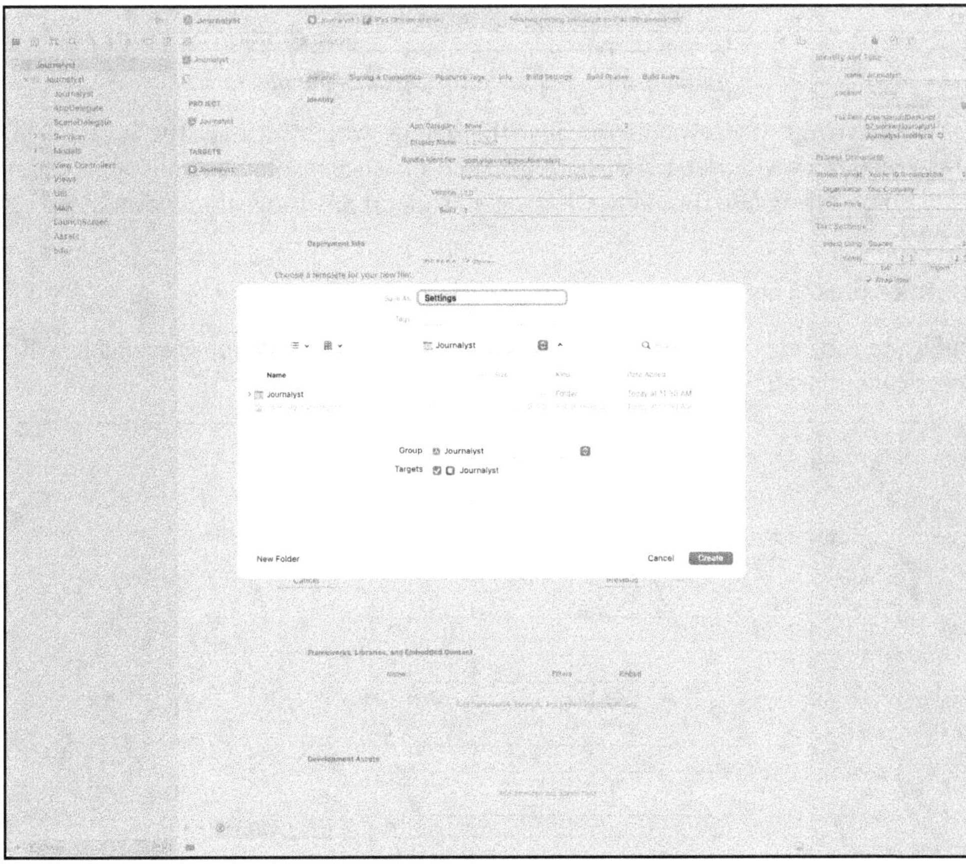

Adding Settings bundle to your app.

Select **Next** then **Create**. You now have **Settings.bundle** in your app's files. There are two files that are created by default for you:

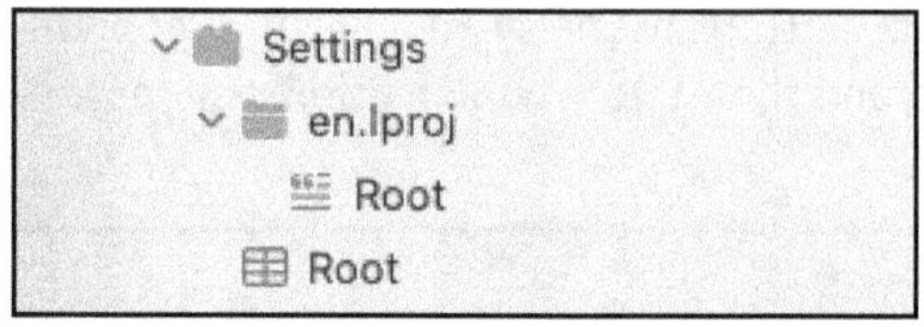

Default files created in the Settings bundle.

1. **Root.strings**: If you want to localize the strings in your settings, the localizations will need to live here. You don't have any access to your app's code within **Settings**, so this allows you to still support any translations your app does.
2. **Root.plist**: This is where your settings will live.

Build and run, and switch back to **Settings**. You'll now see your app is available, with some default preferences.

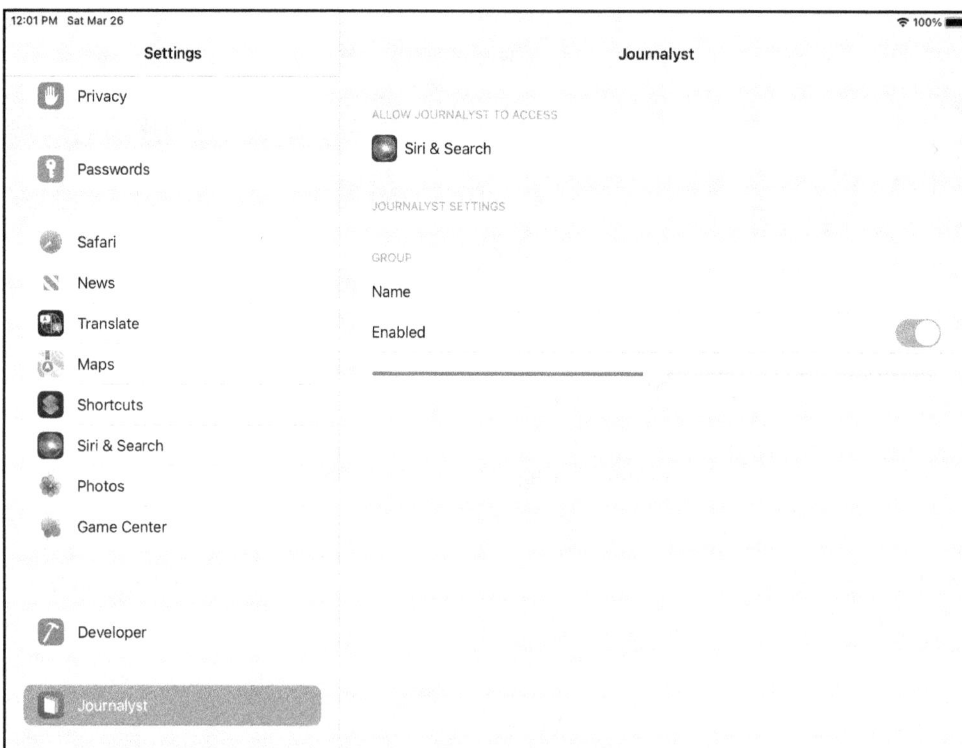

Default settings of your app.

Back in Xcode, open **Root.plist**. Then, expand the entries so you can see all the items under **Preference Items**. Each one corresponds to what you saw in Settings. Delete each item under Preference Items by highlighting one item at a time and selecting **Edit ▸ Delete**.

> **Note**: The plist editor won't let you select multiple items at a time.

Select **Preference Items**, and then from the menu, select **Editor ▸ Add Item**. Repeat this two more times, reselecting Preference Items each time. Since the plist editor can be finicky when attempting to rearrange items, it's easier to add all three items right now. Expand **Item 0**, and use the toggle arrows at the far right for **Type** and change it to **Toggle Switch**:

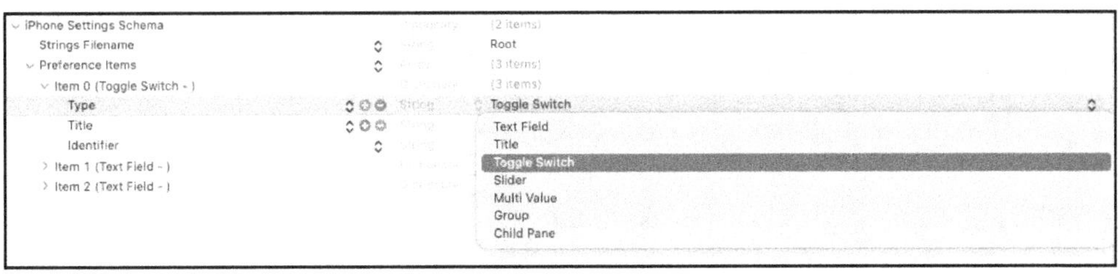

Adding Preference Items.

Set the other values to the following:

- **Title**: Include Signature When Sharing
- **Identifier**: signature_preference

Although you've added a "toggle switch" in the context of settings, the user will see a familiar **UISwitch**. The title you entered will be displayed to the left of the toggle.

In iOS, iPadOS and macOS, your app's preferences or settings can be a property stored within the user defaults. Whenever the toggle value is changed, it will use Identifier to know what key to save the value to in the user defaults.

With Item 0 highlighted, select **Editor ▸ Add Item**. Set the newly added key and value to the following:

- **Key**: Default Value
- **Value**: NO

This will give your user default an initial value, allowing the system to know what to set the toggle to initially.

Next, set the following values for **Item 1** in **Preferences Items**:

- **Type**: Text Field
- **Title**: Name When Sharing
- **Identifier**: name_preference
- **Keyboard Type**: Alphabet
- **Autocapitalization Style**: Words
- **Autocorrection Style**: No Autocorrection

This will add a text field that the user can enter their name in.

And finally add the following items for **Item 2**:

- **Type**: Toggle Switch
- **Title**: Show Entry With Light Background
- **Identifier**: entry_color_preference
- **Default Value**: NO

This setting will allow the user to decide whether or not they want the text view to always be a light color, regardless of whether the system is in dark mode or not.

Build and run, go to **Settings**, and you'll now see all your new items.

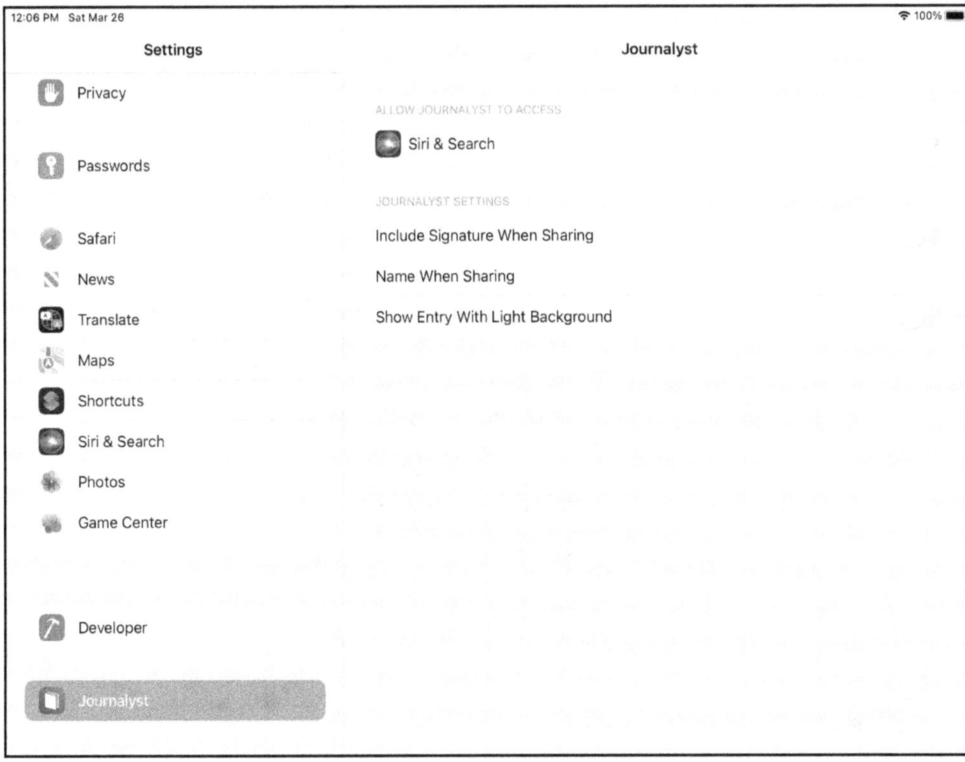

New items created in Settings.

Responding to Change

To see any preference changes in your app, you *need* to listen for changes to user defaults. Open **EntryTableViewController.swift**, and add the following to the end of `viewDidLoad`:

```
UserDefaults.standard.addObserver(
  self,
  forKeyPath: colorPreference,
  options: .new,
  context: nil
)
```

Apple states that changes to a setting must have an immediate effect on the app, so you want to observe when the user defaults change. Here, you've set your view controller to observe when user defaults changes the key `entry_color_preference`.

Next, add the following to **EntryTableViewController**:

```
override func observeValue(
  forKeyPath keyPath: String?,
  of object: Any?,
  change: [NSKeyValueChangeKey: Any]?,
  context: UnsafeMutableRawPointer?
) {
  if keyPath == colorPreference {
    updateEntryCellColor()
  }
}

private func updateEntryCellColor() {
  let overrideColorPreference = UserDefaults
    .standard.bool(forKey: colorPreference)
  if overrideColorPreference {
    entryCell.contentView.backgroundColor = .white
    textView.textColor = .black
  } else {
    entryCell.contentView.backgroundColor = nil
    textView.textColor = .label
  }
}
```

The first method you added will be called when a user changes the toggle for **Show Entry With Light Background**.

The second method checks if the toggle value is `true`. If so, it overrides the text color of the text view to be black, and the background color of the cell to be white. If the value is `false`, it will use the default label and cell background colors.

Build and run. Then still in Xcode, use Environment Overrides by clicking **Debug ▸ View Debugging ▸ Configure Environment Overrides** to change Interface Style to **Dark**.

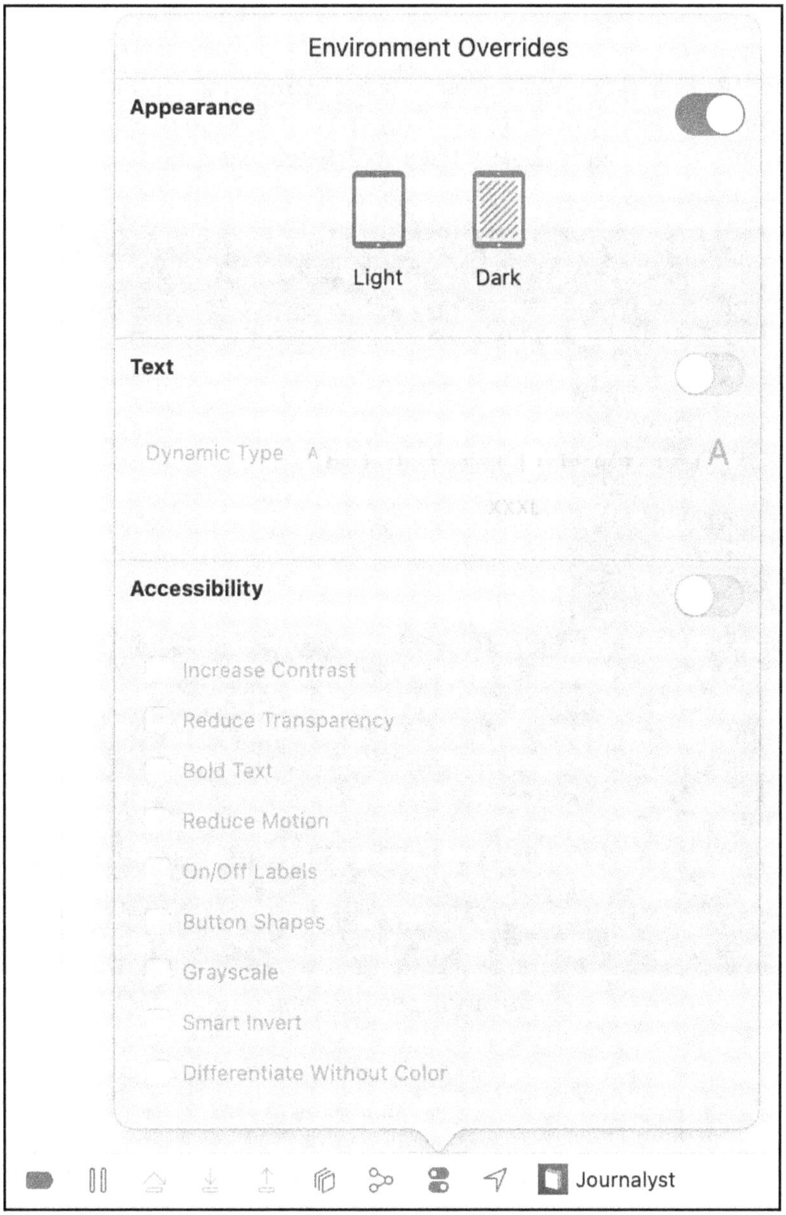

Environment Overrides.

> **Note**: At the time of writing, Xcode 13 didn't show the Environment Overrides window from **Debug**. You can also select **Environment Overrides** from the Xcode's bottom bar.

Now on the iPad simulator, you can go back to **Settings** and set the toggle for **Show Entry With Light Background** to `true`. When you return to the app, your text area appears white. Try changing the interface style toggle back and forth to see how it changes properly.

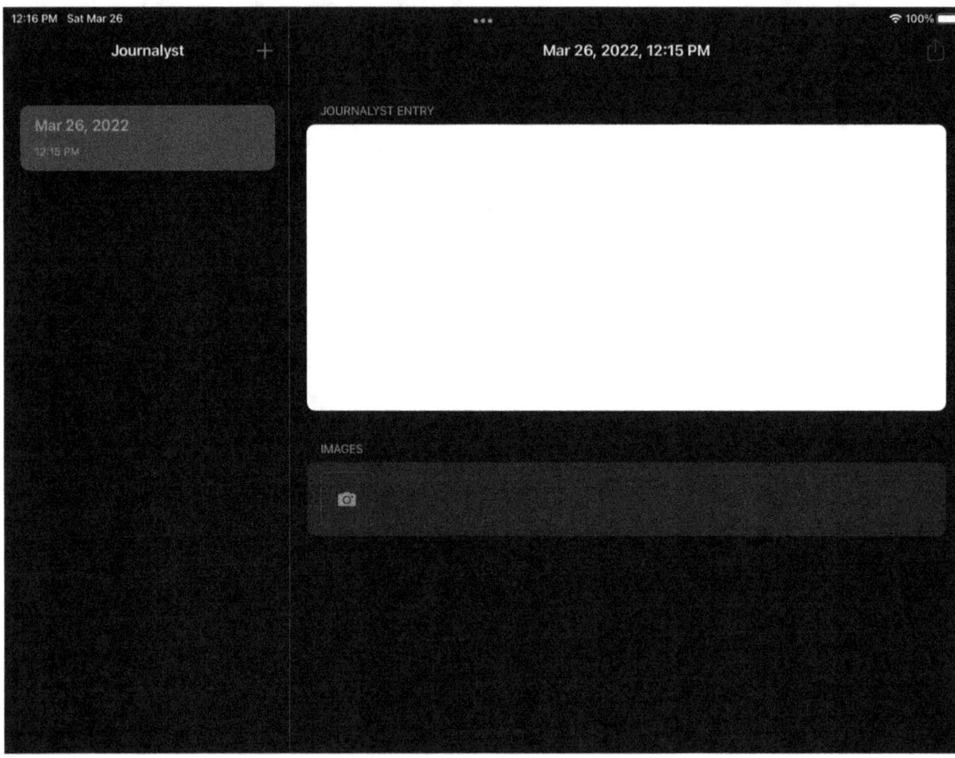

Entry with light background.

Next, back in Xcode, and the following to **EntryTableViewController**:

```
private var shareText: String? {
  guard var textToShare = textView.text,
    !textToShare.isEmpty else { return nil }
  if let namePreference =
    UserDefaults.standard.string(forKey: namePreference),
    UserDefaults.standard.bool(forKey: signaturePreference) {
    textToShare += "\n-\(namePreference)"
  }
  return textToShare
}
```

This creates the string to be shared. If the user has enabled **Include Signature When Sharing** in Settings, the app will append their signature to the text of any entry shared.

Next, replace `share(_:)` with the following:

```
@IBAction private func share(_ sender: Any?) {
  guard let shareText = shareText else { return }
  let activityController =
    UIActivityViewController(
      activityItems: [shareText],
      applicationActivities: nil
  )
  if let popoverController =
    activityController.popoverPresentationController {
      popoverController.barButtonItem =
        navigationItem.rightBarButtonItem
  }
  present(
    activityController,
    animated: true,
    completion: nil
  )
}
```

This method will now use the new text that will be generated by `shareText`.

Build and run. Go to Settings and turn on **Include Signature When Sharing**, and enter your name in **Name When Sharing**. Go back to Journalyst, and enter some text in the entry, then select **Action**. You'll see in the preview that your text now includes your name at the end.

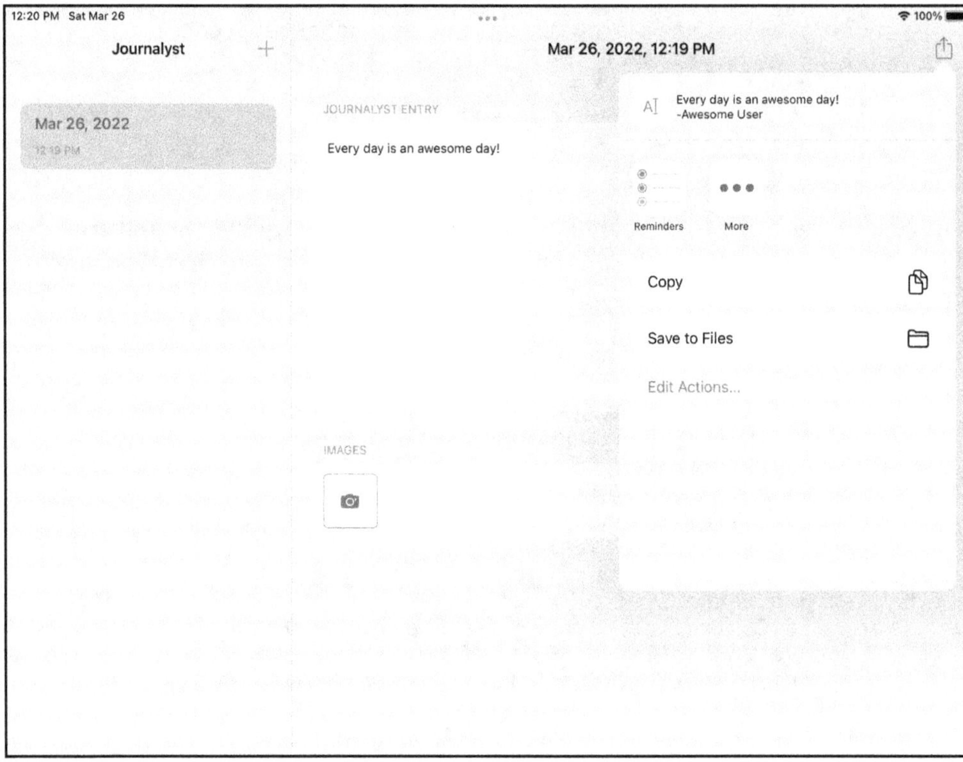

Includes signature when sharing an entry.

Child Panes

Settings.app can do more than *just* show a simple list of items. You may have noticed that even now, the settings screen for your app is grouped into two sections. You can also add groups and even multiple pages. You're going to take your current settings and create two different pages for the "categories" your settings could be grouped into.

In Xcode, select **File ▸ New ▸ File...**, pick **Property List** and name it **Sharing**. Drag the file *into* **Settings.bundle**:

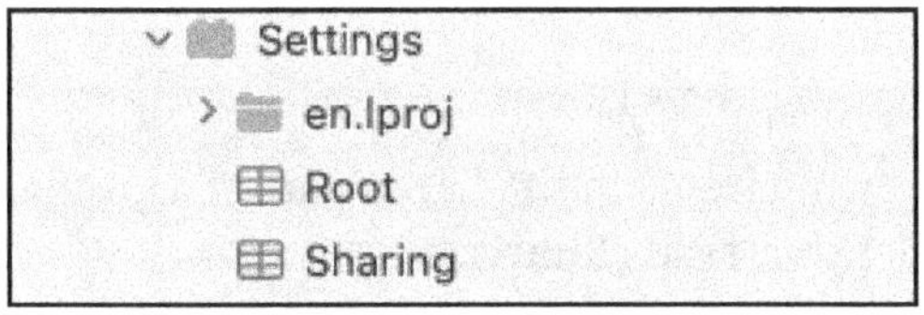

Sharing.plist file created.

Open **Sharing.plist**, and add the following item:

- **key**: StringsTable
- **value**: Root

> **Note**: In the property list, you can right-click **Root**, then select **Property List Type ▸ iPhone Settings plist**. This will let Xcode know that it should show you the appropriate keys and options for a settings bundle. However, it currently will not save the Property List Type after you switch files.

Add another item:

- **key**: PreferenceSpecifiers
- **type**: Array

Remove all the items from `PreferenceSpecifiers` that were added by default, if any.

Next, click the arrow to the left of the new entry you created and add an item to it using the **plus sign** to the right.

> **Note**: When editing a plist, you can use the plus sign to quickly add new items. If you click **plus** next to an item that can't have children, like a string, it will create a sibling entry. If you click **plus** next to an item that *can* have children, it behaves differently depending on whether the current item is "expanded" or "collapsed". When the arrow to the left of the item is pointing right, the item is "collapsed" and the new entry will be a sibling. When the arrow to the left of the item is pointing down, the item is "expanded" and the new entry will be a child.

Change the type of your new entry to **Dictionary** and add the following children:

- **Type**: PSGroupSpecifier
- **Title**: Sharing

This will treat any following items in the list as part of a grouped table view section, with a table view header that reads **Sharing**.

Next, open **Root.plist**, and highlight **Item 0**, then select **Edit ▸ Cut**. Open **Sharing.plist**, collapse and highlight **Item 0**, and select **Edit ▸ Paste ▸ Paste**.

Select the new **Item 0** from **Root.plist**, select **Edit ▸ Cut**, collapse **Item 1** in **Sharing.plist**, and select **Edit ▸ Paste ▸ Paste**.

Now, **Sharing.plist** looks like:

Key	Type	Value
⌄ Root	Dictionary	(2 items)
StringsTable	String	Root
⌄ PreferenceSpecifiers	Array	(3 items)
⌄ Item 0	Dictionary	(2 items)
Type	String	PSGroupSpecifier
Title	String	Sharing
⌄ Item 1	Dictionary	(4 items)
DefaultValue	Boolean	0
Type	String	PSToggleSwitchSpecifier
Title	String	Include Signature When Sharing
Key	String	signature_preference
⌄ Item 2	Dictionary	(6 items)
Type	String	PSTextFieldSpecifier
Title	String	Name When Sharing
Key	String	name_preference
KeyboardType	String	Alphabet
AutocapitalizationType	String	Words
AutocorrectionType	String	No

All items in Sharing.plist.

Last, back in **Root.plist**, add a new dictionary entry to the end of **Preference Items**. Add the following entries to the dictionary:

- **Type**: Child Pane
- **Title**: Sharing
- **Filename**: Sharing

A Child Pane is an option that allows you to specify the name of another plist within Settings.bundle to navigate to. The Filename value must match the file name that has the settings you want to display, without the extension.

To organize everything more clearly, add two groups to **Root.plist**. In **Root.plist**, select **Preference Items** and then **Editor ▸ Add Item**. Set the following entries on the new dictionary:

- **Type**: Group
- **Title**: Viewing

Next, collapse and select **Item 1** and then choose **Editor ▸ Add Item**. Change dictionary to have only the following entry:

- **Type**: Group

Your **Root.plist** now looks like:

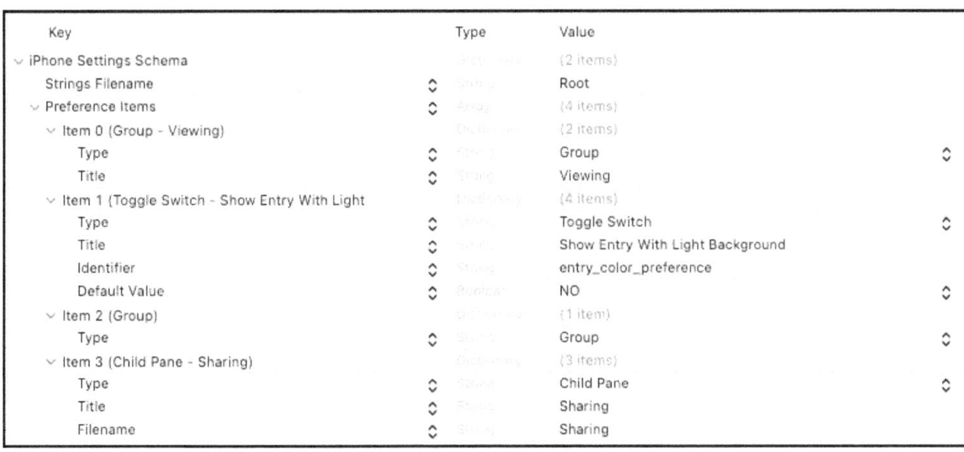

All items in Root.plist

Build and run, then go to **Settings**. You now see two entries at the bottom of the settings list. You'll also see how the groups break out the settings more clearly:

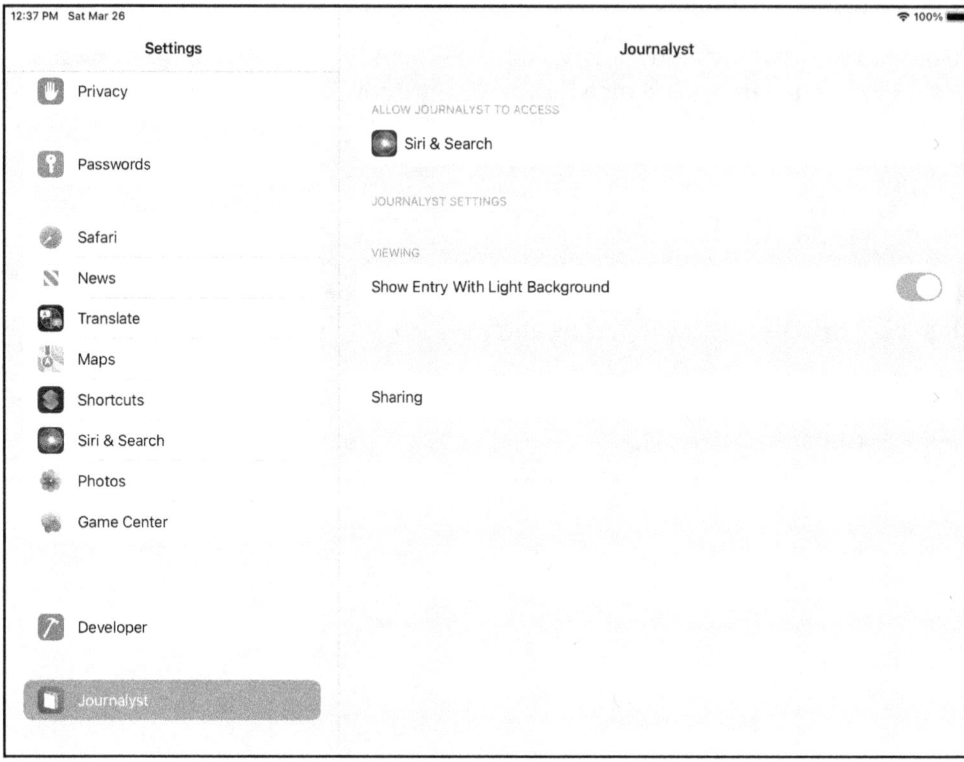

New group created in Settings.

When you select the **Sharing** setting, you'll navigate to another screen where you'll see the specific settings from the corresponding file:

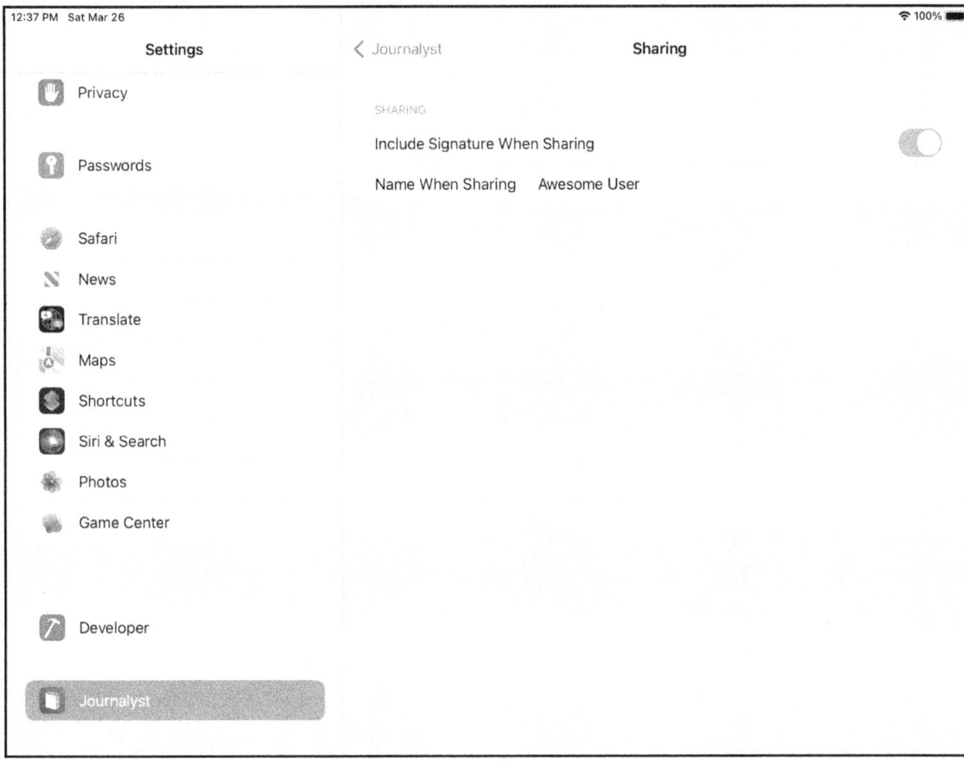

Sharing group in Settings.

Key Points

- Settings and preferences are helpful for your users. For example: Adding your signature when sharing or using a light background for text views.
- Keeping your app's preferences in **Settings.plist** quickly provides a standard way for your users to find available customizations.
- Using multiple plists bring hierarchy and organization to your preferences.

Where to Go From Here?

You can find out about all the other controls available to you in a settings bundle from Apple's Preferences and Settings Programming Guide (https://developer.apple.com/library/archive/documentation/Cocoa/Conceptual/UserDefaults/Preferences/Preferences.html).

You can also learn about Apple's guidelines for settings in the Human Interface Guidelines (https://developer.apple.com/design/human-interface-guidelines/ios/app-architecture/settings/).

Section II: Making a Great Mac App

The good news is that most of your code will be useful for *both* iPad and Mac platforms. But what about the things that are Mac-specific: like mouse support, Touch Bar support and more?

In this section, you'll take your first-rate iPad app and add Mac-specific touches to make it work well on macOS.

Chapter 8: Making Your App Feel at Home on macOS

By Nick Bonatsakis and Andy Pereira

In the previous section, you learned how to turn your iPhone-only app into a great iPad app. As you now know, this is the first step in making a great Mac app.

In this chapter, you're going to take things to the next level by making some adjustments that will really make your app shine when running on macOS via Catalyst. Throughout the rest of this section, you'll go deeper on several other Mac-specific features. When you're done, you'll have the makings of a world-class Mac app.

By the end of this chapter, you'll learn how to:

- Add a Mac-specific icon.
- Take advantage of system colors.
- Enable window-resizing.
- Enhance your Settings bundle for running on Mac.
- Make a handful of other minor Mac-related improvements.

Until now, you've been test running your app on Mac, but have been focused on iPad. That all changes right now. Ready to finally get your hands dirty with macOS? Fantastic, onward and upward!

It Starts With an App Icon

One of the first things you might have noticed about running Journalyst on macOS in previous chapters is that it uses the same icon on the Mac as it does on iPhone and iPad. While the icon style as of macOS Big Sur has skewed more towards the rounded rectangle style found on iOS, you still may want to tweak your app icon for macOS. Many of Apple's stock apps now have rounded rectangle icons on macOS, but they are slightly different and distinctly Mac.

Apple has accounted for this fact and given you the ability to include a Mac-specific icon in your app's bundle. And, it's a pretty straight-forward task to do just that.

Open the starter project for this chapter, then open **Assets.xcassets**. Click **AppIcon** in the assets list, expand the right panel in Xcode if not already visible, then go to the **Attributes inspector** tab (right-most tab). Finally, check the checkbox next to **Mac**.

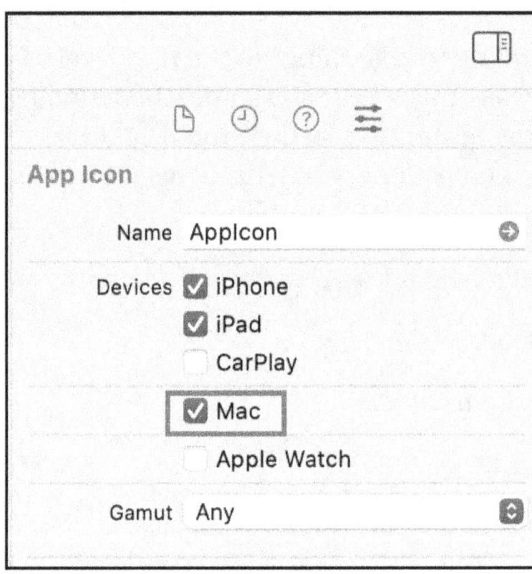

Mac checkbox in the Attributes inspector.

You'll now see several new slots for Mac icon size variants within the main editor. Inside the starter directory for this chapter, you'll find a **Mac App Icon** folder that contains a spiffy new Mac icon in all the required sizes. Drag the appropriately sized icon into each slot to finish.

Set the target device to **My Mac**, then build and run and you'll find that your app now looks much more at home on the Mac, with an icon that has a larger book glyph.

AppIcon changed for Mac.

Adding a Touch of Color

Another thing you may have noticed when running Journalyst on the Mac is that some of the colors seem off. That's because how iOS uses color differs in some key ways from how it's used on macOS.

Mac apps have traditionally adhered to some precise rules around how and where to use colors for standard system UI elements. Since most Mac apps lean heavily on these elements, they tend to have a very consistent look and feel. Conversely, until now, iOS hasn't exposed system standard colors, and so iOS designs have tended to vary much more in their application of color.

In iOS 13, Apple added a consistent set of "system" colors in the form of static `UIColor` properties. Using these new properties will result in rendered colors that are accurate no matter which OS your app is running on. With this in mind, you're now going to update a few key areas in your app to take advantage of these new colors so that your app adopts Mac-like colors when running on macOS.

The first area that looks somewhat out of place on the Mac is the background of the journal entry's right-hand detail screen. Because its table view uses a `grouped` style, its background defaults to the `.systemGroupedBackground` color on all OS's. On the Mac, this color renders as white, and this prevents you from differentiating the background from specific element areas.

To fix this, open **EntryTableViewController.swift** and append the following to `viewDidLoad`:

```
#if targetEnvironment(macCatalyst)
view.backgroundColor = .secondarySystemBackground
#endif
```

Note the use of `#if targetEnvironment(macCatalyst)` ... `#endif`.

This is a **compiler directive** enabling you to include code conditionally — here *only* if you're building for the Mac. Within this `#if` block, you then set the view's background color to `.secondarySystemBackground`. The result is a Mac-appropriate off-white background color that's visually distinct from the primary background color.

Next, notice that the journal entry cells in the left-hand sidebar still include lots of colors. On the Mac, data entry cells like this one typically use colored text sparingly. Additionally, the macOS selected color is user-defined and commonly darker than the standard iOS gray color. Together, these issues add up to journal entry cells that look out of place on the Mac.

Open **EntryTableViewCell.swift** and add the following:

```
private func setupForMac() {
  // 1
  dateLabel.textColor = .label
  // 2
  dateLabel.highlightedTextColor = .white
  // 3
  timeLabel.textColor = .secondaryLabel
  // 4
  timeLabel.highlightedTextColor = .white
}
```

Here's what this does:

1. First, you set the normal color for the date label to the `.label` color, which renders as a dark gray in light mode.
2. Next, you set the highlighted text color for the date label to `.white`. This is the color the label changes to when the cell is selected. Most of the time on the Mac, the system-selected color has a higher contrast, so white makes more sense here than on iOS.
3. Now, you set the time label color to `secondaryLabel`. This is a secondary piece of information, so the color provided by the system will be less pronounced than `.label`.
4. Finally, you set the time label highlighted color to `.white` just as you did for the date label.

Now, add the following to awakeFromNib:

```
#if targetEnvironment(macCatalyst)
setupForMac()
#endif
```

You call your new method when running on a Mac.

Build and run and you'll find the app looks much nicer now:

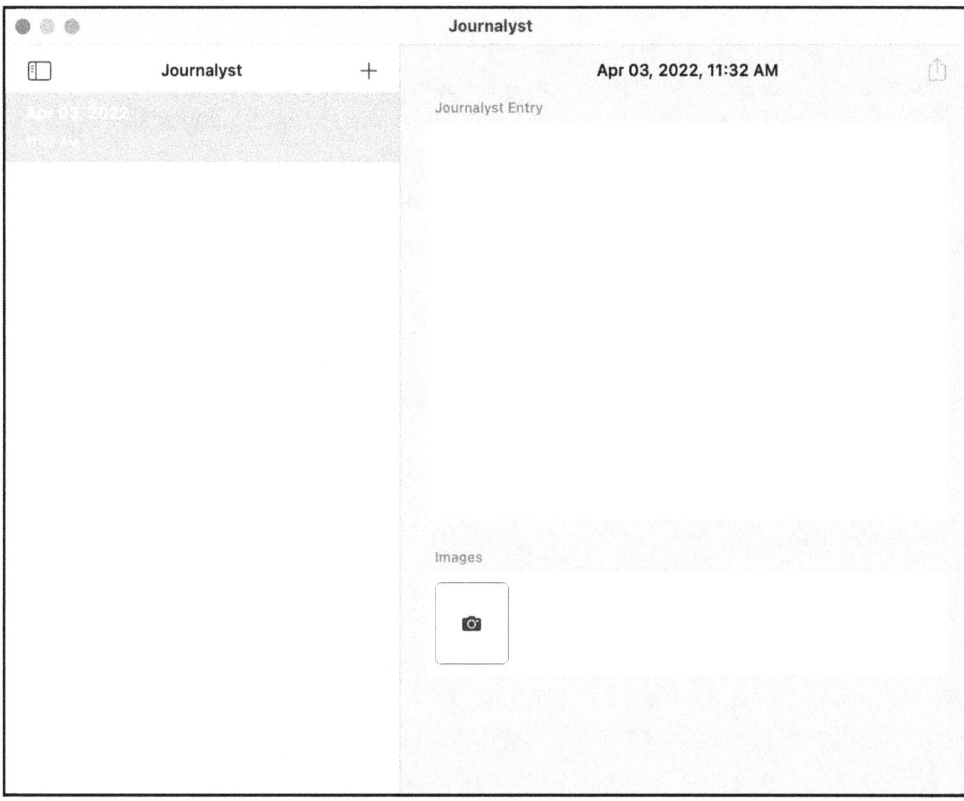

Colors changed in Mac.

A Word on Typography

While there is nothing you need to change to make your app's text readable on the Mac, it's worth noting UI content will be scaled down when running on macOS. According to Apple's guidelines.

> Content scaling. Text in the macOS version of an iPad app looks the same as it does in iOS because SF fonts are available on both platforms. However, the baseline font size in iOS is 17 pt, whereas the most common font size in macOS is 13 pt. To ensure that your text and interface elements are consistent with the macOS display environment, iOS views are automatically scaled down to 77%.

Keep this in mind if you have specific situations where this default scaling may cause issues, and take care to address those potential problems.

Sizing Down Window Resizing

When running on an iPad, you have a few options for how a secondary window is sized. On Mac, freeform window sizing has been a platform feature since Apple *borrowed* multi-windowing from Xerox PARC in the 1980s. It would be a shame to let that historical bit of *borrowing* go to waste, so let's make sure your app supports window resizing properly.

You can already resize the window when running on the Mac, but you'll quickly find that the system doesn't allow you to shrink the window down past a default size. It would be nice to have tighter control over the minimum and maximum window dimensions.

Open **SceneDelegate.swift** and add the following to the beginning of `scene(_:willConnectTo:options:)`:

```
if let scene = scene as? UIWindowScene {
  scene.sizeRestrictions?.minimumSize =
    CGSize(width: 768.0, height: 768.0)
  scene.sizeRestrictions?.maximumSize =
    CGSize(
      width: CGFloat.greatestFiniteMagnitude,
      height: CGFloat.greatestFiniteMagnitude
    )
}
```

`sizeRestrictions` is a property on `UIWindowScene` that allows you to control the minimum and maximum sizes for the window. In the above code, you set the minimum size to 768x768 and the maximum to `CGFloat.greatestFiniteMagnitude` which effectively means "as large as you want to make it."

Now there's one more thing you need to add that will come in handy later in this chapter. Add the following notification definition to the top of **SceneDelegate.swift**:

```
extension Notification.Name {
  static var WindowSizeChanged = Notification.Name(
    "com.yourcompany.Journalyst.WindowSizeChanged"
  )
}
```

And then, add the following to `SceneDelegate`:

```
func windowScene(_ windowScene: UIWindowScene,
  didUpdate previousCoordinateSpace: UICoordinateSpace,
  interfaceOrientation previousInterfaceOrientation:
  UIInterfaceOrientation,
  traitCollection previousTraitCollection: UITraitCollection) {
    NotificationCenter.default.post(
      name: .WindowSizeChanged, object: nil
    )
}
```

The above delegate method gets called whenever the window bounds change. When this happens, you issue the `WindowSizeChanged` notification so that any objects in your app can observe for this event.

Build and run, then resize the window. You'll find that the minimum size has now changed to the custom value you specified above. Through the magic of auto-layout, everything looks fine regardless of whatever window size you ultimately choose.

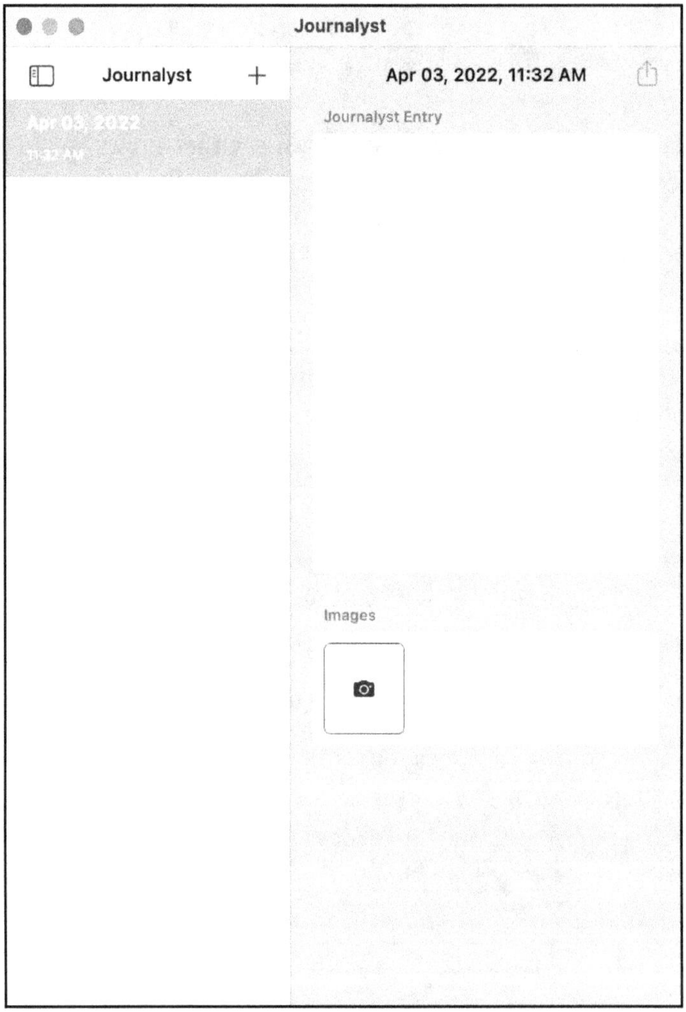

Mac window resizes.

Preferential Treatment

In the previous section, you learned how to add a Settings bundle to expose app preferences to the iOS Settings app. By doing so, you also enabled a default *Preferences* window for your app when running on the Mac, accessible via the **Journalyst ▸ Preferences** menu item. The out-of-the-box screen looks like this:

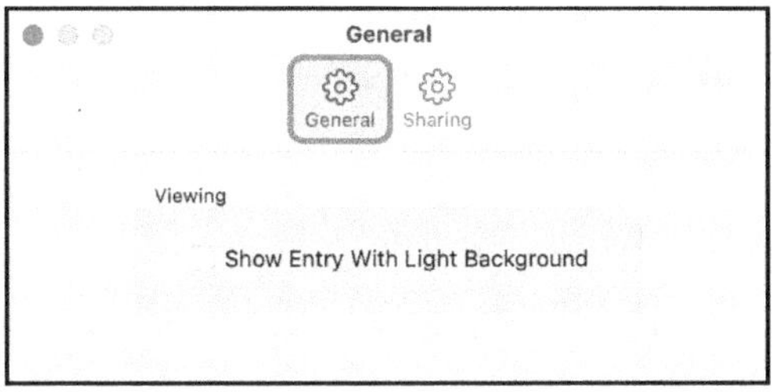

Basic preferences window on the Mac.

Not too bad, *especially* for free. But you can do better!

First, you'll notice that both tabs use the same default icon. The default icon is fine for the *General* tab, but it'd be nice to have a separate icon for the *Sharing* tab. Thankfully, the Settings bundle mechanism now supports adding custom icons, so that you can add some style.

To start things off, find **sharing.png** and **sharing@2x.png** in **starter/Sharing Settings Tab Icon**, and drop them into the top level of **Settings.bundle**. Then, to specify the icon for the *Sharing* tab, do the following:

1. Find **Sharing.plist** inside the Settings bundle and open it.

2. Right-click the Root element and click **Add Row**.

3. Set the key for the new row to `Icon`.

4. Finally, set the value to `sharing`.

It's pretty common for Mac preference panes to have descriptions for checkbox-based settings. Your current app lacks these descriptions, so you'll add them to both Boolean settings.

To add the description on the *General* tab:

1. Open **Root.plist** in the Settings bundle.

2. Expand **Preference Items** and then expand **Item 1**.

3. Right-click **Item 1** and click **Add Row**.

4. Set the key to `Description`.
5. Set the value to `Enable to force a light background on the entry screen`.

Now, add a description to the checkbox on the *Sharing* tab:

1. Open **Sharing.plist** in the Settings bundle.
2. Expand **PreferenceSpecifiers** and then expand **Item 1**.
3. Right-click **Item 1** and click **Add Row**.
4. Set the key to `Description`.
5. Set the value to `Automatically include a custom signature when sharing journal entries`.

The last preference enhancement you'll add is to show a confirmation prompt when the user turns on the journal entry signature setting on the *Sharing* tab. This is another feature that is specific to apps running on the Mac, so the plist entries will be ignored when running on iOS.

To add the confirmation dialog:

1. Open **Sharing.plist** in the Settings bundle.
2. Expand **PreferenceSpecifiers** and then expand **Item 1**.
3. Right-click **Item 1** and click **Add Row**.
4. Set the key to `TrueConfirmationPrompt`.
5. Set the type to `Dictionary`.

Add the following sub-items as `String` key-value pairs to `TrueConfirmationPrompt`, again by right-clicking and then choosing **Add Row** for each:

- `Type` -> `PSConfirmationPrompt`
- `Title` -> `Confirm Share Name`
- `Prompt` -> `Turning this on will share your name with the journal entry`
- `ConfirmText` -> `Enable`
- `DenyText` -> `Don't Enable`

Now, build and run. Then, open the preferences pane by clicking **Journalyst ▸ Preferences**. Your hard work has paid off, and you now have a much more Mac-like preferences window. Try enabling and disabling the various settings to see how things work.

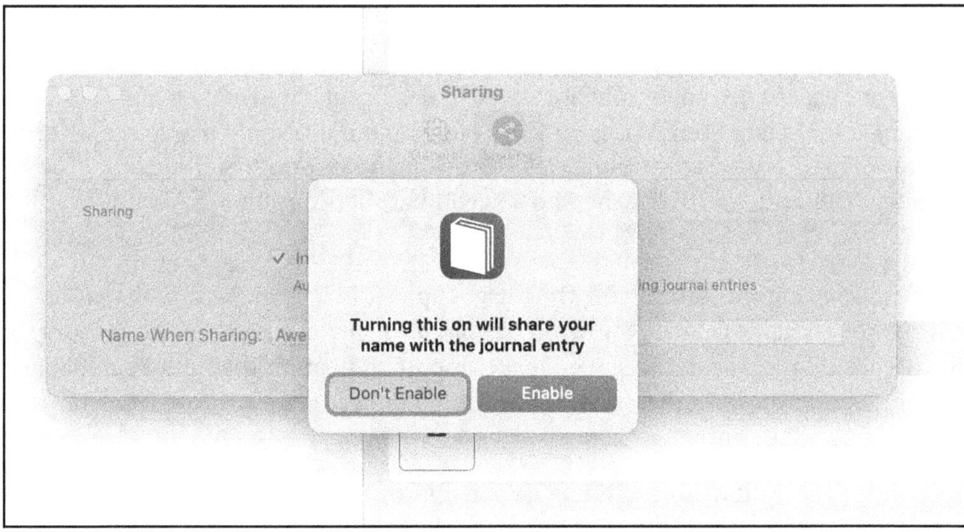

Final preferences window on the Mac.

Pretty slick right? Just a few more odds and ends to take care of and you'll be on your way.

A Few More Odds and Ends

Another thing that may be nagging your better Mac sensibilities is the look of the sidebar. On Mac, sidebars for split views tend to be styled in such a way that they let the content beneath bleed through, applying a blur.

Adding this behavior to your split view's side bar is a simple *one-liner*. Open **RootSplitViewController.swift** and append the following to the end of `viewDidLoad`:

```
splitViewController.primaryBackgroundStyle = .sidebar
```

This one line of code keeps the sidebar unchanged on iOS, but when running on the Mac, it now looks like the standard macOS sidebar.

Next, you have a minor scrollbar-related tweak to make. When any `UIScrollView` instance is used, and your app is running on the Mac, the scroll bars that are only visible on demand on iOS are styled as Mac scrollbars and visible at all times. For example: when someone is actively scrolling.

> **Note**: By default scrollbars will auto-hide on Mac when using a trackpad. You may not experience any scrollbar related issues if you have this setting enabled in System Preferences and don't use a mouse. If you'd like to see what it looks like for your users who use a mouse, open **System Preferences**, choose **General**, and under the **Show scroll bars** setting, choose **Always.**

On the journal entry detail screen, the images appear in a `UICollectionView` that is laid out horizontally. On iOS, the scroll bars aren't really necessary, since the way the list extends off the side of the screen makes it pretty apparent that it is a scrollable element. But on the Mac, there's no touch interaction, so scrollbars are how you typically move the content area.

Open **EntryTableViewController.swift** and update the `#if targetEnvironment(macCatalyst)` code block at the end of `viewDidLoad` to match this:

```
#if targetEnvironment(macCatalyst)
view.backgroundColor = .secondarySystemBackground
collectionView.showsHorizontalScrollIndicator = true
#endif
```

Now, when running on the Mac, the collection view that renders images will have a scrollbar visible if the content extends past the view frame. That's not quite enough to make this work. You still need to let the collection view know when the window bounds change, or else it won't know to update the scrollbar state. For example, if you start with a window that is very wide and can accommodate all the images, but then resize to a much smaller window width, the collection view needs to change from not showing scrollbars to showing them.

Earlier in the chapter, you added a `WindowSizeChanged` notification to `SceneDelegate`. It's now time to make use of it!

Still in **EntryTableViewController.swift**, add the following to `viewDidLoad`:

```
NotificationCenter.default.addObserver(
  self,
  selector: #selector(handleWindowSizeChanged),
  name: .WindowSizeChanged,
  object: nil
)
```

The code above must be pretty familiar, as you have done many times already. You are subscribing to a notification, in this case, `WindowSizeChanged`.

Next, add the implementation for the `handleWindowSizeChanged` handler method like so:

```
@objc func handleWindowSizeChanged() {
  collectionView.reloadData()
}
```

This will force the collection view to reconsider whether it should be showing scrollbars or not, based on its current bounds.

Lastly, there is one more minor tweak you'll want to make to how sidebar cells are rendered. At present, whenever you make changes to the text of a journal entry, the sidebar cell shows a preview of that text. This looks fine on an iPad, where cell heights commonly vary, but on the Mac, they tend to be more uniform, so it would be nice not to show that text preview in this case.

Open **EntryTableViewCell.swift** and add the following code to the `didSet` of the `entry` property:

```
#if targetEnvironment(macCatalyst)
summaryLabel.isHidden = true
#endif
```

Pretty straight-forward! You're again using the `#if targetEnvironment(macCatalyst)` check to only run the code when on the Mac, in this case, hiding the summary label.

Build and run one more time, then bask in the glory that is your app, one huge step closer to being a marvelously Mac-like macOS app. Try saying that ten times fast!

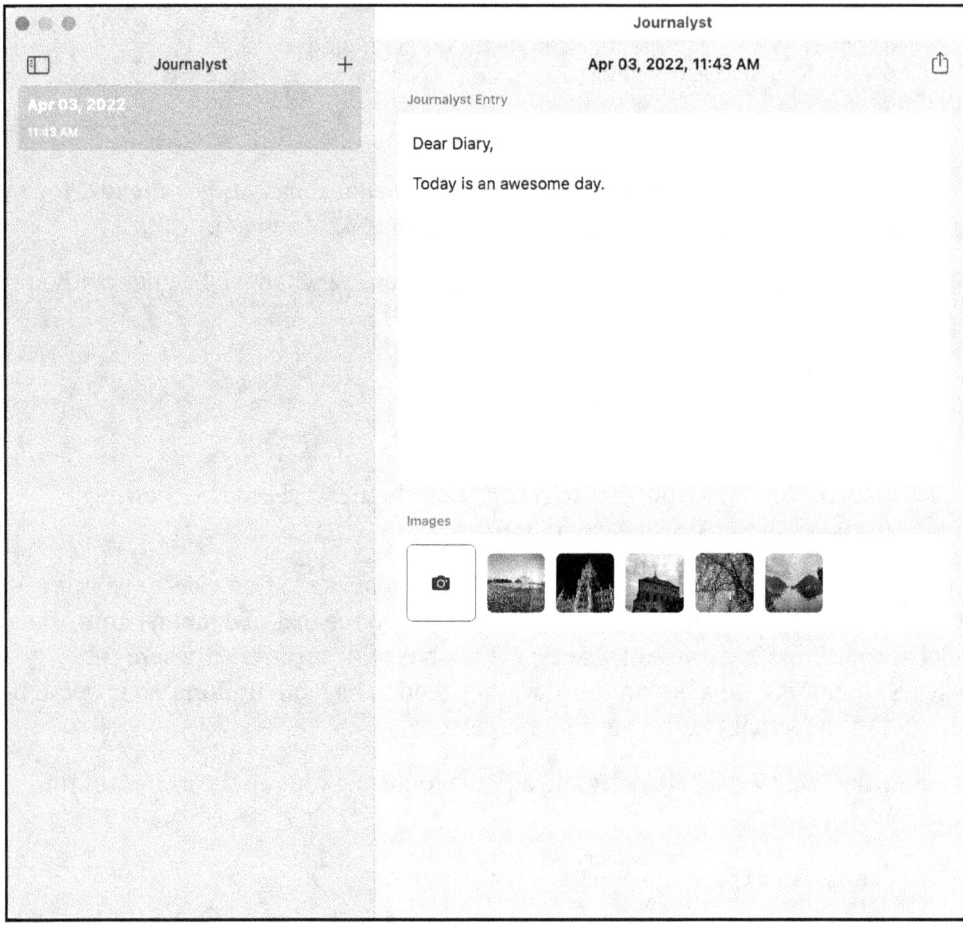

Finally, a Mac-like app.

Key Points

- Including a Mac-specific icon for your Catalyst app is easy and helps make the app feel more at home on the Mac.
- There are many ways to leverage system colors to improve the styling of your iOS app when it runs on the Mac.
- You need to consider window resizing when your app runs on the Mac.
- Mac preferences panels get lots of functionality for free for Catalyst apps, but you can go further with *some* extra effort.

Where to Go From Here?

In this chapter, you took the first steps towards really making your iOS app shine when running macOS, taking advantage of various styling methods, window resizing, preferences, and more. But there are still some glaring omissions, things you'd expect to see in a great Mac app.

In the next chapter, you'll learn how to replace those navigation bars that look so out of place on the Mac, with native Mac toolbars.

Chapter 9: The Mouse

By Andy Pereira

Just like a keyboard, the mouse is a toolset that you may *not* have encountered if you've focused solely on iOS development. Catalyst makes working with the mouse easy since it provides a familiar pattern, and it gives you a great amount of control in the process.

In this chapter, you'll learn to implement `PointerStyleProvider` and `UIHoverGestureRecognizer` to show a shadow effect or to change the default mouse pointer, when hovering over a diary entry in the sample app. You'll also learn to *accessorize* your mouse pointers using `UIPointAccessory` that's new in iOS 15. You'll look at the differences between iOS/iPadOS and touch targets in macOS.

Getting Started

Open the starter project for this chapter. Build and run for iPadOS. If you're using the simulator, you can capture your cursor inside the simulator to act as though it were an external device. Do this by selecting **Capture Pointer** in the simulator toolbar:

Capture mouse in the simulator.

Add a few entries and then move your mouse around the app. Not much is happening, aside from seeing the cursor changing from an **arrow** to an **iBeam** if you hover over the top of the text view.

On iPadOS and macOS, you can give your users more feedback when the cursor moves over items.

Pointer Style Providers

On iPadOS, your cursor behaves a *bit* different from that of macOS. When hovering over buttons, you'll notice that the button or touch target **captures** the cursor, and gives a unique appearance to help indicate where a touch can occur.

Open **EntryTableViewController.swift** and the following block of code inside `supplementaryDataSource`, just before the line that returns `reusableView`:

```
if let button = reusableView.viewWithTag(1) as? UIButton {
  button.pointerStyleProvider = { button, effect, _ in
    var rect = button.bounds
    rect = button.convert(
      rect, to: effect.preview.target.container
    )
    let style = UIPointerStyle(
      effect: effect, shape: .roundedRect(rect)
    )
    return style
  }
}
```

Here, you've added a *very* simple `UIButton.PointerStyleProvider`. Added in iOS 13.4, it allows you to define custom styles and shapes for your cursor on touch areas. Here, you *simply* take the button's shape, have the pointer style take the entire shape of it.

Build and run, and capture the mouse. Then hover your mouse over the **Camera** button to see the effect take place. You see the button fill with a color, like below:

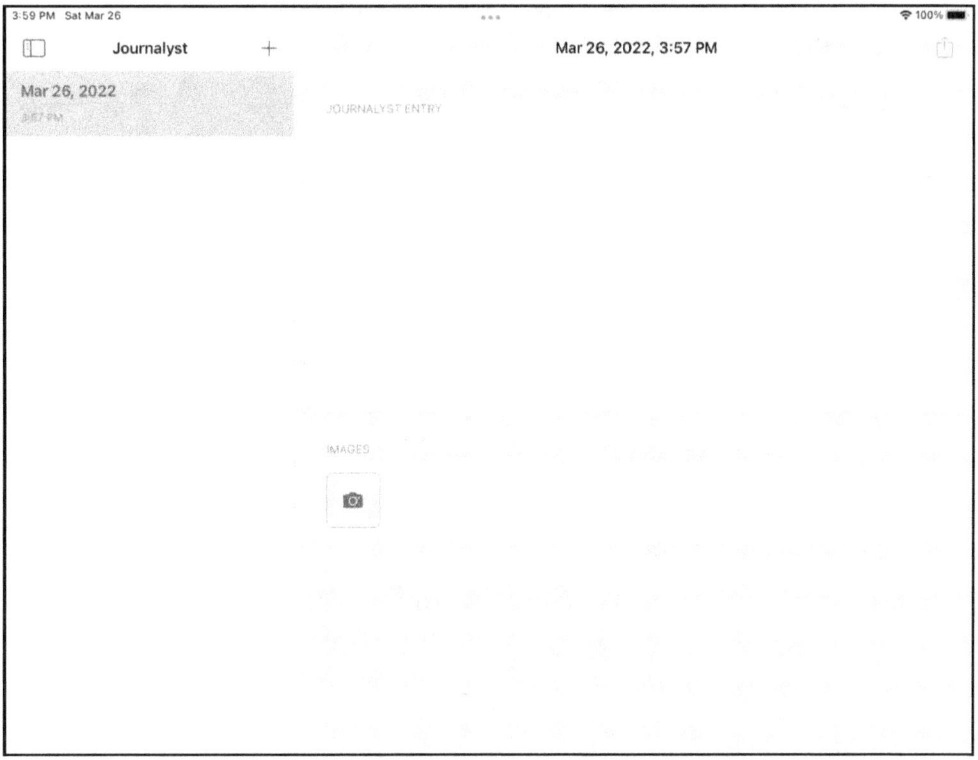

Camera button's effect on hovering mouse over it.

It's a *subtle* effect, but things like this make a difference to your users, even if they aren't thinking about it.

Adding Effects With Hover Gesture Recognizer

Next, you'll use `UIHoverGestureRecognizer` to add some more effects for iPadOS, as well as macOS.

To start, open **EntryTableViewCell.swift**. Add the following to the end of `awakeFromNib`.

```
addHoverGesture()
```

Then add the following to the class:

```
private func addHoverGesture() {
  let hoverGesture = UIHoverGestureRecognizer(
    target: self,
    action: #selector(hovering(_:))
  )
  contentView.addGestureRecognizer(hoverGesture)
}
```

This method does the following:

- It creates a hover gesture recognizer, setting `self` as the target, and an action that you'll set up in the next step.
- It adds the hover gesture to the content view of the cell.

Next, add the following to the same class:

```
@objc private func hovering(
  _ recognizer: UIHoverGestureRecognizer
) {
  // 1
  guard !isSelected else { return }
  // 2
  switch recognizer.state {
  // 3
  case .began, .changed:
    backgroundColor = .secondarySystemBackground
  // 4
  case .ended:
    backgroundColor = .none
  default:
    break
  }
}
```

Here, you can see how you respond to the hover events:

1. This ensures that nothing happens if you've already selected the cell.
2. The gesture recognizer passes itself as a parameter to this method. You check the state of the gesture recognizer.
3. If the hover is starting (`.began`) or moving around (`.changed`), you change the background color of the cell.
4. Once the mouse is no longer hovering over the view (`.ended`), you remove the color you set.

Build and run. Then add a few entries and hover your mouse over the table view. You now see that all the cells, except for the cell you selected, change background color while the mouse is over it. Once the mouse leaves the view, it changes back to having no background color.

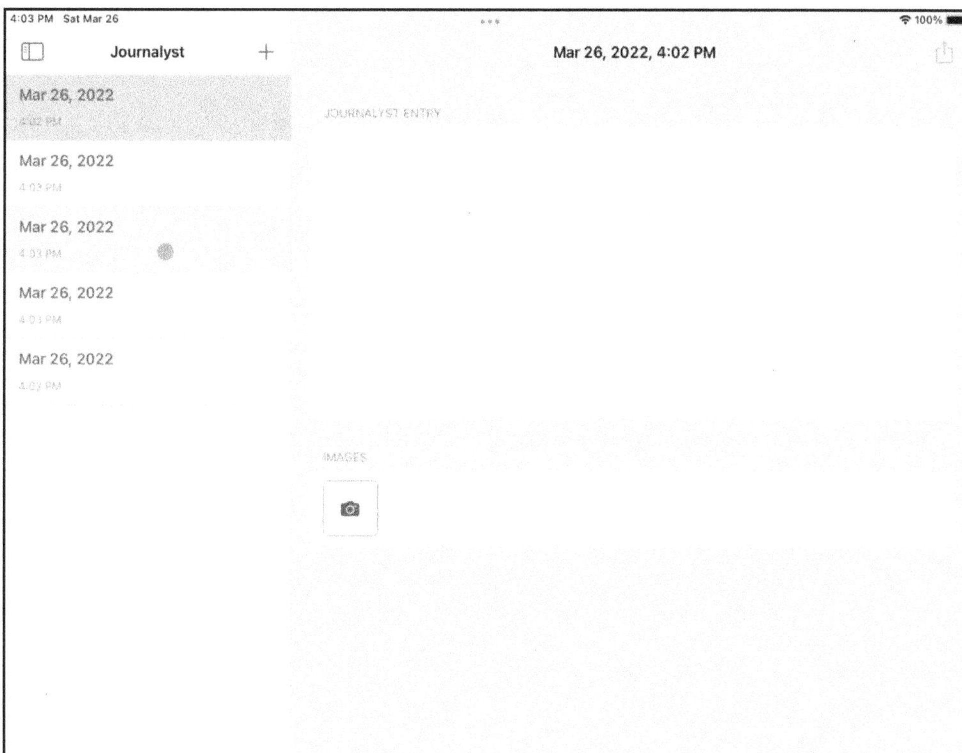

Entry cell's effect on hovering mouse over it.

There's one more place where you can add a hover gesture to give your app more finesse.

Open **EntryTableViewController.swift** and add the following to `supplementaryDataSource`, just before it returns `reusableView`:

```
let hoverGesture = UIHoverGestureRecognizer(
  target: self,
  action: #selector(self.hovering(_:))
)
reusableView.addGestureRecognizer(hoverGesture)
```

Once again, this code creates a hover gesture and adds it to the reusable view that the collection view's header returns.

Next, add the following to the class:

```
@objc private func hovering(
  _ recognizer: UIHoverGestureRecognizer
) {
  #if targetEnvironment(macCatalyst)
  switch recognizer.state {
  case .began, .changed:
    NSCursor.pointingHand.set()
  case .ended:
    NSCursor.arrow.set()
  default:
    break
  }
  #endif
}
```

Here, you respond to the event over the **Camera** button and change the cursor to the pointing hand when above it. It goes back to the default arrow when you mouse away from it. While this code you added in the first section was only for iPadOS, this new code complements your UI on macOS, all without having to write too much code.

Build and run on macOS. Then hover over the **Camera** button in the Entry view. It now changes cursor shapes as you mouse over it.

Camera button's effect on macOS.

A Few Notes on Elements and Haptics

Keep in mind that the interface guidelines for iOS state that you should keep touch targets for interactive elements to a minimum of 44pt × 44pt. The cursor gives you a lot more flexibility when your app is running on macOS. If you're creating macOS-specific UI elements, you can use smaller elements if it makes sense for your app.

You also have access to haptic feedback on both platforms. You could easily set up haptic feedback when mousing over an area if your app requires it. Keep Apple's guidelines in mind, and remember not to overstimulate your users.

Accessorize

New to iOS 15, `UIPointAccessory` allows you to add custom views to the cursor, providing additional context for users. You can use predefined shapes, or custom bezier paths.

Open **EntryTableViewController.swift**. In `supplementaryDataSource`, replace the existing `if let` block with:

```
if let button = reusableView.viewWithTag(1) as? UIButton {
  button.pointerStyleProvider = { button, effect, _ in
    var rect = button.bounds
    rect = button.convert(
      rect, to: effect.preview.target.container
    )
    let style = UIPointerStyle(
      effect: effect, shape: .roundedRect(rect)
    )
    style.accessories = [
      .init(.path(.plusPath), position: .bottomRight)
    ]
    return style
  }
}
```

Here, you add a new accessory to the `UIPointerStyle`. In this case, it is a custom bezier path, a **plus** symbol, which shows at the bottom right of the cursor.

Build and run on iPadOS. Then hover over the **Camera** button to see the new accessory.

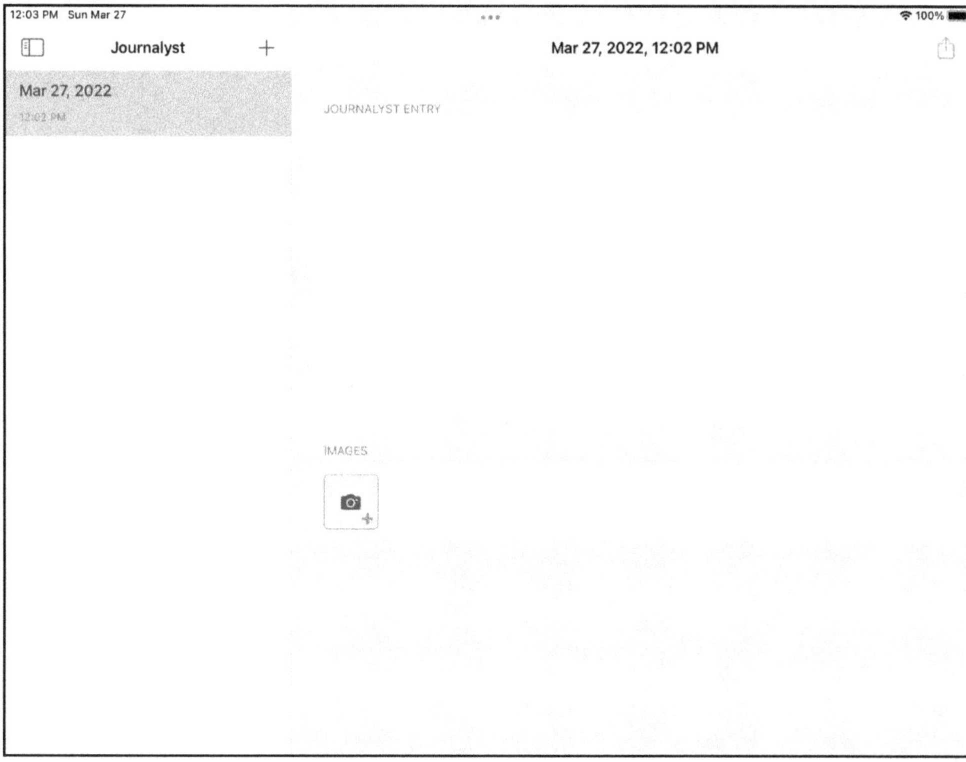

Camera button's new accessory.

Key Points

- You can use `PointerStyleProvider` to respond to cursor events on iPadOS.
- Add hovering to views by adding a hover gesture recognizer to give your user more visual feedback.
- Hover gesture recognizers work similarly to other gesture recognizers.
- You can access `NSCursor` on macOS with Catalyst.
- Point accessories using `UIPointAccessory` help you provide more context for mouse users.

Where to Go From Here?

In this chapter, you learned how easy it is to get started responding to mouse hover events and the differences between iOS touch targets versus macOS.

You can find Apple's Human Interface Guidelines for the mouse and trackpad, here (https://developer.apple.com/design/human-interface-guidelines/macos/user-interaction/mouse-and-trackpad/).

You can read more about `UIHoverGestureRecognizer` from Apple's website (https://developer.apple.com/documentation/uikit/uihovergesturerecognizer).

To learn more about the possible states for a gesture recognizer, refer to the Apple documentation (https://developer.apple.com/documentation/uikit/uigesturerecognizer/state).

Chapter 10: Barista Training: Menu Bar

By Marin Benčević

Welcome to barista training! In the next few chapters, you'll learn all about adding different kinds of bars to your Catalyst app, including the menu bar, toolbars and supporting the touch bar. In this chapter, you'll trim the default menu bar of the Journalyst app to remove some unnecessary items. You'll also add new items to delete, share and add new entries. Get out your beans and your fancy hipster oat milk — it's time to get brewing!

A Free Menu Bar

All Catalyst apps include a default menu bar for free. Open the starter project from the provided materials and run it on macOS. When your app is active, you'll see its menu bar at the top of your screen. All the standard menus like *File*, *Edit*, etc. are already there.

> **Note**: WWDC 2021 introduces a new property in info.plist called `UIApplicationSupportsPrintCommand`. When set to `YES`, in your menu bar, under **File**, it gives you **Print...** and **Export as PDF...** options.

Apple sometimes calls the menu bar the "main menu." That's how you must think about what actions to put in the menu bar. Like in a video game, the main menu includes general actions the user can perform inside your app.

One thing you must keep in mind is that menu bars aren't dynamic. They're built once when the app launches and the items never change during runtime. For more dynamic actions related to specific parts of your app, use context menus as described in Chapter 5, "Adding Some Context."

The menu bar itself is a nested `UIMenu` instance. Each `UIMenu` can contain child menus and **commands**. Commands are the buttons you can press to do something. They can be enabled or disabled, and each command can specify a keyboard shortcut for easier access.

Commands get executed using *something* called the **responder chain**.

The Responder Chain

Open the **Edit** menu, and you'll notice that *Cut*, *Copy* and *Paste* are all greyed out. This makes sense: Since nothing is selected, there's nothing to cut or copy.

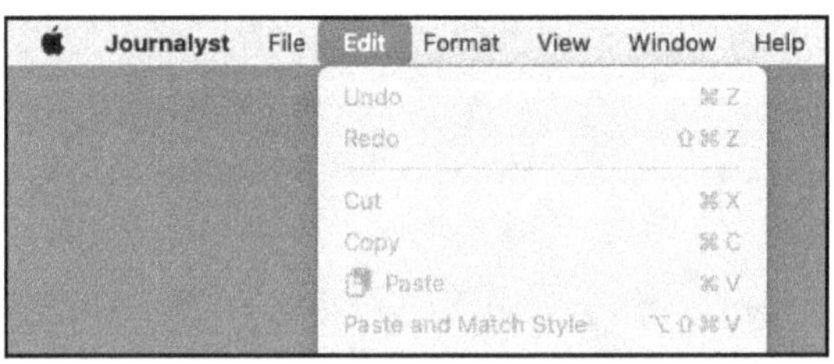

Disabled items in Edit menu.

However, if you type in something in the entry screen and select the text, you'll notice the menu items are now enabled.

`UIKit` disables and enables these items for you using the **responder chain**. The responder chain is built of `UIResponder` instances, which include all views, view controllers and the app itself.

When you click the text view, it becomes the **first responder**. The responder chain starts from the text view and moves up the view hierarchy through all superviews and view controllers, all the way to the app itself.

Menu items use the responder chain to enable or disable themselves. Each menu item has an associated **selector**. When the first responder changes, menu items query the whole responder chain to see if anyone can perform their selector. In the case of *Cut*, the text view can perform the action. *File ▸ Close* is always active because the app handles that one, and the app is always at the far end of the responder chain.

OK, that's enough theory for one day. It's time to get hacking.

Beyond the Default Menu

You'll start by trimming some unnecessary items from the menu bar. The menu bar can be changed either in Interface Builder or through code. In this section, you'll use Interface Builder and, later in the chapter, you'll learn how to do the same in code.

Open **Main.storyboard**, from the **Library** drag over a **Main Menu** anywhere on the storyboard. You see a new scene in the storyboard that looks just like your menu bar:

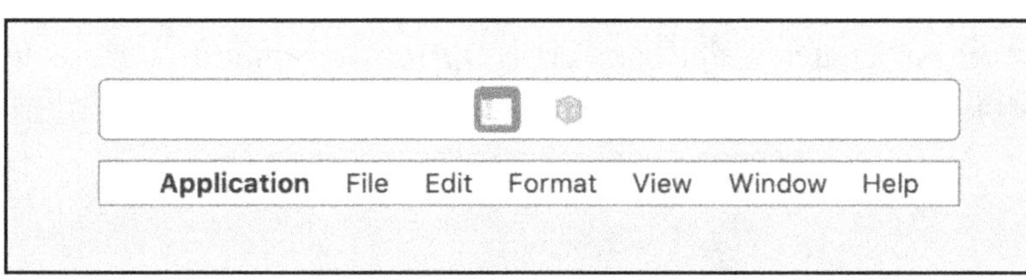

Main Menu in the storyboard.

Select the **Format** menu in the Document Outline and press **Command-Backspace** to delete it. Since you're not using rich text in the app, this menu serves no purpose. Build and run, and you see a menu bar without *Format*:

Menu bar without the format menu.

Now, add a new command for adding new entries. Start by going back to the Library and dragging over an **Inline Section Menu** to the top of the **File** menu in the Outline View.

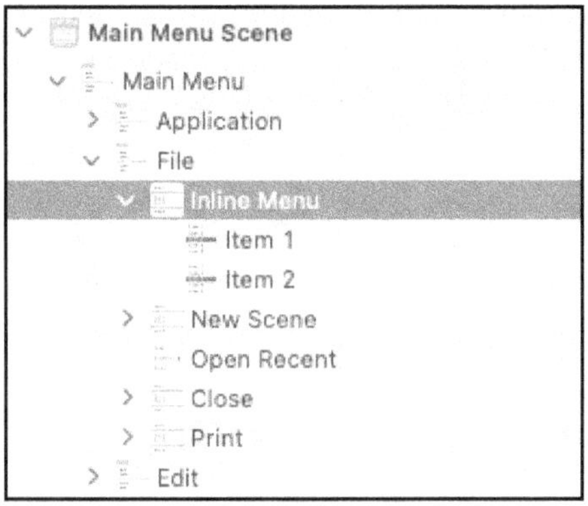

Inline Section Menu in File menu.

This adds an **inline menu** with two commands. Inline menus can't be opened. Instead, all their commands are added to the parent menu, separated with a thin line from other items.

Select **Item 1** and open the Attributes inspector. Change the Title to **New Entry**. Then click the Key Equivalent box and press **Option-Command-N**. This adds a keyboard shortcut to the command.

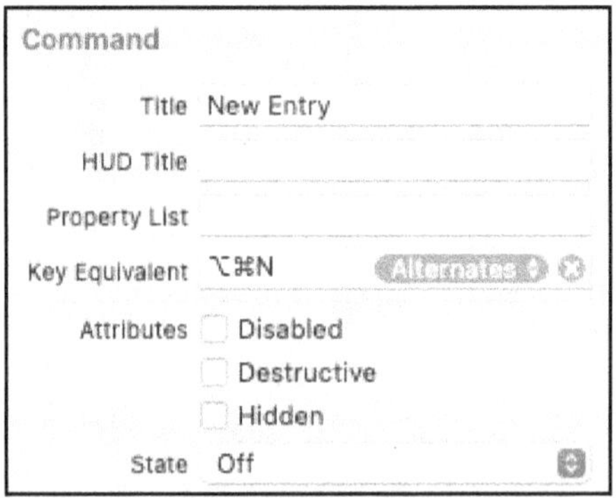

Item 1 Attributes inspector.

Next, in **RootSplitViewController.swift** add the `@IBAction` attribute for `addEntry(sender:)` at the start of it's declaration. It now looks like this:

```
@IBAction @objc private func addEntry(
  sender: UIKeyCommand
) {
```

Then return to the storyboard again, control-drag from the **New Entry** command to the **first responder**, which is the little yellow cube above the menu bar in the storyboard. Select `addEntryWithSender:` as the sent action.

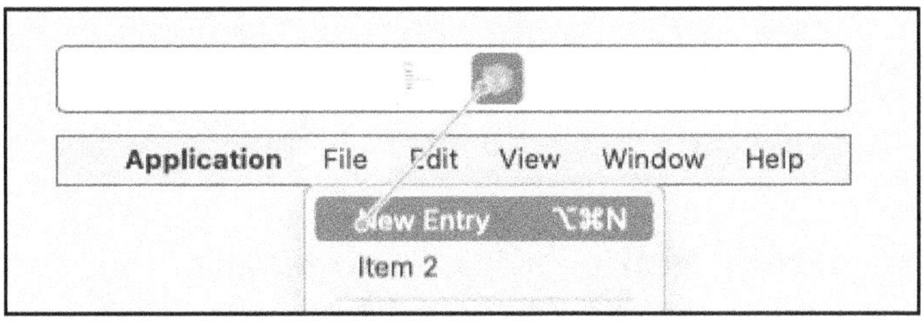

New Entry's first responder.

This connects the `addEntryWithSender:` selector to the command. As discussed earlier, the system will search the responder chain until it finds an object which can perform that selector.

If the method weren't marked as `@IBAction`, Interface Builder wouldn't be able to find the method.

Build and run. Select **File ▸ New Entry** in the menu bar. You'll see a new entry pop-up. You can also press **Option-Command-N** to add new items.

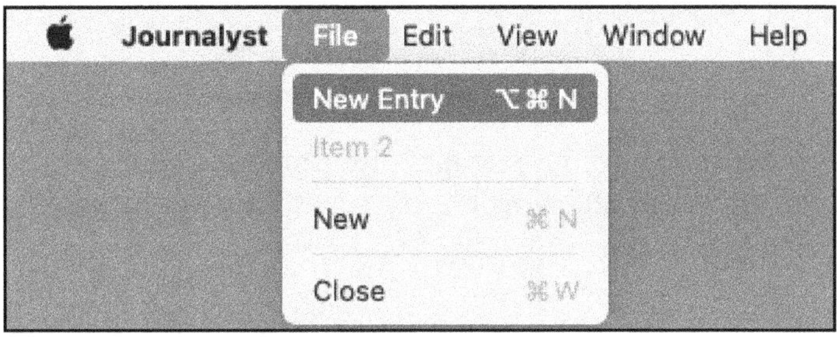

New entry in the File menu.

Congrats, young barista, you just brewed your first menu item. Keep the momentum going by adding a command to delete an entry.

Deleting Entries

Back in **Main.storyboard**, select **Item 2** in the File submenu you added earlier. In the Attributes Inspector, change its **Title** to **Delete Entry** and set the **Key Equivalent** to **Shift-Command-Backspace**.

Open **RootSplitViewController.swift** and add `@IBAction` to `removeEntry(sender:)`:

```
@IBAction @objc private func removeEntry(
  sender: UIKeyCommand
) {
```

Again, the method needs to be annotated with `@IBAction` so interface builder can see it.

Now, back in **Main.storyboard** control-drag from the **Delete Entry** command to the first responder and select `removeEntryWithSender:` as the action.

Build and run, then select the first entry. Select **File ▸ Delete Entry** to delete the entry.

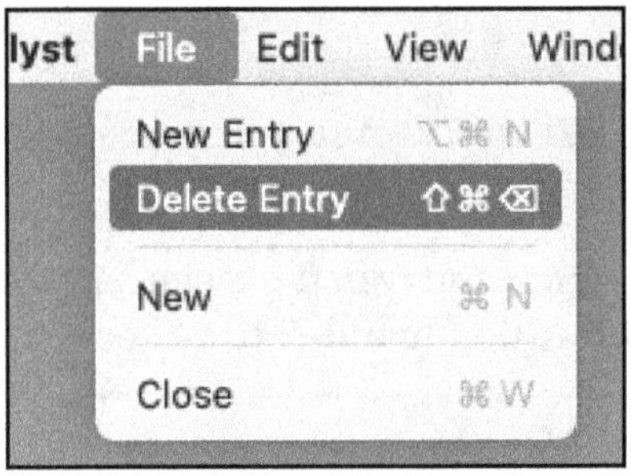

Delete Entry in the File menu.

It might be a good idea to give the user more information about *which* item they're deleting. You can do that by changing the command's title to include the date and time of the currently selected entry.

Open **EntryTableViewController.swift** and override `validate(_:)` once again:

```
override func validate(_ command: UICommand) {
  switch command.action {
  case #selector(share):
    if textView.text.isEmpty {
      command.attributes = [.disabled]
    } else {
      command.attributes = []
    }
  default:
    break
  }
}
```

If the user hasn't entered any text, you're adding `.disabled` to the command's attributes array. Otherwise, you're clearing the attributes so that the command becomes enabled.

> **Note**: You can also disable commands by overriding `canPerformAction` and returning `false`. Keep in mind that by doing so, `validate` won't get called for the disabled command.

Build and run one last time and you'll see *Share* disabled until you type something into the entry's text view.

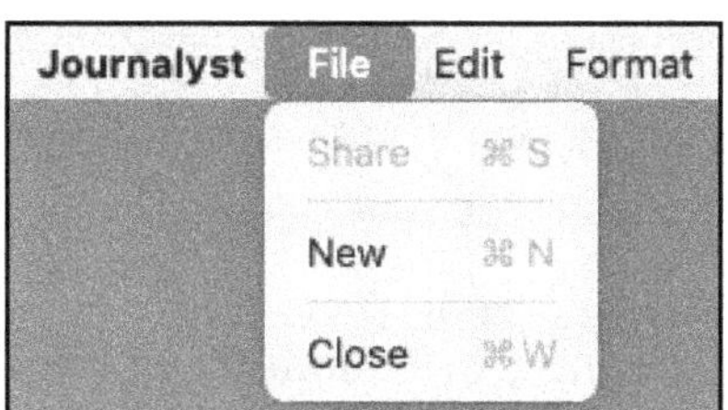

Disable Share in empty text view.

This concludes your barista training for the menu bar! Keep an eye out for any cafe managers bringing you job offers.

Key Points

- Catalyst apps include a default menu bar for free.
- The menu bar consists of nested **menus** which contain **commands**.
- Each command has a **selector** that it calls when pressed, and uses the **responder chain** to enable and disable itself.
- You add or remove items from the menu bar by dragging over a **Main Menu** to your app's storyboard.
- You can make the same changes in code by overriding `buildMenu` in the app delegate.
- Override `validate` in a `UIResponder` subclass to change the appearance of a command.

Where to Go From Here?

The Human Interface Guidelines section on menus (https://apple.co/2EymXZv) has some useful tips of which actions to consider for the menu bar, and where to put them.

To see which options you have when building out a menu bar, check out the documentation for `UIMenuBuilder` here (https://apple.co/33lcUyj). You can also see the different properties of `UICommand` to get a sense of how to further customize commands (https://apple.co/2M6qJvp).

Finally, the WWDC 2019 session Taking iPad Apps for Mac to the Next Level (https://apple.co/33j3CmM) walks you through building a menu bar using the menu builder.

Chapter 11: Barista Training: Toolbar

By Andy Pereira

Toolbars are an essential part of macOS applications. Without a doubt, `NSToolbar` is used so ubiquitously across so many apps that most users may overlook its presence. Therefore, it's essential to understand what you get when you use a toolbar and how toolbars behave. By adopting `NSToolbar` in your app, you have access to almost two decades worth of work from the smart developers and designers at Apple.

Getting Started

Open the starter project for this chapter. Select **My Mac** for the active scheme, and build and run. At the moment, this project has a split view controller and can handle multiple windows:

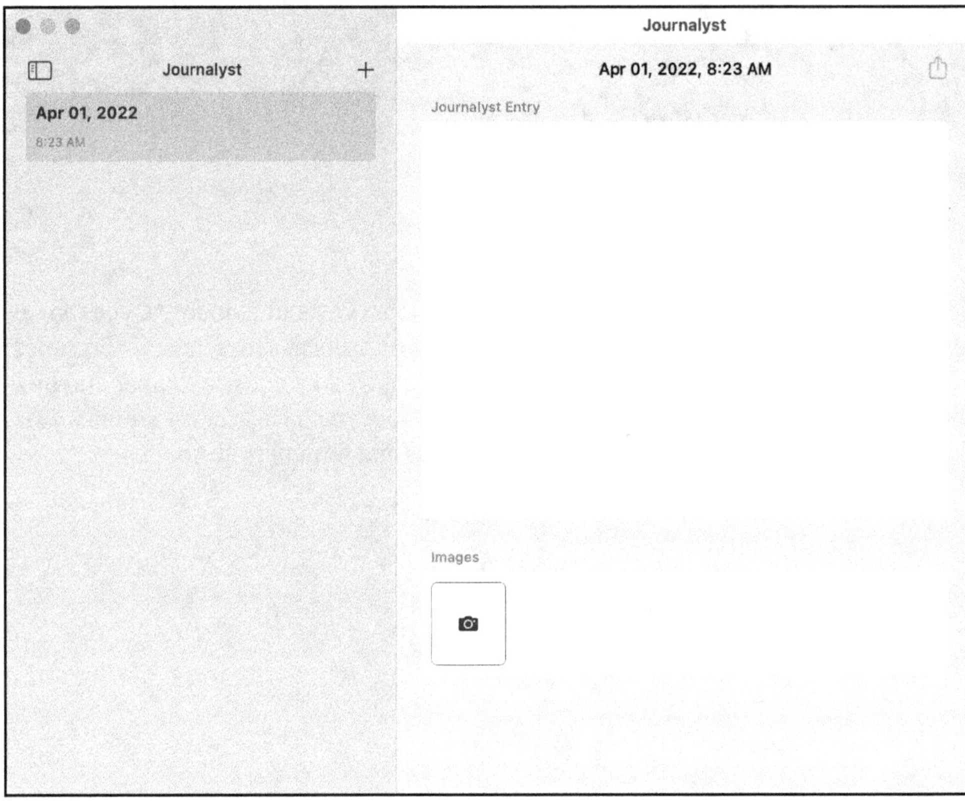

Starter with a split view controller, handles multiple windows.

Adding the Toolbar

`NSToolbar` is a macOS-specific control. In the past, you probably had to use macros or targets to ensure frameworks did not get imported into unsupported builds. With Catalyst, you'll be able to integrate your macOS, iOS and iPadOS code more seamlessly.

To add the toolbar, open **SceneDelegate.swift** and add the following to the end of `scene(_:willConnectTo:options:)`:

```
#if targetEnvironment(macCatalyst)
// 1
if let scene = scene as? UIWindowScene,
    let titlebar = scene.titlebar {
    // 2
    let toolbar = NSToolbar(identifier: "Toolbar")
   // 3
   titlebar.toolbar = toolbar
}
#endif
```

Here's what you've done:

1. You check that the scene has a `titlebar`. This property will be present if the app is running inside a macOS environment.
2. Then you create a toolbar with an identifier. Every one of the toolbars will have the same identifier so that the system synchronizes their state across windows.
3. Last, you set the toolbar on the titlebar.

Build and run, and you'll see a beautiful — albeit empty — toolbar.

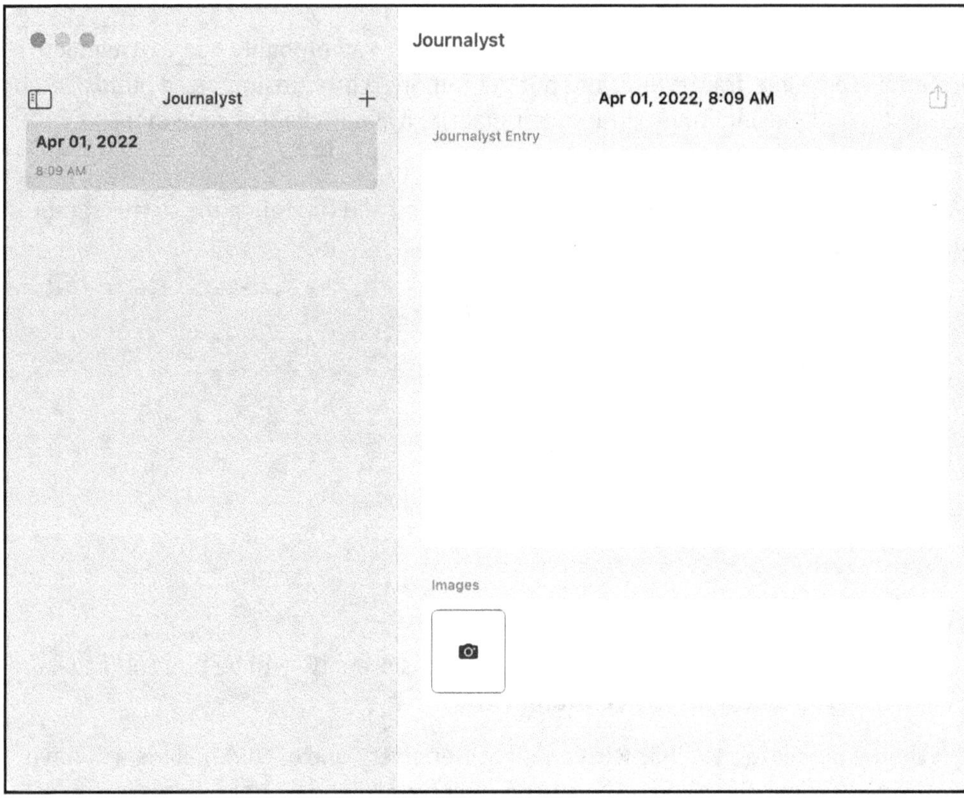

Empty toolbar.

It doesn't make sense to keep the navigation bars around any longer, as the toolbar serves the same purpose.

To get rid of both of the navigation bars, open **MainTableViewController.swift** and add the following to the end of `viewDidLoad`:

```
#if targetEnvironment(macCatalyst)
navigationController?.navigationBar.isHidden = true
#endif
```

Here, you hid the navigation bar when running on macOS.

Then, open **EntryTableViewController.swift** and add the same line of code to the existing macro. Build and run, and now your navigation bars are gone, leaving just a toolbar:

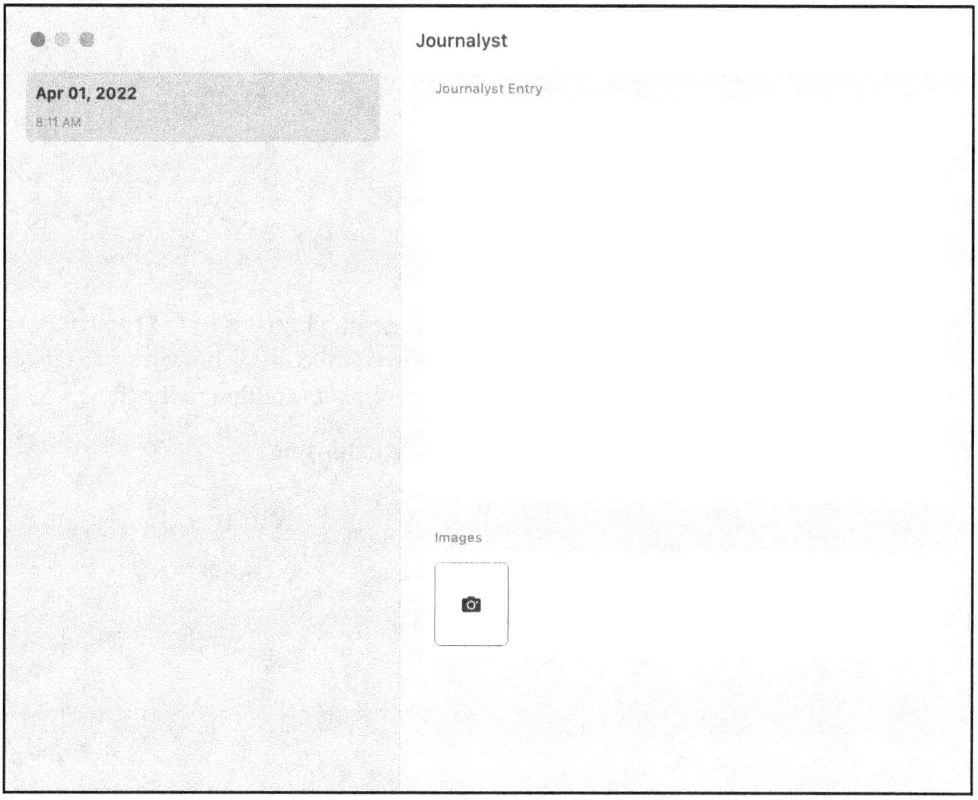

Navigation bars removed.

Adding Buttons

In its current state, the toolbar is providing no functionality to the app. To start adding functionality, you'll add a few buttons.

Open **SceneDelegate.swift** and add the following after setting the toolbar on the titlebar:

```
toolbar.delegate = self
```

Next, at the end of the file, inside the empty macro that checks for Catalyst, add the following:

```
extension NSToolbarItem.Identifier {
  static let addEntry =
    NSToolbarItem.Identifier(rawValue: "AddEntry")
  static let deleteEntry =
    NSToolbarItem.Identifier(rawValue: "DeleteEntry")
  static let shareEntry =
    NSToolbarItem.Identifier(rawValue: "ShareEntry")
}

extension SceneDelegate: NSToolbarDelegate {
}
```

These three toolbar identifiers are needed to start adding buttons to the toolbar. Just like you added an identifier to the toolbar for the system to know how to sync across windows, these identifiers allow the toolbar to know *what* is added to itself.

Next, add the following to the **NSToolbarDelegate** extension:

```
func toolbarAllowedItemIdentifiers(
  _ toolbar: NSToolbar
) -> [NSToolbarItem.Identifier] {
  return [
    .toggleSidebar,
    .addEntry,
    .deleteEntry,
    .shareEntry,
    .flexibleSpace
  ]
}
```

By adding this, you tell the toolbar which identifiers are allowed to be in the toolbar. You'll notice that the three identifiers are what you *just* added in the previous step.

The first item, `.toggleSidebar` is a convenience button for showing and hiding your sidebar. The last one, `.flexibleSpace`, is a system-defined identifier that places a blank item that used to automatically adjust its spacing. As of macOS 11, it just adds a divider line.

Now, add the following method:

```
func toolbarDefaultItemIdentifiers(
  _ toolbar: NSToolbar
) -> [NSToolbarItem.Identifier] {
  return [.toggleSidebar, .addEntry, .shareEntry]
}
```

Adding `toolbarDefaultItemIdentifiers(_:)` informs the toolbar what should initially be displayed in itself. Later, when you start customizing the toolbar, it will provide the user a way to reset the toolbar to the initial state.

You're almost there, but there are a few more steps before you can add the buttons. Add the following methods inside the same extension:

```
// 1.
func toolbar(
  _ toolbar: NSToolbar,
  itemForItemIdentifier itemIdentifier:
  NSToolbarItem.Identifier,
  willBeInsertedIntoToolbar flag: Bool
) -> NSToolbarItem? {
  var item: NSToolbarItem?
  return item
}

// 2.
@objc private func addEntry() {
}

@objc private func deleteEntry() {
}
```

Here's what you've added:

1. This method provides the actual buttons to a toolbar. It's currently incomplete and will be finished shortly.

2. These methods are for convenience right now and will be finished later.

At last, you're ready to add the buttons.

Add the following property to `SceneDelegate`:

```
#if targetEnvironment(macCatalyst)
private let shareItem =
  NSSharingServicePickerToolbarItem(
    itemIdentifier: .shareEntry
  )
#endif
```

Replace `toolbar(_:itemForItemIdentifier:willBeInsertedIntoToolbar:)` with the following:

```
func toolbar(
  _ toolbar: NSToolbar,
  itemForItemIdentifier itemIdentifier:
  NSToolbarItem.Identifier,
  willBeInsertedIntoToolbar flag: Bool
) -> NSToolbarItem? {

  var item: NSToolbarItem?
  switch itemIdentifier {
  // 1
  case .addEntry:
    item = NSToolbarItem(itemIdentifier: .addEntry)
    item?.image = UIImage(systemName: "plus")
    item?.label = "Add"
    item?.toolTip = "Add Entry"
    item?.target = self
    item?.action = #selector(addEntry)
  // 2
  case .deleteEntry:
    item = NSToolbarItem(itemIdentifier: .deleteEntry)
    item?.image = UIImage(systemName: "trash")
    item?.label = "Delete"
    item?.toolTip = "Delete Entry"
    item?.target = self
    item?.action = #selector(deleteEntry)
  // 3
  case .shareEntry:
    return shareItem
  case .toggleSidebar:
    item = NSToolbarItem(itemIdentifier: itemIdentifier)
  default:
    item = nil
  }
  return item
}
```

You add custom buttons to the toolbar by checking the identifier passed in and returning the appropriate button. Here are the buttons you added:

1. **Add**: This adds a new journal entry to the app.
2. **Delete**: Based on the active window, it deletes the selected entry.
3. **Share**: Just like delete, it shares the active window's current entry.

Build and run. Since your default buttons are just **Add** and **Share**, you'll only see two buttons on the right initially:

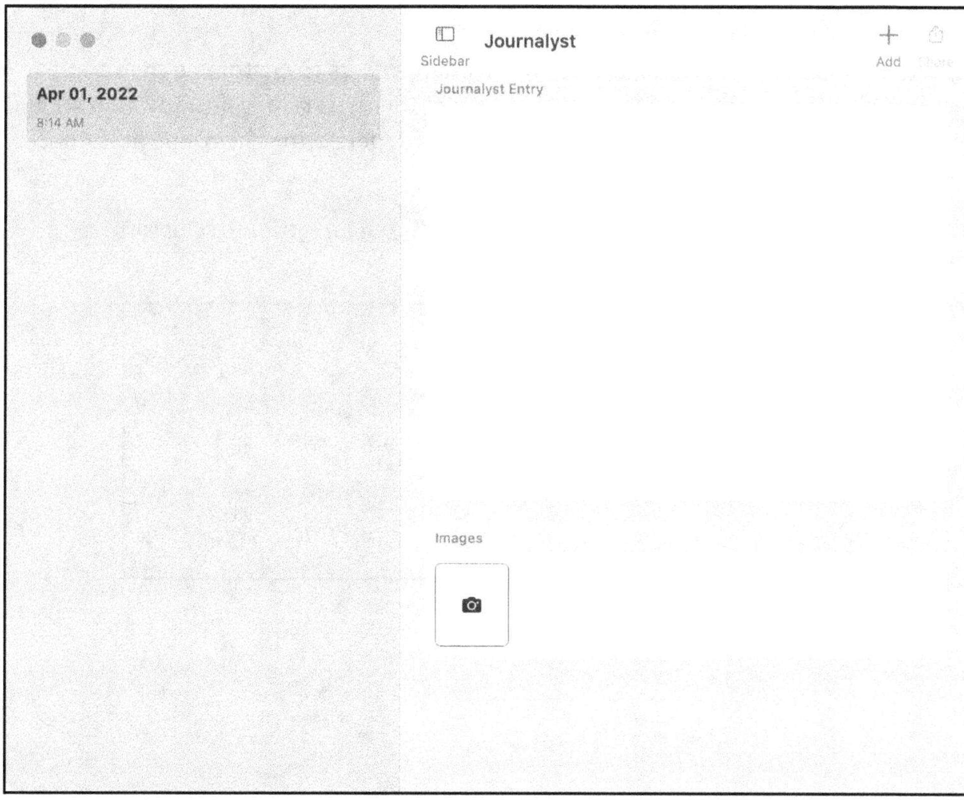

Add and Share buttons.

OK. You're now officially past the toughest part of working with toolbars in this chapter!

Customizing the Toolbar

Toolbars don't always have to contain a fixed set of buttons. Above, you provided a delete button without giving the user a way to see it. You can enable your toolbar to be customized by the user, and save its state between launches.

Still within **SceneDelegate.swift**, add the following lines of code after you set the delegate for the toolbar inside `scene(_:willConectTo:options:)`:

```
toolbar.allowsUserCustomization = true
toolbar.autosavesConfiguration = true
```

By setting `allowsUserCustomization`, you enable users to customize their toolbar by right-clicking it. Also, `autosavesConfiguration` determines if the system should save the toolbar configuration to `NSUserDefaults`, persisting the user's preferences between runs.

Build and run, then right-click your toolbar. You'll see an option to **Customize Toolbar**:

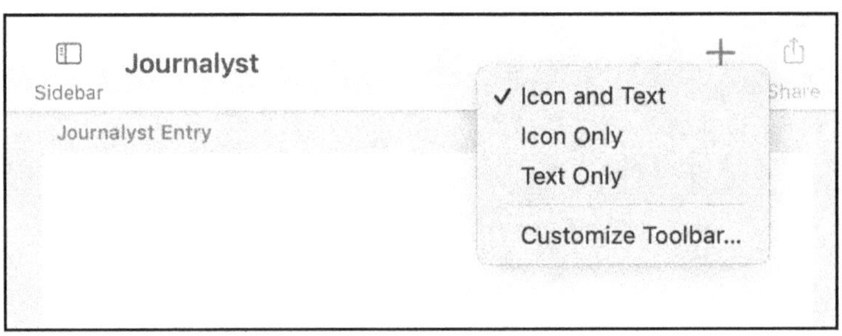

Customize toolbars.

Select this option, and you'll see a modal window in which you can customize the toolbar:

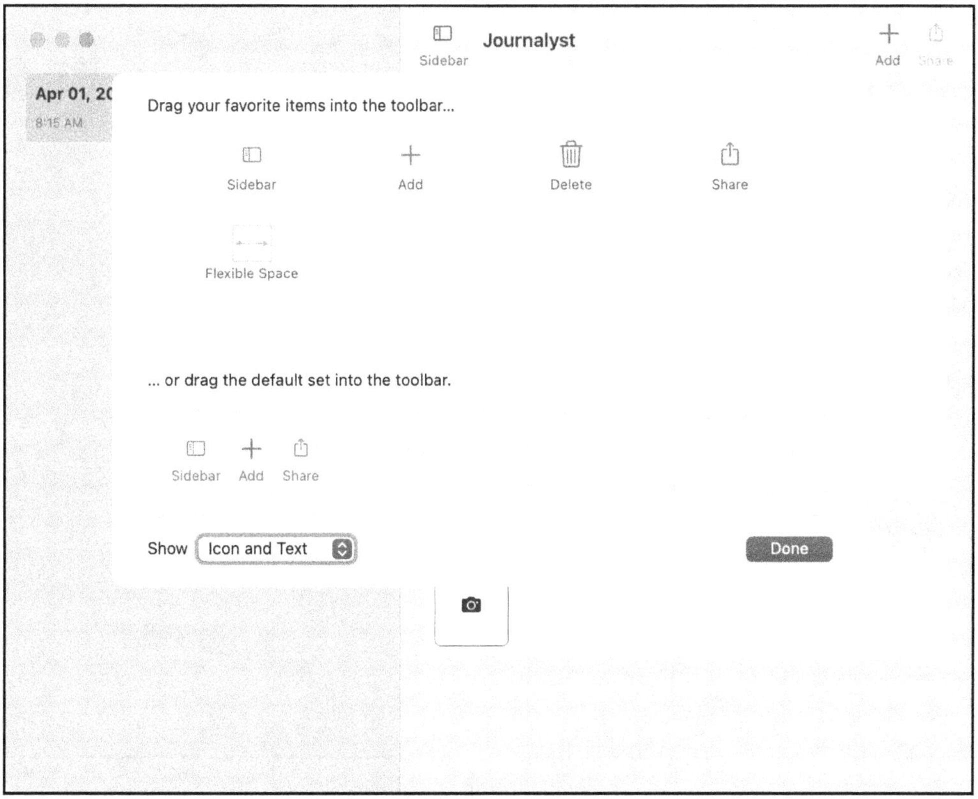

Modal window to customize toolbar.

Try changing the configuration, then quit the application and restart it. Your changes remain between runs.

Finally, you can also remove the title bar from the window, making the toolbar a bit smaller. To test this, add the following to `scene(_:willConnectTo:options:)`, after setting the delegate:

```
titlebar.titleVisibility = .hidden
```

Build and run to see how this looks:

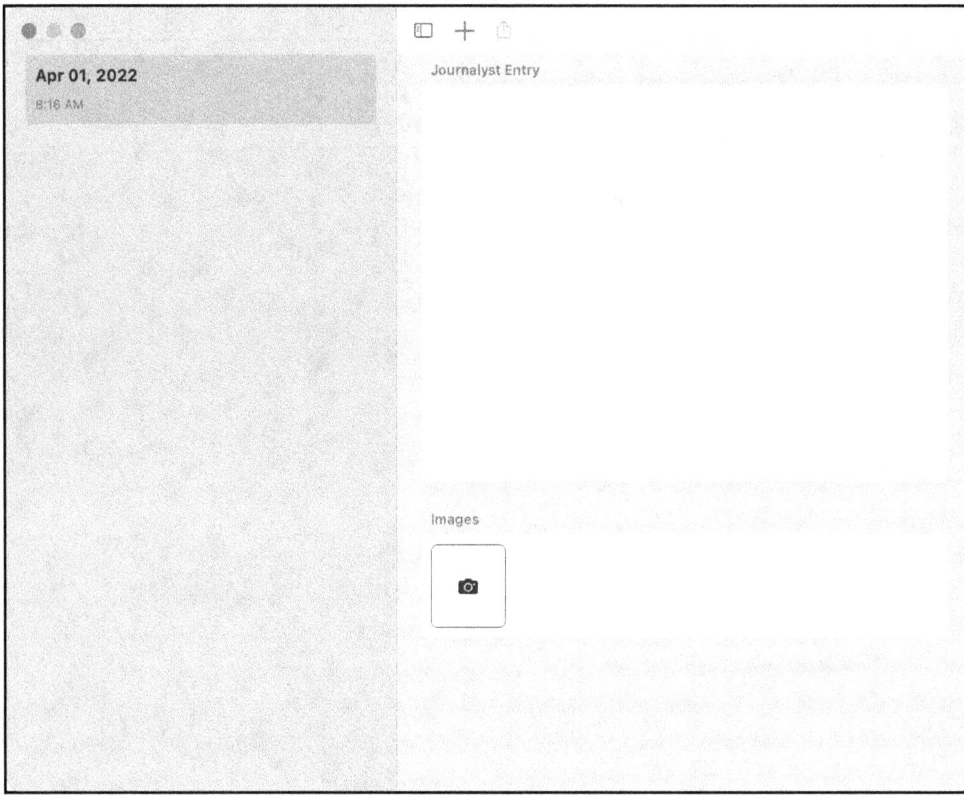

Toolbar without a title bar.

Notice that the labels and the title in the window are now gone. You can remove this line of code for the remainder of the chapter.

Responding to Actions

The last thing you need to do is respond to actions in the toolbar. To add items to the list, replace the empty `addEntry` with the following:

```
@objc private func addEntry() {
  guard
    let splitViewController
      = window?.rootViewController
      as? UISplitViewController,
    let navigationController
      = splitViewController.viewControllers.first
```

```
        as? UINavigationController,
      let mainTableViewController
        = navigationController.topViewController
        as? MainTableViewController
    else { return }
    DataService.shared.addEntry(Entry())
    let index = DataService.shared.allEntries.count - 1
    mainTableViewController.selectEntryAtIndex(index)
  }
```

This code adds a new entry to your data model, and then select it in the list.

Build and run, then click **Add**. You see entries get added to the list:

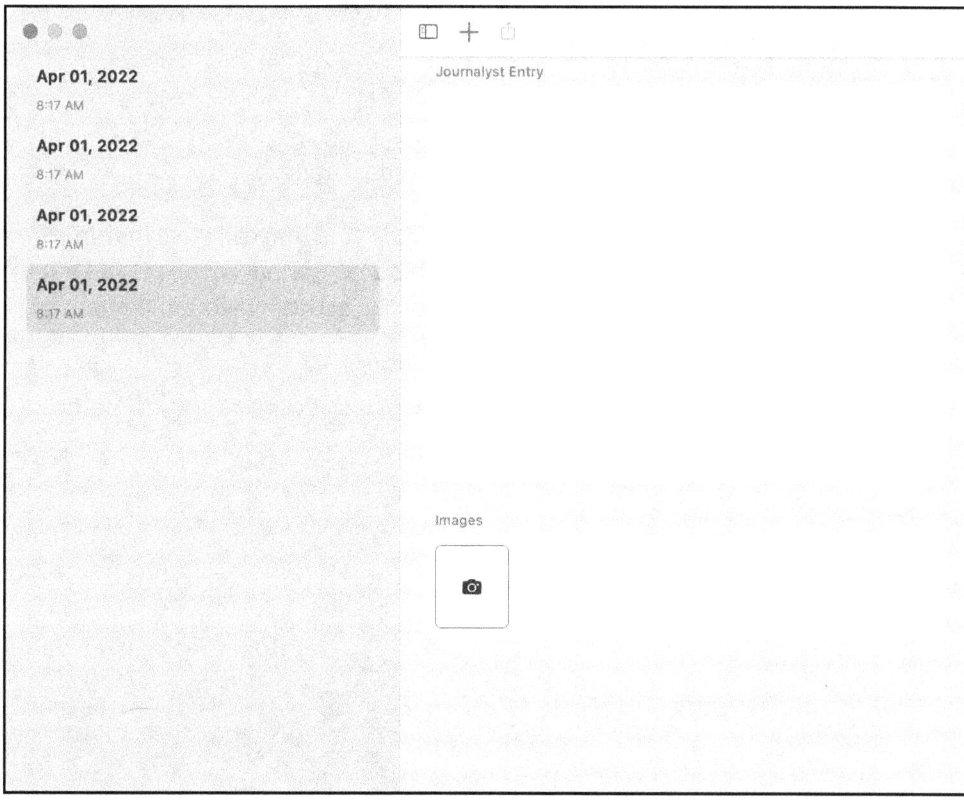

Entry gets added to the list.

Next, implement `deleteEntry` with the following:

```
guard let splitViewController =
  window?.rootViewController as? UISplitViewController,
  let navigationController =
    splitViewController.viewControllers.first
    as? UINavigationController,
  let mainTableViewController =
    navigationController.topViewController
    as? MainTableViewController,
  let secondaryViewController =
    splitViewController.viewControllers.last
    as? UINavigationController,
  let entryTableViewController =
    secondaryViewController.topViewController
    as? EntryTableViewController,
  let entry = entryTableViewController.entry,
  let index = DataService.shared.allEntries
    .firstIndex(of: entry) else { return }
DataService.shared.removeEntry(atIndex: index)
mainTableViewController.selectEntryAtIndex(index)
```

This isn't as complicated as it *may* first appear. Since your app can have multiple windows, you need to check which entry is selected in the window you select **Delete** in. This code simply goes through the hierarchy of the active window and removes the appropriate entry.

Build and run. Ensure you have the delete button in your toolbar, add a few entries, then select **Delete**.

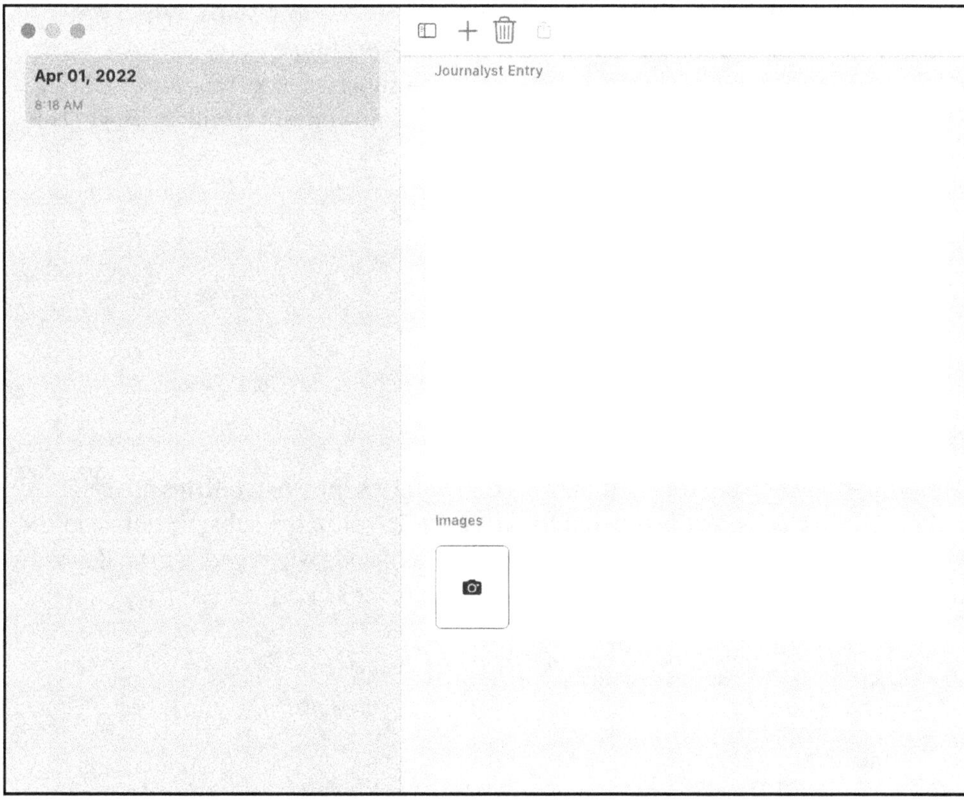

Entry gets deleted from the list.

Sharing

For the final toolbar item, **Share**, you'll need to do a few more steps. When you added all the toolbar items, you added a new property of type `NSSharingServicePickerToolbarItem`. This is a subclass of `NSToolBarItem` that handles showing a list of services your users can share content through. To get this working takes a few steps.

First, import `Combine` in **SceneDelegate.swift**:

```
import Combine
```

Next, add a new property to `SceneDelegate`:

```
private var
  activityItemsConfigurationSubscriber: AnyCancellable?
```

This property will listen for notifications that will be sent when entries are selected in the main list, or as text is entered for an entry. To setup the subscription, add the following in **SceneDelegate.swift**, after the lines of code when you set the delegate for the toolbar inside `scene(_:willConectTo:options:)`:

```
activityItemsConfigurationSubscriber
  = NotificationCenter.default
  .publisher(for: .ActivityItemsConfigurationDidChange)
  .receive(on: RunLoop.main)
  .map({
    $0.userInfo?[NotificationKey.activityItemsConfiguration]
      as? UIActivityItemsConfiguration
  })
  .assign(
    to: \.activityItemsConfiguration,
    on: shareItem
  )
```

If you're unfamiliar with **Combine**, all you need to understand is the following:

- You setup `activityItemsConfigurationSubscriber` to listen for the notification `ActivityItemsConfigurationDidChange`.
- When it receives the notification, handle any actions on the main thread.
- Grab the `activityItemsConfiguration` that was sent in the notification, and assign it to your **Share** button's `activityItemsConfiguration`.

At the moment, your **Share** item is always disabled. It remains disabled until an entry is in a state to be shared.

To handle this behavior, and setup the configuration that your button is expecting, open **EntryTableViewController.swift** and add the following extension to the end of the file:

```
extension EntryTableViewController {
  private func configureActivityItems() {
    let configuration
      = UIActivityItemsConfiguration(objects: [])
    // 1.
    configuration.metadataProvider = { key in
      // 2.
      guard let shareText
        = self.shareText else { return nil }
      switch key {
      // 3.
      case .title, .messageBody:
        return shareText
      default:
        return nil
      }
    }
    // 4.
    NotificationCenter
      .default
      .post(
        name: .ActivityItemsConfigurationDidChange,
        object: self,
        userInfo: [
          NotificationKey
          .activityItemsConfiguration: configuration
        ]
      )
  }
}
```

Here's a breakdown of what you've added:

1. You create a `UIActivityItemsConfiguration` and setup what needs to be provided through the `metadataProvider`. This will inform the service that handles sharing your content what needs to be shared.
2. Ensure that you have text to share, otherwise don't allow content to be shared.
3. Set your entry's text as the content to be shared.
4. Post a notification with the new configuration. This is the notification and configuration content you setup in the previous step.

There's two places you'll want to call `configureActivityItems`. First, add the following to the main body of `EntryTableViewController`:

```
override func viewDidAppear(_ animated: Bool) {
  super.viewDidAppear(animated)
  configureActivityItems()
}
```

This will handle notifying your toolbar item to update whenever you switch entries.

Finally, replace `textViewDidChange(_:)` with the following:

```
func textViewDidChange(_ textView: UITextView) {
  validateState()
  configureActivityItems()
}
```

Now, when you start entering any text for an entry, the share button will be updated with your latest content.

Build and run, add some text to an entry, then select **Share**.

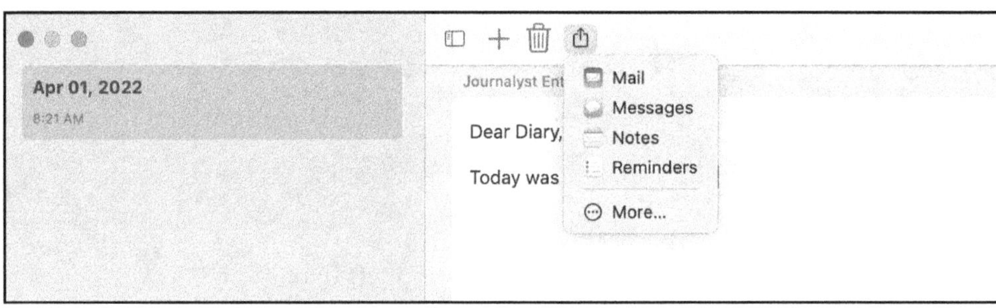

Share entry.

Key Points

- Use Mac style toolbars, not iOS navigation bars in macOS apps.
- Toolbars are for the entire window, not just the specific view controller presented to the user.
- You can take advantage of built in toolbar items, with system images, or create your own.
- Users are used to customizing toolbars in many apps. Ensure you provide this capability, as it makes sense.

Where to Go From Here?

This chapter showed you how quick it is to implement a macOS-centric design in a way that was never so easy. While knowing how to implement your own toolbar items is important, don't forget there are several other system-provided toolbar items provided that you can put to use as well.

You can learn more about these topics from Apple's website (https://developer.apple.com/documentation/appkit/nstoolbaritem/identifier).

Chapter 12: Barista Training: The Touch Bar

By Marin Benčević

You're just one final step away from becoming a true barista master! The one last remaining bar on your journey is... the Touch Bar. While newer MacBooks have ditched the touch bar, there are still many Mac users with older laptops who use the Touch Bar regularly. Since Apple makes supporting the Touch Bar really easy there is no reason why you wouldn't take this step in making your Catalyst app feel completely at home on macOS.

In this chapter, you'll expand the app you've been working on to add a few useful items to the Touch Bar. You'll learn about positioning those items and how to allow your users to customize them.

Before you get started, though, you'll learn how the Touch Bar works under the hood.

Understanding the Touch Bar

While using your Mac, the Touch Bar is continuously changing depending on what's active on the screen. Similarly to the menu bar, the Touch Bar uses the **responder chain** to determine which items to present. Take a look at Chapter 10, "Barista Training: Menu Bar" to learn more about the responder chain.

The gist is that each view controller and view is a **responder**, and one of them is the **first responder**, which is the currently active view. The responder chain works like a tree, going upwards from the first responder all the way to the root window of your app.

Each item in the responder chain can say "Here are the items I want in the Touch Bar." When the first responder changes, the Touch Bar goes up the chain, picking up items as it goes. Of course, not all of these items fit on the Touch Bar, so the Touch Bar prioritizes items closer to the first responder. The ones at the back don't get shown, and wait patiently for their turn to shine.

However, the ones in the back don't necessarily have to take back stage! If you think an item is more or less important, you can set its priority to a higher or lower value. The Touch Bar will take this into account when ordering the items.

The responders suggest their items to the Touch Bar by overriding `makeTouchBar`. That method returns an `NSTouchBar` object. Don't let the naming confuse you: The Touch Bar — the physical bar — displays multiple instances of `NSTouchBar`. In the following screenshot you'll see three distinct `NSTouchBar` instances shown on the Touch Bar:

Notes app Touch Bar.

This is the Touch Bar of the Notes app. Bar 3 is the system bar and it's always there. Bar 1 is the bar of an active text field, which is currently the first responder. Bar 2 bullied through and hid some items from Bar 1 because Bar 1 is deeper in the responder chain.

Note: Since the Touch Bar is only available on macOS, `NSTouchBar` and related APIs are lifted directly from macOS and included in Catalyst, which explains the *NS* prefix. This means that already existing macOS-specific Touch Bar documentation and tutorials are generally applicable to Catalyst apps.

Adding Items

Now that we've, ahem, *touched* on some theory, you're ready to add some new items!

Open the starter project from the provided materials for this chapter and navigate to **RootSplitViewController.swift**. As mentioned before, each view controller is a responder and, since `RootSplitViewController` is always in the responder chain, it makes sense to add entry-related items there.

You'll start by adding a button that adds a new entry. The first step to adding a Touch Bar item is to define its **identifier**. The Touch Bar uses these identifiers to keep track of which items to show and hide. It also uses the identifier to save customization options for specific items. You'll read more about customization later in this chapter.

Add the following extension at the top of the file, right under the `import`:

```
#if targetEnvironment(macCatalyst)
extension NSTouchBarItem.Identifier {
  static let newEntry =
    NSTouchBarItem.Identifier(
    "com.yourcompany.Journalyst.addEntry"
  )
}
#endif
```

It's a good practice to extend `NSTouchBarItem.Identifier` instead of peppering a bunch of hard-coded strings around your codebase.

Since the Touch Bar only exists on macOS, you'll wrap most of the code from this chapter in a preprocessor macro that conditionally compiles the code only if it's running on macOS.

Now you can create the item. As mentioned, each subclass of `UIResponder` can override `makeTouchBar` to add items to the Touch Bar.

Next, override `makeTouchBar` in the class like this:

```
#if targetEnvironment(macCatalyst)
override func makeTouchBar() -> NSTouchBar? {
  let bar = NSTouchBar()
  bar.defaultItemIdentifiers = [.newEntry]
  let button = NSButtonTouchBarItem(
    identifier: .newEntry,
    title: "New Entry",
    target: self,
    action: #selector(addEntry)
  )
  bar.templateItems = [button]
  return bar
}
#endif
```

Here's what you're doing:

First, you create a new instance of `NSTouchBar`. The most important property of the bar is `defaultItemIdentifiers` — an array of all the items' identifiers. If you forget to set this, the items won't show.

Then, you create an `NSButtonTouchBarItem` object, which is a subclass of `NSTouchBarItem`. You define the button's title and set its identifier to the one you just created. Just like menu bar items, Touch Bar items use the target-action pattern to determine what happens when tapped. Finally, you add the item to `NSTouchBar`'s `templateItems` property and return the bar. The `templateItems` property lets you directly manipulate which items the touch bar will show.

If you're running on a Mac without a Touch Bar, you can still test this out. In Xcode, choose **Window ▸ Touch Bar ▸ Show Touch Bar** and it'll show the Touch Bar in a floating window.

Build and run. You see the item in the Touch Bar.

New Entry item shows in the Touch Bar.

Click the Journalyst Entry text field and note how this causes this item to disappear because it's no longer in the responder chain. When you reactivate any cell in the list of entries, this causes the "New Entry" item to reappear once again.

You'll notice that you used a subclass of `NSTouchBarItem`. Generally, you won't use the `NSTouchBarItem` class directly, since Apple provides a selection of pre-built item types for you. These include:

- `NSCandidateListTouchBarItem`: Shows a list of options to pick from.
- `NSColorPickerTouchBarItem`: Lets you pick a color.
- `NSSharingServicePickerTouchBarItem`: Displays a list of ways to share provided data.
- `NSSliderTouchBarItem`: Shows a slider between two values.
- `NSButtonTouchBarItem`: That's the one you used earlier. It displays a regular button.

You can also use `NSCustomTouchBarItem` to show a custom view in the Touch Bar item.

Unfortunately, most of these items are exposed in a limited way in Catalyst, and several of them are completely unusable. Of the above items, the only fully usable ones are `NSButtonTouchBarItem` and `NSColorPickerTouchBarItem`.

There are also higher-level subclasses that can contain multiple items. These are `NSGroupTouchBarItem`, which holds a group of items, and `NSPopoverTouchBarItem`, which expands to show more items when tapped. You'll use `NSGroupTouchBarItem` later in the chapter.

Going back to what you did in the code. You created your item by adding it to the bar's `templateItems` property. This is the easiest way to create Touch Bar items. But it comes with a drawback. Since the Touch Bar has a direct reference to the item, it stays loaded in memory, even when not shown. That's why you must use `templateItems` *only for lightweight items.*

Implementing the Delegate

To avoid this memory issue, you'll implement `NSTouchBarDelegate`. Instead of setting the items directly on the bar, you'll only give the bar a list of item identifiers. The bar then asks the delegate for the item only when it's needed. This is similar to how table views work: Cells are created *on-demand* instead of being loaded automatically.

First, change the implementation of makeTouchBar. Remove the lines where you create and set the button on the bar, and add a new line to set the bar's delegate to self. When finished, your method's code looks like this:

```
let bar = NSTouchBar()
bar.delegate = self
bar.defaultItemIdentifiers = [.newEntry]
return bar
```

Next, at the bottom of the file add the following extension to implement the delegate:

```
#if targetEnvironment(macCatalyst)
extension RootSplitViewController: NSTouchBarDelegate {
  func touchBar(
    _ touchBar: NSTouchBar,
    makeItemForIdentifier identifier: NSTouchBarItem.Identifier
  ) -> NSTouchBarItem? {
    switch identifier {
    case .newEntry:
      let button = NSButtonTouchBarItem(
        identifier: identifier,
        title: "New Entry",
        target: self,
        action: #selector(addEntry)
      )
      return button
    default:
      return nil
    }
  }
}
#endif
```

This is similar to tableView(_:cellForRowAt:). The method asks the delegate to create an item based on the provided identifier. In the method, switch on the identifier and, if it matches the one you created earlier, create the item in the same way you did in makeTouchBar.

Build and run, you see the same item you saw earlier.

New Entry item again shows in the Touch Bar.

So, you just changed a bunch of your code, and absolutely nothing changed in the bar. Pretty heady stuff, right? :]

Seriously, in spite of a lack of fireworks, the important thing is that your new code is now more *memory-efficient*. While this might seem like overkill for a single button, in practice you'll typically have a lot more items in your app. Adding items this way from the start saves you from potential headaches down the road.

One more thing: You probably noticed that the Touch Bar automatically positioned your item on the left-hand side. In the next section, you'll see how to position Touch Bar items in a better way.

Grouping Items

It's time to add three more items to the Touch Bar: "Delete," "Next Entry" and "Previous Entry." Since all these three items relate to the currently selected entry, you put them all in a single group item, instead of adding them individually.

First, add the following property to the `NSTouchBarItem.Identifier` extension:

```
static let entryOptions = NSTouchBarItem.Identifier(
  "com.yourcompany.journalyst.entryOptions"
)
```

You'll use this identifier for the group item. Add it in `makeTouchBar` by changing the array of item identifiers to this:

```
bar.defaultItemIdentifiers = [.newEntry, .entryOptions]
```

Now that the Touch Bar is instructed to display the item, you can create it in `touchBar(_:makeItemForIdentifier:)`. Start by adding a new case inside the switch statement, right before the `default` case, and inside this case, create an item for each of the three actions you'll add:

```
case .entryOptions:
  let next = NSButtonTouchBarItem(
    identifier: .init(identifier.rawValue + ".next"),
    title: "Next Entry",
    target: self,
    action: #selector(goToNext)
  )
  let previous = NSButtonTouchBarItem(
    identifier: .init(identifier.rawValue + ".previous"),
    title: "Previous Entry",
    target: self,
    action: #selector(goToPrevious)
  )
  let delete = NSButtonTouchBarItem(
```

```
    identifier: .init(identifier.rawValue + ".delete"),
    title: "Delete",
    target: self,
    action: #selector(removeEntry)
  )
```

In this code, you've created these three new items in the same way that you added the "New Entry" button item earlier. Note that the starter project already includes methods for each of these items to call.

Next, you'll create a spacer item and place it between "Previous Item" and "Delete." This is small user experience improvement that helps ensure that your users don't tap on "Delete" accidentally.

To do this, add the following line to the case after the delete item:

```
let spacer = NSTouchBarItem(identifier: .fixedSpaceLarge)
```

Spacer items are built-in Touch Bar items that are created by assigning one of two predefined identifiers to the item: `.fixedSpaceSmall` or `.fixedSpaceLarge`.

While all other item identifiers *must be unique*, you can use as many spacer items with the same identifier as you like.

Finally, create a group item and return it by adding the following code to the end of the case:

```
let group = NSGroupTouchBarItem(
  identifier: identifier,
  items: [spacer, next, previous, spacer, delete])
return group
```

Build and run, and you see your new items, including a small space between "Previous" and "Delete."

Entry items with spacing in the Touch Bar.

Since a group contains these items, the Touch Bar treats them all as a single composite item. They will always be shown and positioned together.

While using a MacBook with a Touch Bar, you might have noticed that some items are centered in the Touch Bar. You'll add one final *touch* to your group by centering it.

Each `NSTouchBar` can define one centered item, and it's called the **principal item**. The good news is that designating an item as principal is very easy. Modify your code now by adding the following line to `makeTouchBar`, just before its `return`:

```
bar.principalItemIdentifier = .entryOptions
```

Build and run again. You'll now see the group item centered inside the Touch Bar.

Group item centered in the Touch Bar.

By the way, the reason you work with identifiers rather than actual items is that whether items are displayed isn't always up to you. In fact, you can do something here that many developers dread: Give control of this decision directly to your users. In the next section, you'll see how to let users add and remove items from the Touch Bar.

Customizing the Touch Bar

If there's one thing nerds like us enjoy, it's customization options. Apple clearly had this in mind when they created the Touch Bar, as they added app-specific Touch Bar customization. As a developer, it's relatively easy to add support for this.

Apps that support Touch Bar customization have an additional option called **Customize Touch Bar...** inside the **View** menu of the menu bar. To add this option, head over to **AppDelegate.swift** and add the following line at the start of `application(_:didFinishLaunchingWithOptions:)`:

```
#if targetEnvironment(macCatalyst)
NSTouchBar.isAutomaticCustomizeTouchBarMenuItemEnabled = true
#endif
```

Take a moment to savor that supersized property name and read it out loud: "Is automatic customize Touch Bar menu item enabled." It's quite the mouthful, but the benefit of this verbosity is that the property name certainly does explain itself. :]

In spite of its length, enabling this property isn't enough to enable user Touch Bar customization. You'll need to do three more things:

1. Add a customization identifier to the `NSTouchBar` instance.

2. Enable customization for each item you want to be customizable.

3. Add a customization label to each of those items.

Head back to **RootSplitViewController.swift** to do this.

Fist, add an extension at the top of the file, inside the `#if` macro:

```
extension NSTouchBar.CustomizationIdentifier {
  static let journalyst = NSTouchBar.CustomizationIdentifier(
    "com.yourcompany.journalyst.main"
  )
}
```

Just like the item identifiers, the customization identifier has to be unique for each `NSTouchBar` instance.

Now, set this identifier and make your two items customizable by adding the following two lines to `makeTouchBar`, right before you return the bar:

```
bar.customizationIdentifier = .journalyst
bar.customizationAllowedItemIdentifiers
  = [.newEntry, .entryOptions]
```

That takes care of steps 1 and 2.

Next, you'll deal with step 3 by adding a customization identifier to each item you created. In `touchBar(_:makeItemForIdentifier)`, add the following line before `return button`:

```
button.customizationLabel = "Add a new entry"
```

Finally, do the same for the other case by adding this line before `return group`:

```
group.customizationLabel = "Entry Options"
```

These labels show on the customization screen. If you don't set them, you'll see an ugly warning instead of the labels.

Build and run, then select **View ▸ Customize Touch Bar...**

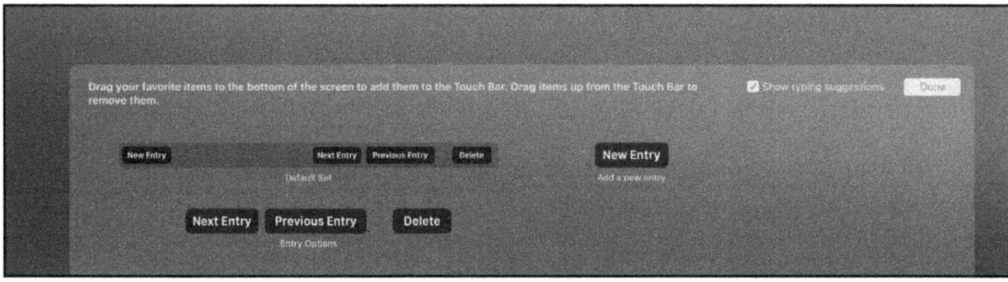

Customization Screen.

You'll see a screen where you can drag and drop each of your items to and from the Touch Bar. It feels kind of magical to drag an item to something *outside* the screen. Your settings will be saved, so the Touch Bar will stay the same each time you run the app.

> **Note**: If you're using the Touch Bar simulator, you won't drag and drop directly to the floating window. Imagine you have a Touch Bar below your screen — you'll drag to the bottom of the screen as if the Touch Bar was down there.

Congratulations, the Touch Bar was the final bar in your training journey. You're now a certified "bar"ista — feel free to add that to your resume! :]

This also completes Section 2 of this book. By now, your app looks like a native macOS citizen, while also running on iOS devices. How cool is that?

Key Points

- The Touch Bar is made of `NSTouchBar` instances.
- The Touch Bar uses the responder chain to determine which items to show.
- Each view and view controller can add items to the Touch Bar by overriding `makeTouchBar` and returning an `NSTouchBar`.
- Use `templateItems` only for lightweight items.
- For other items, implement `NSTouchBarDelegate`.
- Allow customization by enabling the customization menu item, making items customizable, and adding customization labels to the items.

Where to Go From Here?

To see some other Touch Bar items in action, check out here (https://bit.ly/2kxqPjs), the `NSTouchBar` tutorial written by Andy Pereira, one of the authors of this book.

Each Touch Bar item can be further customized by adding images and changing the fonts or colors of the item. You can read how to do this from Apple's documentation (https://apple.co/2k8Dx8c).

If you consider yourself a pro-level barista, keep in mind that items can be custom views and even include gesture recognizers. Try to think outside the box and make the Touch Bar a unique part of the way users interact with your app.

Section III: Distributing Your App

Congratulations! You now have a Mac app. But getting that app, first to your testers and then to your users can be a *little* different than on iOS.

In this section, you'll learn learn to roll out your app for beta testing using TestFlight. You'll then learn the options for distributing your app and how those options work.

Chapter 13: Releasing on the App Store

By Marin Benčević

If you're reading this book in order, you have a pretty good grasp of how to bring an iPhone or iPad app to macOS. Now it's time for the next step: getting your app into the users' hands.

Fortunately, once you have a Mac app, you can use Catalyst to choose how to distribute it. There are four ways to distribute your app:

- **The App Store**: The Mac App Store works almost like the iOS store. Since iOS apps already follow Apple's app review guidelines, you shouldn't have any issues going through app review. You can either release your app as a standalone Mac App Store product or offer a **universal purchase** so that your customers can buy your app on one Apple platform and have it everywhere else.
- **Third Party Distribution**: As long as you sign the app and have it notarized by Apple, anyone can simply download and launch it. The distribution, in this case, is up to you.
- **Developer Signing**: Similar to third-party distribution, you must sign your app with a development certificate. You can't use this option for distributing to the general public because the certificate includes an allowlist of specific devices that can install the app. In the past, this was your best bet for testing the app in development because macOS didn't have TestFlight support until 2021.
- **Test Flight**: Towards the end of 2021, Apple finally included TestFlight support for macOS apps. Test Flight is a service you can use to distribute beta versions of your app to your testers. Before you release your app, you can collect valuable feedback from the testers and improve your app.

If you made your Catalyst app in Xcode 11.3 or earlier, there are a few steps you need to take to get your app up to speed.

Updating Existing Catalyst Apps

Before Xcode 11.4, Catalyst apps had an automatically-assigned bundle ID with a *maccatalyst.* prefix. If you want to offer a universal purchase or just want a custom bundle ID, you'll have to make a quick change.

Go back to your main target's settings and open the **Build Settings** tab. Scroll down to the **User-Defined** section and set **DERIVE_UIKITFORMAC_PRODUCT_BUNDLE_IDENTIFIER** to **NO**. This setting tells Xcode to stop generating a bundle ID automatically and let you change the bundle ID in the **Signing & Capabilities** tab.

From there, you decide how you want to distribute your app.

The App Store vs. Third-Party Distribution

Since developer signing is only for testing, you're probably trying to decide whether to use the App Store or distribute the app independently. Each approach has pros and cons. The App Store has several benefits, including:

- Apple manages the app's storage and distribution.
- Apple handles payments, including the initial purchase of the app, in-app purchases and subscriptions. They also manage complaints and refunds.
- You can offer a universal purchase and make your app available on iOS and macOS with a single purchase.
- There's a chance that Apple might feature your app, giving you access to many users who otherwise might not hear of the app.
- You get access to the App Store's analytics and crash reporting with no additional effort.
- TestFlight is built-in and lets you easily beta test your app internally and with outside beta testers.

That said, distributing on the App Store does come with downsides:

- Most notably, Apple takes a cut from all App Store sales. This includes 15% or 30% of app sales and in-app purchases of digital goods, as well as 30% of subscriptions in the first year and 15% after that.
- You tie the app's destiny to Apple's. If they decide to move the App Store in a different direction or change their guidelines, you have no say. Apple could potentially hurt your sales or make your app unavailable.
- It limits your business model options. Offering dynamic or tiered pricing, enterprise deals or other more creative business models can be difficult or impossible.

While Apple takes a sizable cut of your income, it gives you the most convenient way to sell your app. It's your choice whether to invest significant effort to be the master of your destiny or save time by having Apple take care of distribution for you and take a cut of your profits.

If you really can't decide, Apple lets you simultaneously sell your app on your own and on the App Store.

This chapter teaches you how to distribute your app on the App Store, test it with TestFlight and offer a universal purchase. The next chapter deals with distributing your app on your own. If you need help deciding, read both chapters and see how you feel once you know what goes into both approaches.

Adding Your App to the App Store

Distributing your app via the App Store is tedious but straightforward. All you have to do is click a bunch of things! Before you get started, take note of some basic terminology you'll need while going through this process.

Code Signing

Xcode does an excellent job of automatically **code signing** your app. As the name suggests, code signing is a way of verifying that you wrote the code inside the app and that it hasn't changed since you wrote it. Code signing is required before a user can install an app on a device. Your signature is a **distribution certificate** that you get from Apple and is unique to your developer account.

However, the certificate alone is not enough. You also need an **App ID**, a value that uniquely identifies your app among all other apps on the App Store.

Your App ID and distribution certificate make up a **provisioning profile** that you include in the app's binary. The profile verifies that (a) this is your unique app, and (b) you signed it and didn't change it after that signing.

You can see all these parts in Xcode. Open this chapter's starter project or the app you want to distribute. In the **Project navigator**, click the name of the project and then the app target. Open the **Signing & Capabilities** tab.

You'll find all the relevant information for signing your app under **Signing**. The **Provisioning Profile** is the same for iOS and macOS, making macOS distribution much simpler.

Setting up an App ID

First, you need to create your app's app ID. You'll do that in Apple's developer portal.

Head to developer.apple.com, and click **Account** in the top-right corner. Log in with your Apple Developer ID.

Once logged in, navigate to **Certificates, IDs & Profiles** and then to **Identifiers**.

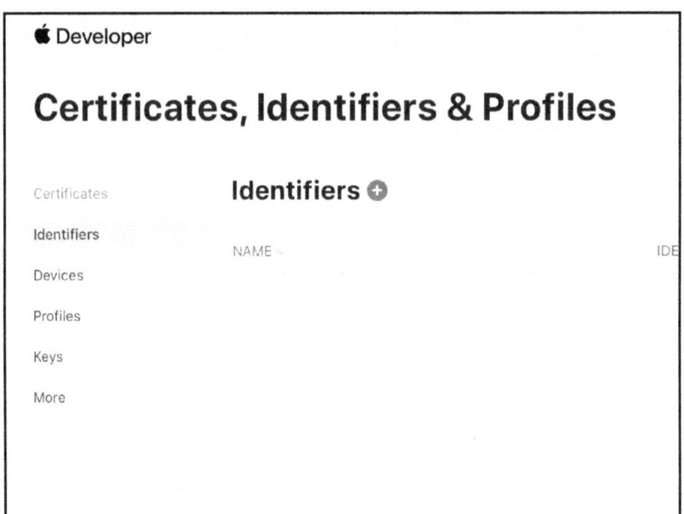

Creating an app identifier.

Click the + button next to the header to add a new app ID. Select **App IDs** and click **Continue**.

On the next screen, select **App** as the type. For the **Bundle ID**, enter the one you saw earlier in Xcode. The **Description** isn't public but helps you remember which identifier is which, so pick something memorable. Click **Continue**.

> **Note**: If you're using features like CloudKit, push notifications or other capabilities, you must enable them on this screen. Most are self-explanatory, and if you don't know what they are, you probably don't need them. You can also enable these later.

The next screen is an overview of the App ID. If everything looks good, click **Register**. Now you have a new App ID that you can use to create a new app on App Store Connect.

Adding an App Entry

> **Note**: If you already have an existing app entry on App Store Connect, skip to the next section.

App Store Connect is where your app's binary meets the App Store. You can create new App Store apps and add data like the app title, description or screenshots. Most importantly, it's where you upload, test and release the app.

Go to App Store Connect (https://appstoreconnect.apple.com) and click **My Apps**. Click the + button in the top-left corner and select **New App**.

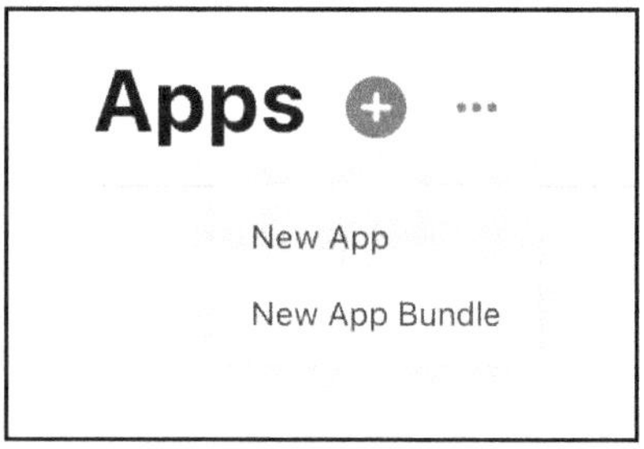

Creating a new app in App Store Connect.

For **Platforms** select **macOS** and, optionally, **iOS**. Here comes one of the most important decisions of your app's life: its name.

This is the name that appears on the App Store. Call upon your inner Don Draper and enter something short but catchy. Enter **"Journalyst, An app to remember"**. See what you did there?

The **Primary Language** determines in which language the App Store will display the app's name and description if there's no localization for the user's locale. For the **Bundle ID**, choose the one you just created in the Developer Portal.

You might be thinking, "What the heck is an **SKU**?" SKU is short for **Stock Keeping Unit**. It comes from the retail world, where each product has a number to identify it. All you need to know is that this should be a value that's unique among your apps. Your bundle ID will do just fine, but feel free to use whatever identifying system you like.

User Access refers to the members of your development team. It determines which of your colleagues can edit the app's information. Consider choosing **Full Access**, especially when you have only one developer on the team. :]

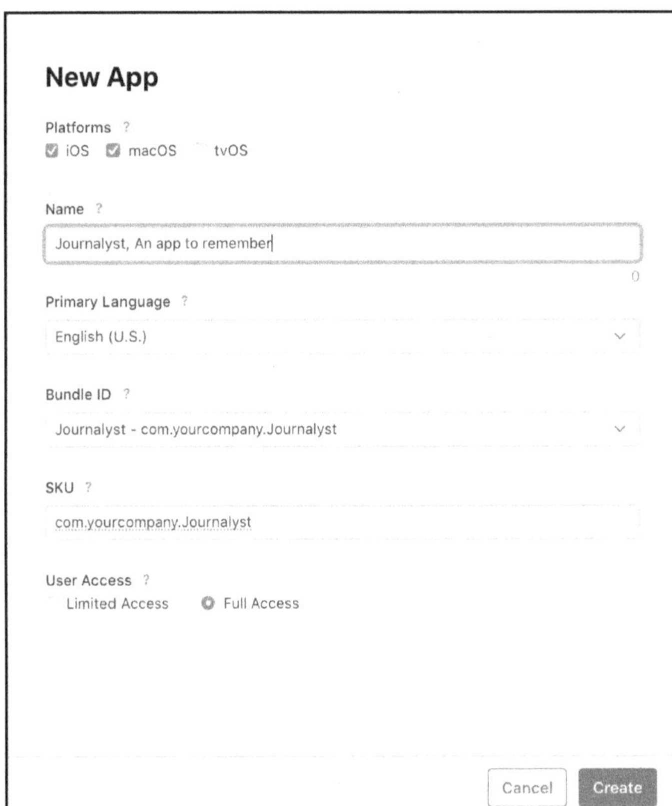

Filling new app information.

> **Note**: Don't worry about getting something wrong. You can change everything except the SKU later.

Finally, click **Create** to make a new app entry.

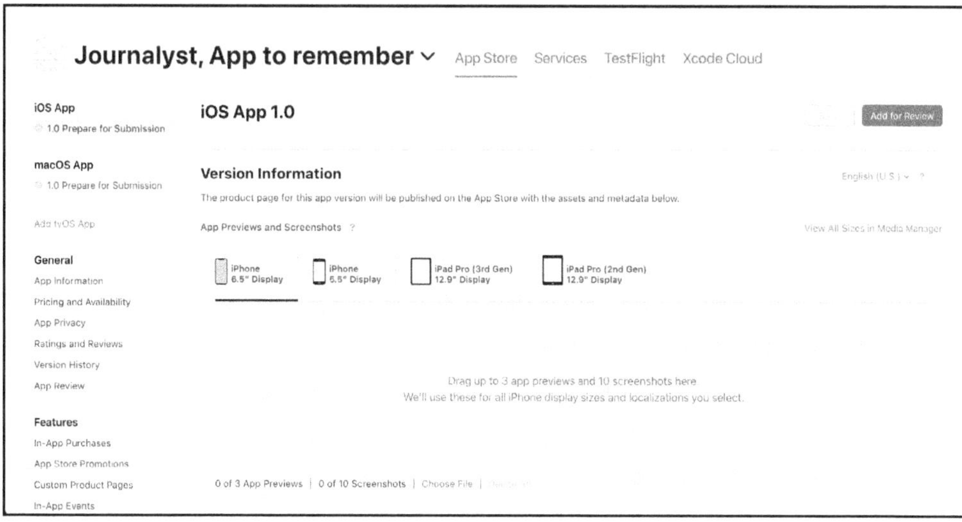

App Store Connect page.

Welcome to your app's dashboard!

There are four tabs at the top of the dashboard:

- **App Store** contains everything related to your app's presentation on the App Store, including the app's title and description, keywords, prices and released app versions.
- **Services** is where you add information related to different app services, like game center groups, encryption information and promo codes.
- **TestFlight** lets you manage beta versions of your app and distribute them to your testers.
- **Xcode Cloud** lets you make automatic builds in the cloud.

Next, you'll upload your 1.0 build.

Uploading a Build

Your app entry can hold apps for multiple platforms and versions of each of those apps. You'll see a new **macOS App** section and a new version called **1.0 Prepare for Submission**. Now you have a place to upload your app.

> **Note**: If you didn't add the macOS platform earlier, add it now. Click **Add macOS App** in the sidebar on the left of your app's dashboard, and you'll see the **macOS App** section.

Next, go back to **Xcode** to upload a new build of your app to App Store Connect.

First, make sure your project compiles without any errors. Then, in the menu bar, go to **Product ▸ Destination** and make sure you've selected **My Mac**. Click **Product ▸ Archive** to compile your app and create an executable to upload to the app store. Depending on the size of your app, this process might take a few minutes, so make sure to bring snacks! :]

Once it finishes archiving, Xcode will open the **Organizer** and show your app's archives. Select the one you just created.

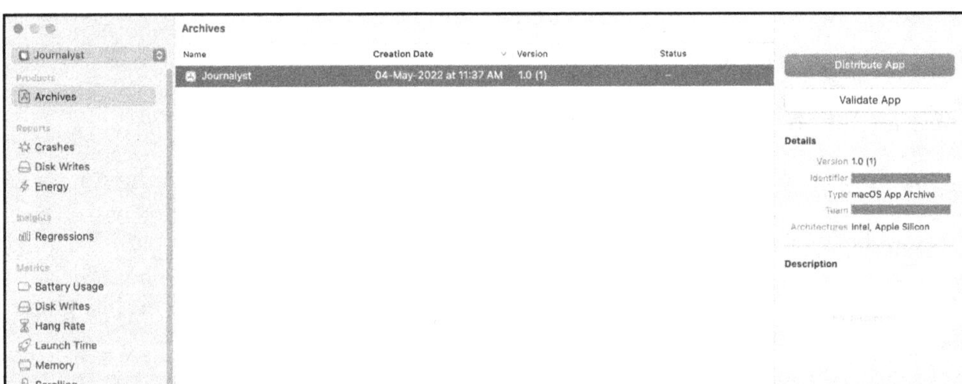

Xcode Organizer.

First, click **Validate App**. Make sure you check the check mark for uploading symbols and click **Next**. Select **Automatically manage signing** and click **Next** again. Xcode will ask you to generate a Mac Installer Distribution certificate on the next screen. Check that checkbox and click **Next**.

Xcode will create a new Mac Distribution certificate and store it in your Keychain. It's recommended you click **Export Signing Certificate...** and save it somewhere secure so you or your colleagues can make builds from other machines. Click **Next.** Make sure you checked **Generate an Apple Distribution certificate** and click **Next** again. Export that one, and — you guessed it — click **Next.**

Finally, you'll see an overview screen of your app's package. Click **Validate** to ensure there aren't any issues with the app.

Now you're back to where you started, in the organizer window. Upload the app by clicking the big blue **Distribute App** button. Select **App Store Connect** and click **Next.** Then select **Upload** and click **Next** again.

Uploading to the app store *is* just clicking a bunch of buttons, isn't it?

Make sure you check the checkbox for uploading symbols and click **Next.** Select **Automatically manage signing.** On the next screen, click **Upload.** Depending on your connection, this might take a while, so give your clicking finger some rest.

Once uploaded, go back to **App Store Connect** and open your newly created app. In the sidebar, click **1.0 Prepare for Submission** under **macOS App.** This is where you'll edit all the information about the 1.0 version of your app.

Editing your app's information.

There are several fields to fill out here. Here's some basic information about the most important fields:

- **App Preview and Screenshots**: These are videos and screenshots of your app. For macOS, the screenshots need to be 16:10 and can only be a specific set of predefined resolutions, as described in the Screenshot specifications (https://apple.co/2KcRFZK) under **Mac**. App previews must be 1920 x 1080 pixels videos with additional requirements described on the App store connect help page (https://apple.co/2twCcJL).
- **Promotional Text**: This bit of text displays under your app's title. It's a short description of what the app does. Aim for something that will make the user click your app.
- **Description** and **Keywords**: These are very important for **ASO** or **App Store Optimization**. If you describe your app well and choose suitable keywords, your app will show up more prominently when users search for related terms.
- **Build**: This is where you select which of your app's uploaded binaries you want to release. Click the + button, select the 1.0 build you uploaded earlier and click **Done**.
- **App Review Information**: This is where you write notes for the person reviewing your app. Look at the App Store Review Guidelines (https://apple.co/1lz8Lit). If your app does things that would make a reviewer suspicious, explain why you're not breaking any guidelines. Also, if your app has login functionality, create a fake user and provide the username and password to save the reviewer time and reduce the chance they'll reject your app for silly reasons.

The rest of the fields are self-explanatory. It may seem like a lot of information, but investing time in getting your metadata right could be the difference between a hit and an app nobody has ever heard of.

Testing Your App With TestFlight

Now that you have everything filled out, it's good practice to make sure everything works as intended before releasing your app to the world. This is where **TestFlight** kicks in.

Apple's TestFlight lets you test your apps and invite outside testers to check out beta versions of your apps. The process is streamlined to make it easy, both for you and your testers.

TestFlight distinguishes between two types of testers, **internal** and **external**. Internal testers are part of your team, and they can test builds almost immediately after you upload them. On the other hand, your app needs to go through an app review before being released to external testers. Thankfully, Apple seems to be more lenient and faster when reviewing beta apps, so the review shouldn't take too long.

Beta Testing Inside Your Team

Go to the **TestFlight** tab, where you'll manage all your beta testing. Here, you'll see a list of your builds available for testing. Each build is available for testing for **90 days** after uploading. Usually, that won't be an issue since there's no need to test old builds!

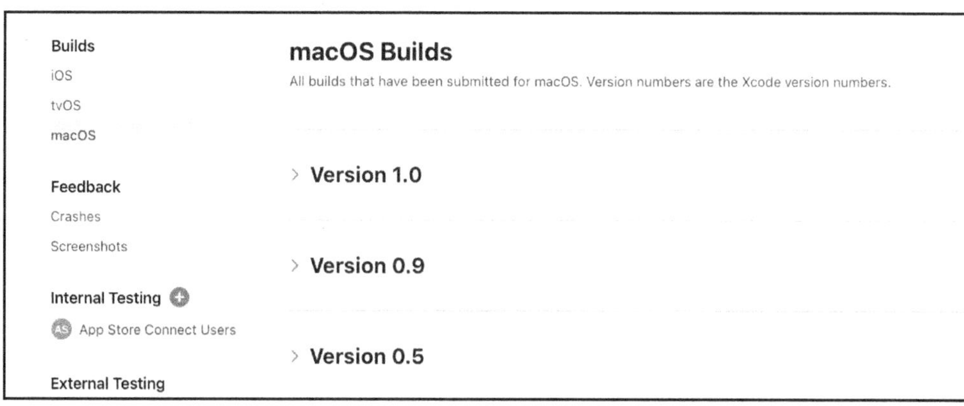

Test Flight builds.

Click the + button next to **Internal Testing** and create a new group to add testers. Give it a descriptive name. If you check **Enable automatic distribution**, whenever you upload a new build from Xcode, it'll automatically invite the people in the group to test your app without you clicking any buttons. This automation is especially handy for internal testing.

Click the + button next to **Testers**to invite a new tester. You'll see a list of your team members. Invite them by checking the checkbox next to their name and clicking **Add**.

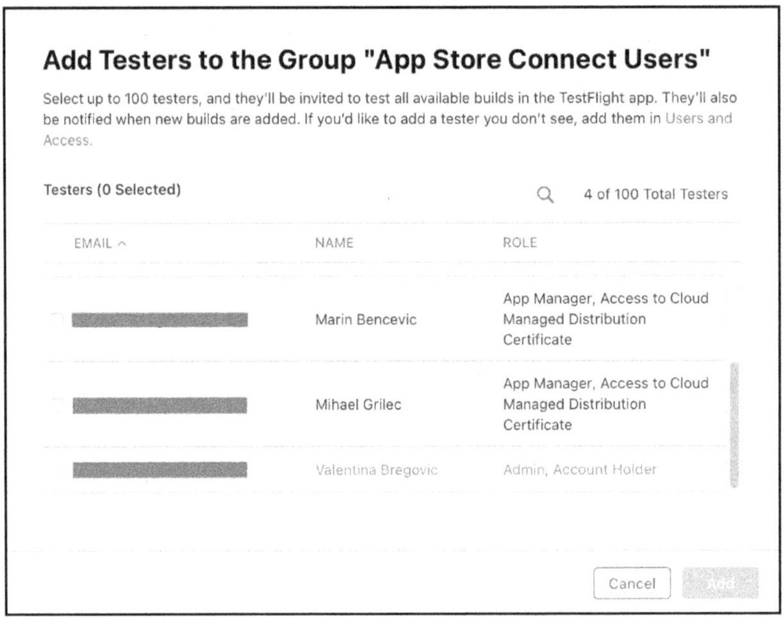

Inviting internal testers to TestFlight.

Once invited, the testers will get an email instructing them to download the TestFlight macOS app and a link to test the app.

Now your teammates can test the app, but what about people outside your company?

Adding External Testers

Before you add any external testers, there are a few things you have to fill out.

In the sidebar, click **Test Information.** First, write your app's **Beta App Description**. In this field, in addition to describing your app, it's helpful to mention which features are in development or any known issues you're having so that your testers are aware of these while checking your app. Other fields are self-explanatory.

Beta App Review Information is not available to testers; It's used for Apple's App Review.

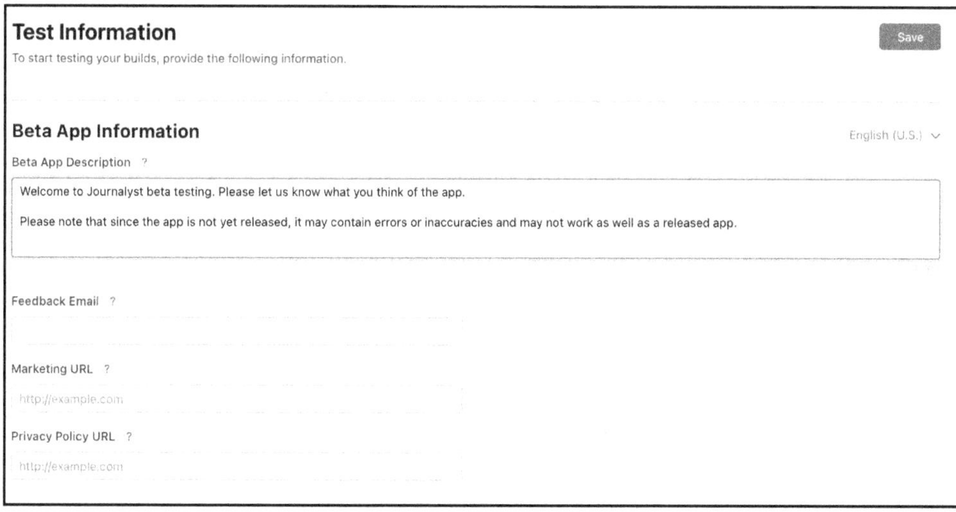

Test information in TestFlight.

Next, create a new tester group under **External Testing** as you did for internal testers.

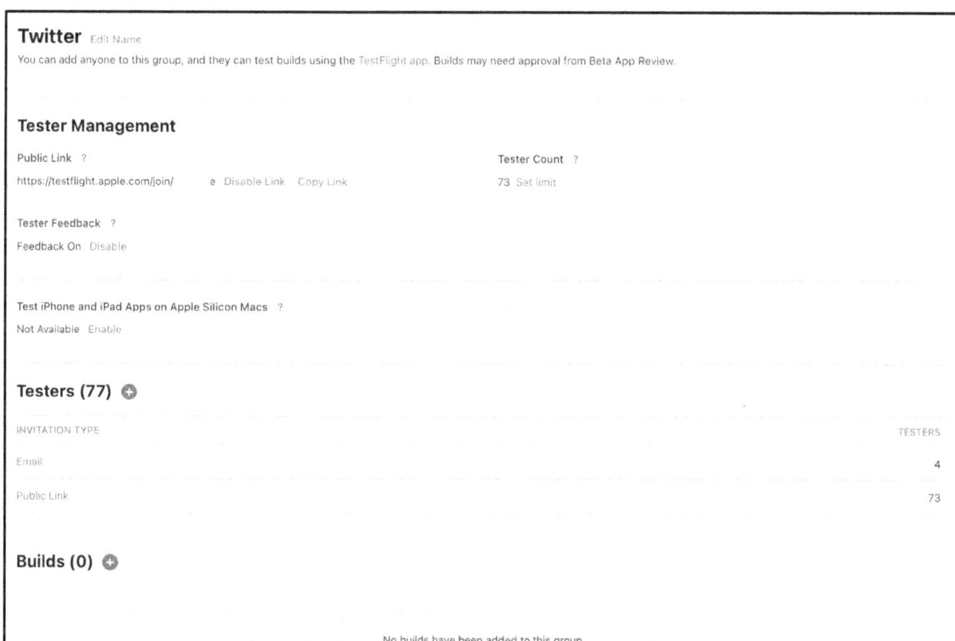

Adding external testers to TestFlight.

There are two ways to invite new testers, either via a public link or private email. The public link lets anyone that clicks the link test your app. This is especially useful if you want to share your app on social media or other public channels.

If you'd like to keep your testing more private, you can also invite someone by entering their email. Click the + button next to **Testers** and then click **Add New Testers**. Type in their emails and, optionally, their names and click **Add**.

While internal testers can receive builds automatically, you must manually add builds to external tester groups. Click the + button next to **Builds** and select the build you uploaded. The first time you do this, your build will go to Apple for App Review. Once it goes through, all your testers will receive an email inviting them to test your new build.

Releasing Your App

You uploaded your build, filled out all the necessary metadata and even tested to make sure it works. All that's left is to release your app to the App Store masses.

Pricing Your App

In the **App Store** tab, go to **Pricing and Availability** in the sidebar. Set the price of your app under **Price Schedule**. You can choose from almost 100 different pricing tiers for your app. Each of the tiers has a roughly similar price in all currencies. Once you select a price, click **Other Currencies** to see the exact values in each territory.

You can also make your app available for pre-order, which makes your app appear in the App Store even before you release your first version.

If you want to charge a subscription price or offer in-app purchases, do that under **In-App Purchases** in the sidebar.

Submitting for Review

Once you've filled everything out, click **Save** in the top-right corner and click **Submit for Review**. A reviewer from Apple will look at your app to ensure you followed the guidelines. This may take a few hours to a few days.

There's something *quite* annoying about having a completed app that's sitting there waiting for review. Be patient and hang in there!

Once your app passes the review, you'll get an email notification and the name of the version changes to **1.0 Pending Developer Release**. In the top-right corner, you'll see a new button titled **Release This Version**. Click this button and pop a bottle of champagne! You just released an app!

> **Note**: Your app version changes to **1.0 Pending Developer Release**if you select **Manually release this version** under **Version Release** of your App Store page.

Keep in mind, the App Store might need a few hours to propagate your app, so make sure to wait a while before you start telling all your friends.

> **Note**: Your app won't be available for universal purchase until you fully release your app on at least two platforms.

Selling Your macOS App Separately

By default, Xcode sets up your project to offer a universal purchase, meaning that users buying your app on the iOS app store get it for free on macOS. With this approach, you might forego the income you'd usually get from a single user, but you give your users a better experience and value for the same price. If your macOS and iOS apps are the same and there's a reason to expect users to want to have both versions, consider offering a universal purchase.

Instead of offering a universal purchase, you can also separately sell your macOS app by using a different bundle ID for your macOS app. Go back to **Xcode** and, from the **Project navigator**, click the project's name and then the app target. Open the **Signing & Capabilities** tab. Uncheck the **Use iOS Bundle Identifier** checkbox and enter a new bundle identifier for your macOS app.

> **Note**: You may have to delete the build setting **DERIVE_UIKITFORMAC_PRODUCT_BUNDLE_IDENTIFIER** to change the checkbox.

macOS as a separate bundle.

Using this new bundle ID, you can distribute your app on the Mac App Store by repeating the steps described in the previous section.

Key Points

- You must sign each app with a **provisioning profile**, which combines a **certificate** with an **app ID**.
- You create app IDs in Apple's **Developer Portal**.
- Manage the app on the App Store by going to **App Store Connect**.
- Upload **new builds** from Xcode.
- Test beta versions of your app with internal and external testers using **Test Flight**.

Where to Go From Here?

To ensure you're not violating any of Apple's guidelines, carefully read through Apple's App Store Review Guidelines (https://apple.co/1lz8Lit). Apple also provides a helpful list of common app rejection reasons. Use it as a checklist (https://apple.co/2ltWgeB) before submitting.

Now that you understand how to upload new builds, think about automating this for **continuous integration** using tools like Jenkins and Fastlane. You'll find an example of how to do this for iOS apps in our Continuous Integration tutorial (https://bit.ly/2YT52pa).

Since you uploaded your app to the App Store, it's time to think more about optimizing it for the App Store's search. Apple provides valuable tips on their site (https://developer.apple.com/app-store/search/).

Finally, make sure to spread the word about your app anywhere you can! App-making is a tricky business, so good luck out there. This entire Book Team is rooting for you! :]

Chapter 14: Third-Party Distribution

By Marin Benčević

If you're reading this chapter, you're probably considering taking destiny into your own hands and releasing your app without the App Store.

It's dangerous to walk that road alone! Take this chapter as a guide. It will talk you through preparing your app so anyone can download it and install it. You'll learn how to notarize your app, how to create a DMG file for your app and also some tips on surviving the harsh world of 3rd party macOS app distribution.

> **Note**: In case you're wondering, push notifications and CloudKit will still work, even if you're not distributing your apps on the App Store.

Before you get started with distributing apps, you'll need an Apple ID enrolled in the Apple Developer Program. Yes, even though you're not using the App Store, you still need a developer account.

The process of distributing apps is complicated by an annoying but useful macOS feature called Gatekeeper. Gatekeeper constantly checks the apps you're running, making sure there's nothing shady inside of them. Have you ever launched an app only to be surprised by an alert telling you the app is from an unidentified developer? That's Gatekeeper.

You've probably noticed not all apps cause this alert to pop-up. It usually happens with less-popular or non-native apps. The ones that don't pop-up the alert are properly **signed** and **notarized**. In the next section, you'll do that for your app to make sure Gatekeeper lets your users run it.

Signed, Notarized and Delivered

> **Note**: To learn more about what code signing is and how it works, look at Chapter 13, "Releasing on the App Store".

For other people to run your app, you'll need to sign it with a **Developer ID** certificate. That's a special kind of certificate that lets you distribute your app outside the App Store. Only the **Account Holder** of your Apple Developer account can create this certificate.

If you have a *personal* Apple Developer account, you're already the Account Holder. If you're in a team, check your role by going to **App Store Connect**'s **Users and Access** section here (https://apple.co/2Da59iB). If you see yourself in the **Account Holder** tab, you're good.

If you're not the Account Holder, you'll have to ask the Account Holder to export a **macOS Developer ID Application** certificate for you. They can do that from Xcode. Apple provides easy-to-follow instructions on how to export certificates (https://apple.co/2mj29Mh).

Signing, however, is not enough. You also need to notarize the app. Notarization is a process where you send your app to Apple and let them perform automatic checks on it to make sure it's not doing anything malicious. Once Apple confirms the app is okay, they give your app a ticket. This ticket tells Gatekeeper to relax when a user opens your app, because Apple checked it.

Think of notarization as an airport security check: Your app needs to go through *Transport Security Administration* before it can fly across the world to your users' Macs.

In the last chapter, you learned code signing guarantees, you made your app and *haven't changed it since you signed it*. The latter part is important for notarization: Whenever your app changes, you need to renotarize the app's binary.

Keep in mind that notarization is an automatic process that usually takes a couple of minutes. It's much more relaxed than App Review and you should expect your app to go through notarization without any issues unless you're doing something very suspicious.

Apple made notarization easy; you can do everything in **Xcode**. Open the starter project of this chapter, or the app you want to distribute, in Xcode.

The first thing you need to do is make an archive of your app. Before you do that, make sure your project compiles without any errors. Then, in the menu bar go to **Product ▸ Destination** and make sure you've selected **My Mac**. Click **Product ▸ Archive**. This compiles your app and creates an executable that you can notarize. Depending on the size of your app, this process might take a few minutes — you can think of a cool website domain while you wait. :]

Once it's finished archiving, Xcode will open the **Organizer**. In the sidebar, you should see your app under **macOS Apps**. If you just created an archive, your app is selected, but you can come back here later and select the app and all your archives will be listed.

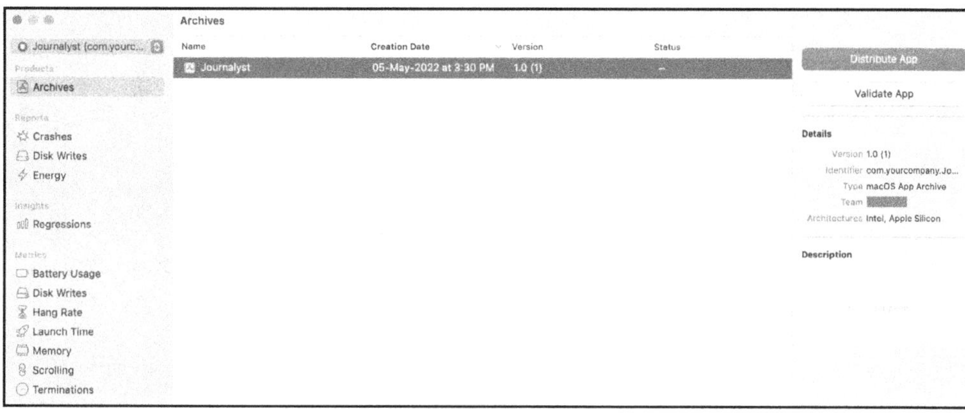

Xcode Organizer.

Now that you have an archive, the next steps are signing and notarization. Xcode automatically does this in one fell swoop.

> **Note**: To notarize your app, you need to have **Hardened Runtime** enabled. The Hardened Runtime locks down the app and protects your users from exploits. It's enabled by default for Catalyst apps, so unless you disabled it manually, you're fine. You can see it in Xcode in the **Signing & Capabilities** tab of your app target's settings.

Click **Distribute App**. In the screen that pops-up, select **Developer ID** and click **Next**. Select **Upload** and click **Next**. In the next screen, select **Automatically manage signing**.

> **Note**: At this point, Xcode might show an error saying that you either don't have a Developer ID certificate or you don't have its private key. If that's the case, contact your Account Holder and make sure they export a new Developer ID Application certificate by following Apple's instructions (https://apple.co/2mj29Mh).

Once signed, you'll get a summary.

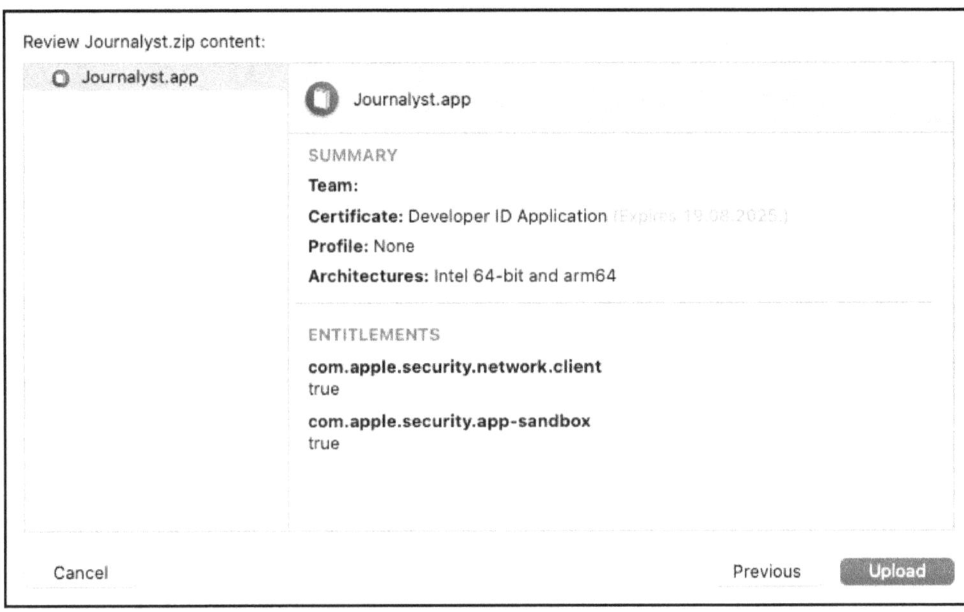

Notorization summary.

Click **Upload** and Xcode will start uploading the archive to the notary service.

Now you wait. If you've decided on your domain, maybe you can brainstorm some website design ideas at this point. :]

You can check your app's status in the Organizer. If you closed the window, you can open it by selecting **Window ▸ Organizer**. You'll see the status under the **Status** column. You can also click **Show Status Log** to see what's been going on.

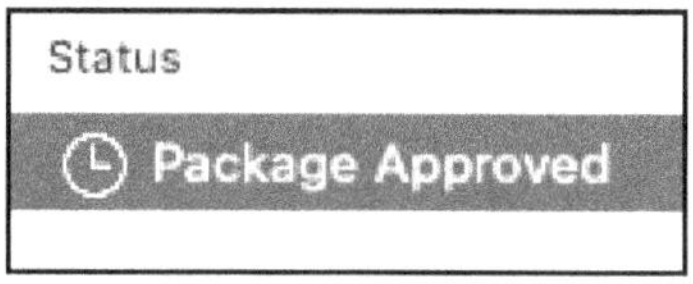

Notorization status.

Once notarization completes, it will change to **Ready to distribute**. If something goes wrong, the status will change to **Rejected**. In that case, you can click **Show Status Log** to see why the notarization service rejected your app.

Now that you have a notarized app, you can export the binary you'll share with your users. Click **Export Notarized App** from the right sidebar. Select a location on disk and you'll have your app!

Your exported app.

While you *could* distribute this app as it is, most developers choose to distribute their apps as compressed disk images, aka DMG files. In the next section, you'll see how and why you'd do that.

Creating a DMG File

If you've ever downloaded a macOS app, chances are it came in a .dmg file, which is short for **Disk Image**. When you double-click a .dmg file, it mounts a new disk that contains the app and sometimes additional files like a read-me document.

Packaging your apps in .dmg files has several advantages:

- It lets the user easily install the app by dragging and dropping it to Applications.
- Since apps (.app files) are something between a file and a folder, packing them up into a .dmg makes sure they appear as a single file to web browsers.
- You can password-protect .dmg files.
- .dmg files can contain additional files like read-me documents, licensing information etc.

.dmg files often contain an alias to the user's Applications folder. This lets users easily drag your app right into Applications without having to look for the folder. Apple heavily recommends that you *instruct users to move your app to Applications*. Running the app straight from the DMG might lead to unexpected behavior and could compromise the user's security.

Disk images often include a custom background image to instruct the user to drag and drop the app. In this section, you'll make your very own disk image with an alias to the Applications folder, as well as a custom image.

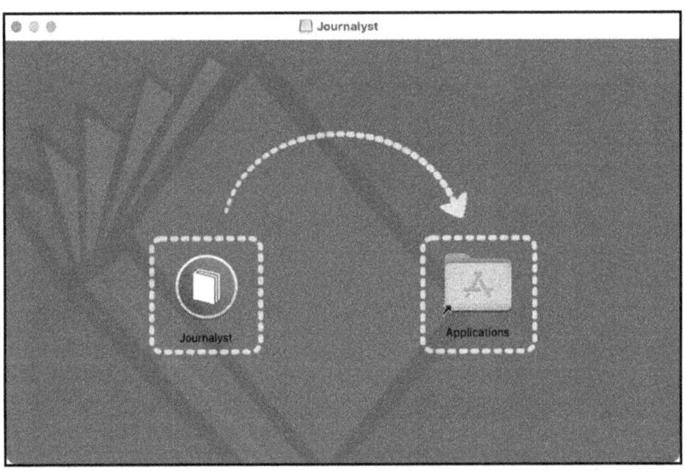

Creating a .dmg file.

To make a new disk image, open **Disk Utility**. Click **File ▸ New Image ▸ Blank Image...**. Enter a file name and fill out the **Name** text field. Usually, these two values are the same. Next, for the **Size**, enter a size that is slightly larger than your app. You'll trim the extra size later. You can leave the default values for the other settings and click **Save**.

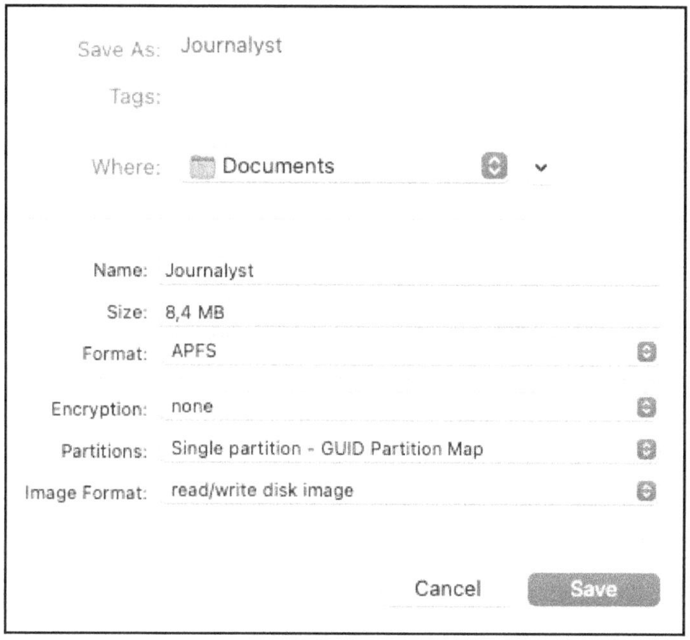

Disk utility settings.

If you go into **Finder**, you'll see that your new disk image has been mounted. Click your disk image in the sidebar.

Any Finder settings that you change for this disk image will get saved and loaded when users mount your disk image. This includes things like the size of the window, which Finder views and tabs the app shows and other view options. This is all saved on the disk image in a hidden file called **.DS_Store**.

Cleaning up Your Window

First, let's clean up the window. Press **Command-1** to view the disk image as a grid of icons. Then, in the **View** menu, hide everything that isn't already hidden by clicking **Hide Toolbar**, **Hide Path Bar** and **Hide Status Bar**. You should see a completely blank window.

Blank image.

> **Note**: Depending on your Finder defaults, some of these may already be hidden. Just make sure all the bars are hidden and your window looks like the screenshot.

The next step is to add a custom background image. Press **Command-Shift-.** to show hidden files. Create a new folder in the disk image named **.background**. If a dialog pops-up saying the folder will be invisible, click **OK** — an invisible folder is exactly what you need.

If you don't have a background image, you can find one in this chapter's materials. In a new Finder window, navigate to the **starter** folder of this chapter's materials. Copy **background.png** to the newly-created **.background** folder.

Next, click **View ▸ Show View Options**. Make sure you've checked **Always open in icon view**. Set the **Icon size** to **80×80** and slide the **Grid spacing** slider all the way to the right. For **Background**, select **Picture** and, from a new Finder window, drag **background.png** from the **.background** folder. While dragging, make sure the disk image is the currently active window.

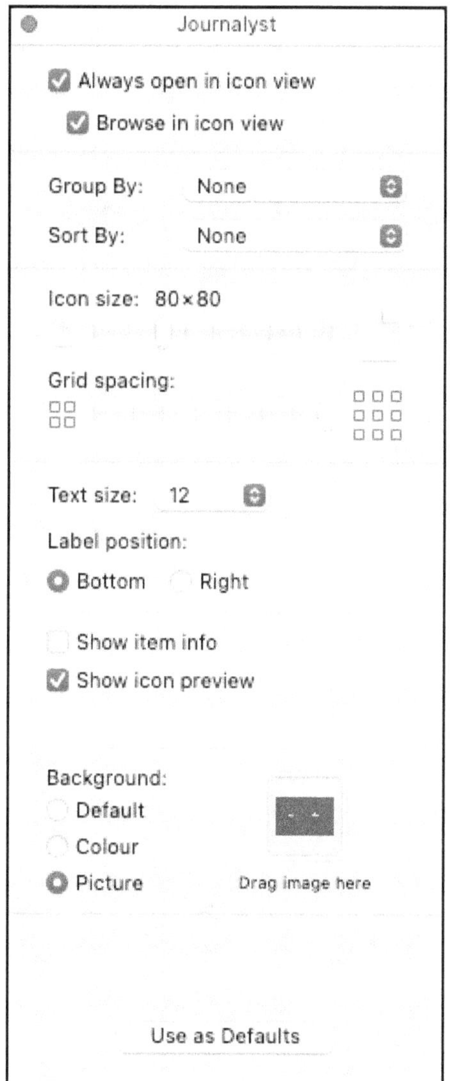

View options.

Close the view options window and resize the disk image window so you can't see the edges of the background picture. Press **Command-Shift-.** again to hide the files.

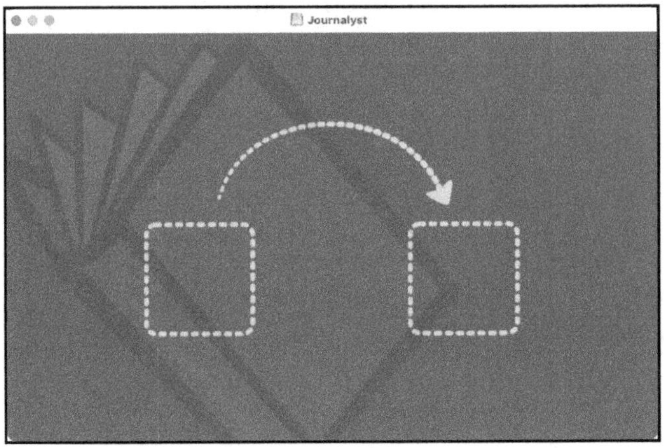

Background image.

Adding Your App

Now that the window looks nice, it's time to add your app and an alias to Applications. From a different Finder window, copy your exported app to the disk image and position it in the left box.

Next, navigate to the root directory of your macOS disk. You can do this from **Terminal** by typing `open /`. Right-click **Applications** and click **Make Alias**. This creates a new folder that acts as a pointer to Applications. Copy the alias to the disk image and position the icon inside the box on the right.

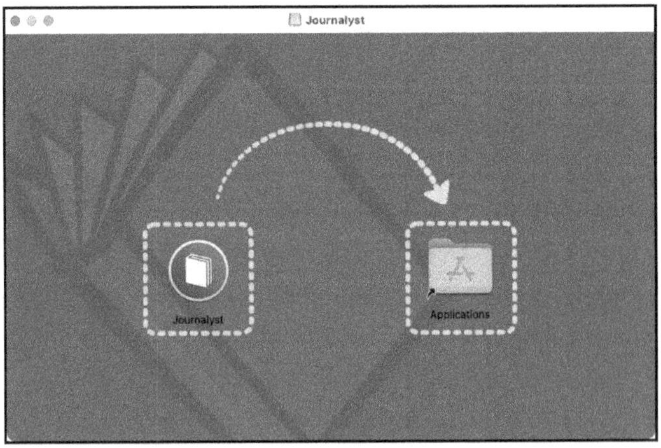

Adding your app in .dmg.

Hey, that's a nice looking .dmg you made! Since you worked hard on setting everything up perfectly, you wouldn't want those pesky users changing things. That's why the next step is to make the image read-only.

Go back into **Disk Utility** and eject your disk image by clicking the little eject button next to the image in the sidebar. Then, in the menu bar, click **Images ▸ Convert...** and select the image you just set up. Name the file anything you like — you can change this later. For the **Image Format**, select **read-only** and click **Convert**. This makes sure nobody can change the image and also trims all the excess space.

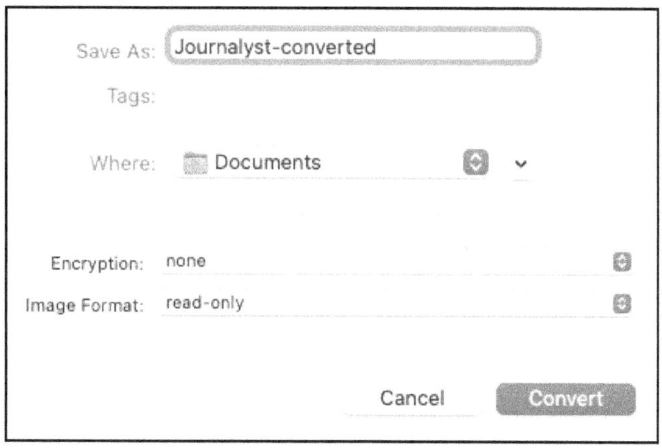

Converting to read-only.

You now have a DMG that you can share with your customers! But unfortunately they won't get far with this DMG. Your users won't be able to run unsigned software. If you're thinking, "I *just* signed my app!" — you're right. But, the .dmg file is *also* a piece of software and needs to be signed and notarized just like your app.

Notarizing Disk Images

You can sign and notarize a .dmg file pretty quickly, just by using the command line. You'll begin by signing the .dmg file.

Before you start, open **Keychain Access** and, in the top-right corner, search for "developer id". You should see a certificate named "Developer ID Application: Team Name (ID)". Click the certificate and copy the whole name in bold at the top of the window, including the team ID.

Certificate in Keychain Access.

Now, open **Terminal** and use `cd` to navigate to the folder where you saved your converted disk image. Enter the following command to sign the disk image:

```
codesign \
  -s "Developer ID Application: Your Name (Your Team ID)" \
  Journalyst-converted.dmg
```

Replace the text inside the quotation marks by pasting the name of your certificate; make sure the file name matches your disk image. If everything goes correctly, you won't see any output.

For this next step, you'll need an app-specific password for your Apple ID. Head over to appleid.apple.com and sign in with your Apple ID. Under **Sign-In and Security**, click **APP-SPECIFIC PASSWORDS**. Click the + button next to **Passwords** and name it **altool**. Click **Create**, confirm your password with Apple and then click **Continue**. Copy your app-specific generated password to a secure location, you'll need it for the next step.

Now, you can upload the disk image to Apple's notarization service. Instead of using Xcode like before, you'll do it from the command line. Run the following command:

```
xcrun altool --notarize-app \
  -f Journalyst-converted.dmg \
  --primary-bundle-id com.yourcompany.Journalyst \
  -u you@yourcompany.com
```

Pre-empting your commands with `xcrun` makes sure the commands run from your developer directory. The tool you'll use to notarize your .dmg file is Apple's `altool`, a command-line tool that lets you interact with the App Store and Apple's notary service.

Replace "Journalyst-converted.dmg" with the name of your disk image, then replace the bundle ID with the one for your app. Finally, unless you're literally the CEO of "yourcompany.com", replace the email with the Apple ID that you use to log into App Store Connect.

You'll see a prompt for a password. Enter the app-specific password you just copied and wait a few moments for the disk image to upload. Once uploaded, you see a message similar to this one:

```
No errors uploading 'Journalyst-converted.dmg'.
RequestUUID = 66accdd9-7d26-4173-8e88-ea53f61b37b0
```

This confirms that the disk image was uploaded, but it doesn't automatically mean it was notarized. To check the notarization status, run the following command again, replacing the email with your Apple ID:

```
xcrun altool --notarization-history 0 \
  -u you@yourcompany.com
```

This shows a table of notarization requests and their statuses. Enter your app-specific password. After waiting for a while and running the command again, you see the "Status" column change to "success" and "Status Message" change to "Package Approved":

```
Date  RequestUUID Status  Status Code Status Message
----- ----------- ------- ----------- ----------------
(...) (...)       success 0           Package Approved
```

Note: If notarization failed, you can see more information by entering the following command:

```
xcrun altool --notarization-info 66accdd9-7d26-4173-8e88-
ea53f61b37b0 -u you@yourcompany.com
```

Replace the email with your Apple ID and the ID with the `RequestUUID` that was output from the `--notarize-app` command. You'll see a log file URL that you can open to see a list of issues with your disk image.

A "success" status means that Apple has notarized your disk image and stored a ticket on their servers. You also need to include this ticket in your .dmg file. You can do that by **stapling** it to the file. Run the following command:

```
xcrun stapler staple Journalyst-converted.dmg
```

You see a message saying, "The staple and validate action worked!". The message makes it sound like Apple itself is surprised the action worked. :]

You now have a signed and notarized disk image that contains a signed and notarized app.

Key Points

- To distribute macOS apps without the App Store, you need to sign the app with a **Developer ID** certificate.
- Apps and other software packages need to be **notarized** to verify they're malware-free.
- You can use Xcode to notarize apps.
- You package apps inside disk images (.dmg files) for easier downloading and installation.
- Sign .dmg files using the `codesign` command-line tool.
- Notarize .dmg files using the `altool` command-line tool.
- After notarization, make sure to staple the ticket to the .dmg file by using the `stapler` utility.

Where to Go From Here?

Unfortunately, unless you want to distribute your app via email, you'll also need a website to host and show off your app. If you're making a paid app, you'll need to deal with payments and managing licenses. This *may* sound little scary, but there are some tools to help you.

Here are a few tools you can use to manage customers and billing:

- Paddle (https://paddle.com/solutions/mac/) lets you manage billing customers both in-app and on your website.
- Even though it's not specific to macOS apps, Gumroad (https://gumroad.com) lets you easily sell stuff online and manage your customers.
- Braintree (https://www.braintreepayments.com) is a company owned by PayPal and also offers an easy way to set up payments.

All of these have ways to integrate them into existing websites and, in some cases, macOS apps.

If you're not a web developer, don't fret. There are plenty of tutorials, courses and website builders to get you started. First of all, you already know Swift, so why not use it to build your website? Vapor, a server-side Swift framework, offers a templating engine called Leaf that you can use to build a landing page for your app. Here are three different resources on Vapor and Leaf:

- Templating Vapor Applications with Leaf tutorial (https://bit.ly/2kKUfL2).
- Server Side Swift with Vapor video course (https://bit.ly/2kdhaOK).
- *Server Side Swift with Vapor* book (https://bit.ly/2FI9wAR).

If you're not into the idea of building out a website with code, you can use website builders like Squarespace (https://www.squarespace.com) or Webflow (https://webflow.com). Aside from letting you build a website without knowing anything about web development, these tools also host your website — one less headache to worry about.

As you can see, exporting your app is not enough. You also need to deal with building websites, managing customers and marketing your app. Nobody ever said it would be easy, but indie app development is *extremely rewarding*. Your success is in your own hands, for better or for worse. The authors and editors of this book are all rooting for you. Good luck out there! :]

15 Conclusion

You made it! Congratulations on finishing the book. We hope you've enjoyed your journey from iPhone to iPad to Mac - to a whole new field of users!

In this book, you learned how to take an iPhone app and add the features that make it work great on both iPad and Mac. That's the great thing about Catalyst - most of your efforts will be useful on multiple platforms now!

You also learned about those things that are specific to the Mac platform, and how to take advantage of them in your app.

In the end, you have a codebase that works great on iPhone, iPad and Mac! That's living the dream!!

Now, you're ready to go out on your own - take your iOS apps to the Mac, and make them insanely great!

If you have any questions or comments about the projects in this book, please stop by our forums (https://forums.raywenderlich.com).

Thank you again for purchasing this book. Your continued support is what makes the books, tutorials, videos and other things we do at our site possible.

We truly appreciate it!

The *Catalyst by Tutorials* team

www.ingramcontent.com/pod-product-compliance
Lightning Source LLC
LaVergne TN
LVHW080042210926
848481LV00011B/3255
9781950325702